Law and Society
Recent Scholarship

Edited by Melvin I. Urofsky

A Series from LFB Scholarly

Muslim and American? Straddling Islamic Law and U.S. Justice

Mark E. Hanshaw

LFB Scholarly Publishing LLC
El Paso 2010

Library of Congress Cataloging-in-Publication Data

Hanshaw, Mark E., 1964-
Muslim and American straddling Islamic law and U.S. justice / Mark E. Hanshaw.
p. cm. -- (Law & society : recent scholarship)
Includes bibliographical references and index.
ISBN 978-1-59332-394-3 (hardcover : alk. paper)
1. Islamic law--United States. 2. Muslims--Legal status, laws, etc.--United States. 3. Justice, Administration of (Islamic law) 4. Justice, Administration of--United States. 5. Jihad. 6. Terrorism--United States--Prevention. I. Title.
KBP69.U6H36 2010
340.5'9--dc22

2010010234

ISBN 978-1-59332-394-3

Printed on acid-free 250-year-life paper.

Manufactured in the United States of America.

For my parents who are not with us
to see the publication of this volume,
my wife who has given me support throughout,
and my son who forever keeps me laughing.

Table of Contents

Acknowledgements

I express gratitude for all those who contributed to this work, and especially John Lamoreaux, Ph.D. He inspired me to carry this project forward. I also express my appreciation for the contributions of Robin Lovin, Ph.D., Serg Frolov, Ph.D., Richard Cogley, Ph.D., Rubin Habito, Ph.D., Michael Provence, Ph.D., Yusef Soddiq, Ph.D., and Ellen Pryor, J.D. Finally, I express my sincere appreciation for the support provided by the communities of Southern Methodist University and Texas Wesleyan University.

Introduction

> *If they can kill each other during Ramadan, they can appear before the grand jury, all they can't do is eat before sunset. I believe Mr. Al-Arian's request is part of the attempted Islamization of the American Justice System. I am not going to put off Dr. Al-Arian's grand jury appearance just to assist in what is becoming the Islamization of America.*[1]

Despite the incendiary words attributed to U.S. Attorney Gordon Kromberg, the relationship between America and its Muslim community often appears to be marked more by confusion and mistrust than the sort of subversion of the Justice system this court official seemed to imagine and fear. Routinely in the U.S., newspapers, magazines and the nightly news are filled with examples of cultures caught not in a grip of conflict, but of misunderstanding. Differences in cultural norms, political views and moral priorities often fuel this divide. The result may be interactions clouded by erroneous or

---

[1] Statement of U.S. Attorney Gordon Kromberg in response to a motion to delay a judicial proceeding involving Defendant Sami Al-Arian to time after Ramadan. See Meg Laughlin, "Al-Arian Attorney Charges Bias," *St. Petersburg Times* (Nov. 10, 2006).

unsupported assumptions and marked by suspicion.[2] This anxiety may spill even into the legal arena, where Muslim religious practices and ideals may come under often unusual scrutiny or challenge. In effect, then, individual efforts to adhere to religious strictures may result in conflict, pitting the religious practitioner against social institutions.

For Muslims, such conflicts present potentially serious personal challenges. Often, Muslims may feel that they face a forced choice between loyalty to their own religious tradition and secular social demands. The commonality of such conflicts has prompted many Muslims, living as minorities in the West, to re-think the manner in which they seek to balance their perceived religious obligations with the demands of Western secular society.

Indeed, a specific dialogue has developed related to the experiences of Muslims who are living in countries where they constitute only a minority. Some of the frustrations of Muslims living in the West, particularly, have been expressed through the charged reflections of Muslim teacher and thinker Sayyed Muhammad Hussein Fadlallah, who has observed:

> The problem which a Muslim faces in himself and his family, in his private and public life, in the West, is one of the most complicated problems in his Islamic existence, in the nature of affiliation and in its details. The matter is not limited to some negative, aspects that they face in the shortcoming of the social reality to which they have emigrated and lived in their present period, or the opposing conditions in individual and family habits and customs, the nature of freedom that governs people in their lives and the laws that contradict some Islamic obligations so that Muslims stand puzzled between religion

---

[2] As a brief primer on popular views of Islam in the U.S., see generally Paul Steinhauser, "Poll: Few Americans have Favorable View of the Muslim World," from the website CNN Online (June 2, 2009), http://www.cnn.com/POLITICS/06/02/us.muslims.poll (accessed June 2, 2009). The poll of more than 1,000 Americans is reported to have indicated that about 20 percent of U.S. citizens view "Muslim countries" favorably, while some 46 percent view them negatively. It also suggested that 80 percent of those polled believed that Muslims had an unfavorable opinion of America. Ibid.

> and the law. The matter is, rather, in the whole of the environment which they breathe into their minds, hearts and feelings and extend, unconsciously, to the movement of their internal and external life, exactly like the air they breathe and the odor they smell in their body pores with all their negative and positive consequences.[3]

While the comments of Fadlallah may be read to suggest certain generalized negative perceptions of Western culture, they also underscore a more specific concern. In particular, many Muslims living in the West have grown to feel they are regularly placed into the untenable situation of having to choose between zealous adherence to their own faith tradition and their desire to be participatory residents of the region they inhabit.

The question that may be raised, then, is how such Muslims, estranged by geography from religious communities of familial origin, are affected by the relocation of their spiritual practice to a region where they constitute a minority and where their system of faith is often broadly misunderstood.

Taha Jabir Al-Alwani, Ph.D., President of Cordoba University,[4] has experience working with Muslims in the West who have been separated from traditional religious and cultural institutions. Based upon this experience, he has argued that such relocation of the faithful has led to the "alienation of [Muslims] from their roots."[5] In this estranged status, he would argue, Muslims suffer from the deterioration of religious priorities and the loss of authoritative relationships. These are slowly replaced by new social relationships and practical norms. The result of this process is that the Muslim practitioner becomes increasingly disenfranchised from his or her own religious faith. By the

---

[3] "Confronting Challenges," From the website Bayynat.org, http://English.bayynat.org.lb/islamicinsights/7.htm (accessed June 10, 2009).

[4] Cordoba University highlights its encouragement of Muslim and Christian dialogue, noting on its website that it is "the first Muslim school to join a consortium of Christian seminaries…." See "Welcome to Cordoba University," from the website of Cordoba University, Asburn, Virginia, http://www.cordobauniversity.org/welcome.asp (accessed June 12, 2009).

[5] See *Toward a Fiqh for Minorities: Some Basic Reflections* (London: The International Institute for Islamic Thought, 2003), xv.

"third or fourth generation" of residence in a minority Muslim environment, Al-Alwani argues, the vital connections between practitioners and their faith may be completely severed through a continuing process of growing alienation.

If Al-Awani is correct in his assessment, it should be asked, what are the primary contributors to this process of estrangement? As well, how may such instances of estrangement affect the broader global Muslim perception of the West or the U.S., in particular? Finally, how may this process of estrangement be addressed by the global Muslim community and, to what extent is this a challenge that demands the attention of Western governments? These are perplexing questions, but they underscore the broad nature of issues affecting relations between Western societies and minority Muslim communities residing therein.

At the heart of Al-Awani's statement lies a concern related to the implementation of that set of ritual and ethical norms, rooted in Islam, that are generally referred to by Western commentators as "Islamic law." The same corpus of ethical and social norms is often identified by Muslims through the use of the Arabic terms *shari'a* or *fiqh*, though these two terms are not entirely synonymous.[6]

Islamic law, rooted in the *Qur'an* and *Hadith*,[7] may be said to provide a comprehensive and practical behavioral guide to Muslim practitioners. As John Esposito has observed, "Islamic law has remained central to Muslim identity, for it constitutes the ideal social

---

[6] In general, the term *shari'a* may be said to relate to the materials derived from the Qur'an and the *Sunnah* of the the Prophet Muhammad, while the term *fiqh* is generally understood to refer to the practice of interpreting these foundational materials and applying them to particular situations confronted by members of the Muslim community.

[7] The employment of the term *Hadith* in the present context may be viewed as being too narrow by some and preference may be given for the utilization of the term *Sunnah*. Broadly, *Sunnah* may be understood as the complex of words, actions and deeds undertaken by the Prophet Muhammad and the associated interpretations of these behavioral models. Preserved in the *Hadith*, Muslims will observe that these traditional articulations of the statements and actions of the recognized founder of Islam provide a foundational ethical pattern to be followed by all subsequent Muslims. It, then, serves as a primary source for identifying the ethical obligations of Muslims, standing in a secondary position only to the Qur'an, itself.

blueprint for the good society."[8] It is Islamic law that provides structure to the lives of Muslims. This structure is broad, touching almost every aspect of human endeavor.

The comprehensiveness of the Islamic system of religious law stems, at least in part, from the origins of the Muslim tradition itself. It is broadly, though not universally, accepted by scholars that, with the emergence of Muhammad as a transformative political and religious leader on the Arabian Peninsula, the populace of the region moved away from their historical embrace of tribal custom as the primary governing social structure. Over time, in its place, an identifiable new social contract was crafted. This social contract was rooted in the revelation claimed by Muslim faithful to have been received by Muhammad from Allah, transmitted through an angelic being. That revelation, of course, is said to be a body of material that has come to be known as the Holy *Qur'an*.[9] This scriptural document is, then, understood to serve as the foundation and principle source for the ethical system of Islamic law.

Admittedly, not all would agree with even this elementary summary statement concerning the development of the Muslim religious tradition and its integrated ethical content. Some, pointing to various pieces of archeological and historical evidence, have attempted to segregate the institution of Islamic law from the life and prophetic activity of Muhammad.[10] Still, regardless of one's interpretation of the

---

[8] *Islam* (Oxford: Oxford University Press, 1988), 75.

[9] *See* Noel J. Coulson, *A History of Islamic Law* (Edinburgh: Edinburgh University Press, 1964), at pp. 11-13; Ignaz Goldziher, *Introduction to Islamic Theology and Law*, Andras and Ruth Hamori, trans. (Princeton, N.J.: Princeton University Press, 1981).

[10] In addition to Goldziher, cited above, examples of those who have contributed to this line of thought may include Richard Bell, who argued that much of the content of the Qur'an stemmed from ancient Christian narrative; Abraham Geiger, who pointed to the inter-relationship between certain Muslim scriptural themes and those of ancient Judaism; and John Wansbrough, who proposed that the materials underlying the system of Islamic law may have been the product of the coupling of a vast array of prior sources over a period of decades. *See* Richard Bell, *The Origin of Islam in its Christian Environment* (London: Routledge, 1968); Abraham Geiger, *Judaism and Islam*, F.M. Young, trans. (New York: Ktav Publishing House, 1970); John Wansbrough, *The*

foundational events giving rise to Islamic law, it appears difficult to deny that this ethical system has played a central role in the lives of Muslims, in some form, for most of the history of the religious movement associated with the Arab prophet Muhammad.

At the same time, whatever role Islamic law has played for Muslims throughout history, its appearance in the modern West has frequently proved controversial, often inciting challenge. It is the recognition of this challenge and the desire to identify a pathway for Muslims to move past such controversies that seemed to be at the heart of the thoughts of Muslim-American legal scholar Louay Safi when, in a 2004 speech, he offered these observations:

> *Fiqh* of minorities is a concept borne out of the needs of Western Muslims who want to ensure that they can apply the rules of *shari'ah* (Islamic law) in a predominately non-Muslim society. The notion itself underscores the new realization by an increasing number of Muslims that they cannot adhere to the same *fiqh* rules adopted by their co-religionists in Muslim societies.[11]

Safi's comments point to the perception among many Muslims living in the West that the demands of their faith tradition simply cannot be fully reconciled with the social expectations they shoulder by virtue of their presence within a predominantly secular environment.

The label "*fiqh* of minorities" is a term cultivated by modern Muslims. It broadly acknowledges the perceived conflict between Islamic religious norms and the expectations of secular society. It also points to an effort by some, such as Safi, designed to aid Muslims living in the West in overcoming this perceived conflict through a re-consideration of aspects of Islamic law. In particular, for those Muslims living in countries lacking specific accommodations for practitioners of Islam, the exercise of the faith may prove cumbersome and

---

Sectarian Milieu (Oxford: Oxford University Press, 1978); and Patricia Crone and Michael Cook, *Hagarism: The Making of the Islamic World* (Cambridge: Cambridge University Press, 1977).

[11] Louay Safi, "The Creative Mission of Muslim Minorities in the West," a paper presented at the Conference *Fiqh Today: Muslim as Minorities*, Westminister University, London, England, February 21, 2004.

practitioners may meet with identifiable uncertainties. The effort to develop a *fiqh* of minorities is typically rooted in an apparent willingness to re-assess the content and mode of implementation of Islamic ethical norms, with the aim of establishing a system that is more responsive to the practicalities of life for Muslims living in regions where they constitute only a minority. Yet, the very suggestion that Islamic law should or could be reformed, likewise, generates conflict within the Muslim community. For, if the affected ethical norms are understood to derive in pristine condition from the original revelations received by the prophet Muhammad and constitute an indispensable component of the larger Muslim system of faith, then how can they be tampered with? Moreover, by modifying aspects of this ideal system of religious practice, it may be argued, the very institution being protected winds up being emasculated.

The clash between Muslim ethical practice and secular law seems to affect principally religious adherents living in those regions where Islam represents only a minority faith and where other specific religious traditions (often Christianity) have tended to dominate the cultural landscape. In large measure, then, the countries of most obvious concern for the purposes of this analysis tend to be located in Western Europe and North America, though these are not the exclusive geographic regions of interest. Nevertheless, it is true, then, that this analysis will focus predominantly upon these regions, with the bulk of the analysis concerned with events in the United States.

The Employment of Islamic Law

As a tradition strongly embracing a detailed system of religious law, the Muslim faith has evolved as a rule-based religious methodology; and the adherence to its legal strictures has been viewed by many within the tradition as an essential ingredient in the practice of Islam, itself. Even today, in many parts of the world, the most vibrant dialogue within the Muslim community relates to the implementation and interpretation of Islamic law.

Part of the difficulty associated with any consideration of this topic as it affects the Muslim community is the very complicated nature of Islamic law itself. Even across the Muslim world, Islamic law is not employed evenly and its content is not wholly agreed upon. Depending upon whether the local government is secular, strictly Islamist, or somewhere in between, varying treatments of Islamic law may be witnessed.

According to U.S. government estimates, there are about 1.3 billion Muslims in the world.[12] From this group, the vast majority of about one billion live in forty-four predominantly Muslim countries around the world. Of these forty-four majority-Muslim nations, about ten identify themselves constitutionally as Islamic states, according to a 2005 report by the U.S. Commission on International Religious Freedom.[13] These countries, which tend to be located in the regions surrounding the Arabian Peninsula and extending into South Asia and Africa, typically recognize and employ, through the state judicial apparatus, some form of a system of Islamic law.

At the same time, twenty-two nations recognize some constitutional role for Islamic law.[14] Often, however, these provisions are limited to specific areas of law, such as standards relating to family relationships.

There are still other approaches to the recognition of Islamic law even within majority-Muslim states. In certain countries, specific aspects of the Islamic law system have been outlawed, perhaps, the most obvious example being polygamy. One country taking such a path is Tunisia and, as such, stands as an exemplar of those states employing what may be termed a redacted version of Islamic law. As well, even in certain of the predominantly Muslim countries, constitutions or other executive or legislative enactments identify the

---

[12] U.S. State Department Annual Report on International Religious Freedom (September 15, 2004), www.state.gov/g/drl/rls/irf/2004/ (accessed August 1, 2008).

[13] Tad Stahnke and Robert Blitt, *The Religion-State Relationship and the Right to Freedom of Religion or Belief: A Comparative Textual Analysis of the Constitutions of Predominantly Muslim Countries* (Washington D.C.: U.S. Commission on International Religious Freedom, March 2005). The ten countries that officially recognize themselves as Islamic states are Afghanistan, Bahrain, Brunei, Iran, Maldives, Mauritania, Pakistan, Qatar, Saudi Arabia and Yemen. Ibid., 9.

[14] Ibid. These countries are Afghanistan, Algeria, Bahrain, Comoros, Egypt, Gambia, Iraq, Iran, Jordan, Kuwait, Libya, Malaysia, Maldives, Mauritania, Oman, Pakistan, Qatar, Saudi Arabia, Sudan, Syria the United Arab Emirates and Yemen. Ibid.

states as officially secular. One example of such a country is Turkey. Yet, even within these countries, legal codes often bear evidence of influences stemming from Islamic law. Thus, Islamic law in such countries may become a sort of invisible partisan, affecting the content of legal codes even though it is not officially recognized.

Still others, such as Nigeria and India, allow Islamic law to be utilized in certain instances or in particular regions. Thus, Islamic law is recognized based upon local or personal circumstance. Often, however, in states such as India, Islamic law is interpreted and implemented by secular judges.

In other words, there is a sort of patchwork quilt of systems[15] employed around the globe focused upon the implementation of Islamic law. In some ways, this presents challenges for the Muslim practitioner. While traveling between even predominantly Muslim states, there may

---

[15] In a statement before the United States Senate Committee on the Judiciary, Dr. Khaled Abou El Fadl asserted that there have been four predominant strategies undertaken by majority Muslim countries in dealing with the question of the extent to which Islamic law should be incorporated into the broader codified legal structure of the country. The first of these he refers to as the "Strict-Separationist Model," wherein civil codes do not refer to or incorporate aspects of Islamic law. He includes Turkey, Mauritania and Albania as examples of countries following this tack. Secondly, there is the "Accommodationist Model," wherein Islamic law is generally excluded as a formal source of law, but certain aspects of the legal arena, most particularly with regard to family law issues, are left to be decided pursuant to Islamic law and often by Shari'a courts. Among the countries identified with this system are Syria, Algeria, Tunisia and Iraq. Third, is the "Integrationist Model," wherein efforts are made to incorporate aspects of Islamic law into the larger legal system of the country and Islamic law is specified as an official source of moral inspiration within the country's legal system. Countries following this path include Egypt, the United Arab Emirates, Kuwait, Oman and Pakistan. Fourth, is the "Requisitionist Model," wherein the state identifies the doctrinal requirements that it believes accurately reflect correct Islamic ritual and moral expectations and adopts and enforces this set of norms. The countries which are identified as followers of this model are Saudi Arabia and Iran. "Constitutionalism, Human Rights and the Rule of Law in Iraq," statement of Khaled Abou El Fadl, professor of law at UCLA, before the United States Senate Committee on the Judiciary, June 25, 2003.

be significant differences in the observed content and the method of application of Islamic law.

Even beyond these issues associated with the implementation of Islamic law, there is no universally recognized and consistent body of ethical norms that may be identified as Islamic law. There are at least four surviving schools of interpretive thought regarding Islamic law from within the Sunni movement alone, which are the Hanifi, Maliki, Shafi'i and Hanbali.[16] The dominant schools of thought in the Shia system are the Ja'faris and the Zaydis. Each of these systems interprets the ethical demands associated with Islamic law in different ways. The result is that, between these systems, there are certain disagreements concerning the precise obligations imposed upon Muslim practitioners. Still other schools of interpretive thought may be recognized from the past history of Muslim society.

Despite these complications, however, within specific jurisdictions, one may argue that there is typically established a reasonable expectation of the ethical and moral obligations that will be confronted by Muslim practitioners and enforced by religious and secular authority. And it is this recognizable system of religious and ethical norms that many Muslims often desire to maintain, even as they relocate from one political and social environment to another.

A second difficulty related to the application of Islamic law within the context of a Western setting is the expansive nature of this ethical system. Because provisions of the *shari'a* relate to many aspects of life typically left to secular political and judicial regimes in the West, ranging from marriage and divorce to contractual relationships, the intersection between these systems is rife with the potential for conflict. Muslims attempting to abide by norms understood to be an integral part of their religious system, may find that their actions are subject to challenge in the West precisely because there exists a legal code addressing, on secular terms, the same events and episodes of life. This potential for conflict has been felt by Muslims living in countries ranging from Europe to North America, and beyond.

---

[16] Ira M. Lapidu, *A History of Islamic Societies* (Cambridge: Cambridge University Press, 1988), 102-103.

American Muslims and Islamic Law

Based upon these preliminary observations, a picture emerges of Muslims facing significant hurdles as they attempt to practice their faith and conform to obligations imposed by the system of Islamic law, while living in countries such as the United States.[17] Not unlike the religious code of the Muslim faith, the secular legal system of the U.S. extends deep into the very fabric of daily life, making conflicts between the two systems inevitable. The main questions to be weighed here, then, concern the ways in which such conflicts manifest themselves in the lives of Muslims residing in the United States and whether there are avenues available through which these conflicts may be addressed or overcome. Put another way, how have American Muslims endeavored to negotiate their own attempt to be faithful to their religion even while adhering to an often-conflicting state regulatory scheme?

This inquiry necessarily raises a number of important sub-issues. Amongst these is whether it is possible to maintain allegiance to the demands of Islamic law and to a comprehensive secular legal code simultaneously. Also, does secular law, as constituted in the United States, inhibit free and full practice by Muslims of their personal faith? Finally, to the extent that American Muslims have modified their own practice to accommodate the demands of U.S. secular society, have their actions resulted in the establishment of a new brand of Islam, responsive to the popular Western expectations, but divergent from traditional ideals and norms?

There is a practical dimension to this set of questions that will be explored in this work. In particular, it is important to consider how and to what extent the religious practices of Muslims have been affected by the treatment their community has received. There is also an ethical dimension to this set of questions. In terms of the interaction between Muslims and Western institutions, it is important to ask whether these exchanges have been consistent with notions of justice. In other words, have Muslims been treated equitably?

---

[17] Since 1990, estimates of the number of Muslims residing in the United States has ranged from slightly over 1 million to about 8 million. See Karen Isaksen Leonard, *Muslims in the United States: The State of Research* (New York: Russell Sage Foundation, 2003), 4.

These questions will be entertained through the exploration of specific data. In particular, attention will be given to the inter-relationship between the American judiciary and American Muslims through examination of judicial decisions focused upon conflicts rooted in exchanges between the two legal systems. This relationship seems particularly important because it is the judiciary, as the enforcer of codified social norms in the U.S., which tends to play the most visible role in any challenge to the legitimacy of Muslim religious activity. As well, the response of Muslims living in the West, generally, and the U.S., in particular, to such perceived social conflicts will be considered. Such responses will be gleaned from varying sources produced by and for members of the Muslims community in the West, including interviews, magazine and journal articles and Internet resources. Finally, this work examines the responses of varying Western governments to situations of conflict pitting Muslim religious law against secular obligations by considering legal, governmental and popular sources, seeking to identify creative solutions. This work is divided into several sections, each delving into a particular aspect of this larger set of inquiries.

Inside the American Courtroom

The first major section of this work includes an examination of case decisions issued by U.S. courts that impinge upon public perceptions associated with the characterization of Muslims or Islamic religious law, itself. In relation to this investigation, it should be observed that U.S. courts are not required to enforce rights claimed under a foreign legal system, such as Islamic law, but there are instances when court officials may choose to entertain such claims of right.[18] Especially during recent decades, a substantial number of decisions rendered by varying U.S. state and federal courts have focused attention upon questions related to the claim of rights by parties pursuant to Islamic law, producing often conflicting results.

---

[18] See Hilton v. Guyot, 159 U.S. 113 (1894), pp. 163-64. The decision about whether to recognize a legal right of foreign origin depends upon the balancing of perceived international duty and the desire to maintain regularity within international law against the interests of citizens or those under the protection of U.S. laws. Ibid.

In many instances, courts have displayed great reluctance to enforce claims of right rooted in Islamic law. With regard to matters related to personal status, U.S. courts have frequently been willing to recognize rights and duties derived from Islamic law only where they are deemed consistent with "public interest." Thus, courts have refused to recognize unilateral divorces (*talaq*) awarded to parties by courts of other jurisdictions in compliance with Islamic law, arguing that these offend requirements of notice demanded by Western notions of justice.[19] Similarly, with regard to child custody, claims supported by principles of Islamic law are frequently dismissed when they are determined to be in conflict with the "best interests of the child."[20] Such reasoning can be witnessed even in the commercial arena.[21]

There are, meanwhile, many cases in which U.S. courts have enforced rights claimed under Islamic law. Often, at least on their face, these cases have presented factual situations that seem to offer striking similarities to those matters in which decisions have been rendered against the enforcement of Islamic law. In the end, due to this apparent contradictory treatment of Muslim litigants with regard to their claimed ethical and religious obligations, religious practitioners may often be left with significant uncertainties related to when and under what circumstances aspects of Islamic law may be recognized or enforced by U.S. courts.

As well, it may asked whether the availability of the U.S. secular court system as a potential vehicle for the resolution of disputes affects the manner in which Muslim religious leaders counsel their community members. Indeed, it is important to consider whether the dismissal of basic obligations and expectations rooted in Islamic law by courts on grounds of perceived conflict with American public policy priorities serves to diminish the authority of the religious system as a whole for its practitioners residing in the U.S.

---

[19] See Ali v. Ali, 279 N.J. Super. 154, 652 A.2d 253 (1994); Malik v. Malik, 182 Cal.App.3d 1018 (1986).

[20] Noordin v. Abdulla, 88 Wash.App. 746, 947 P.2d 745 (1997).

[21] Nakhleh v. Chemical Construction Co., 359 F.Supp. 357 (S.D.N.Y. 1973). In this contracts case arising in New York, where a litigant claimed rights under Islamic law principles recognized by the Saudi Arabian government, the court reasoned that regardless of the foreign validity of such law, no New York judge could enforce rights that violate the "public policy" of the state. Ibid.

At the same time, U.S. court decisions raise questions related to the manner in which Muslims are depicted and characterized. In effect, this analysis seeks to determine whether the courts have adopted language, rooted in apparent stereotype, which appears to affect negatively the broader image and self-identity of Muslims living in the U.S. In some respects, this analysis leans on earlier academic works which have asserted the existence of a broad Western effort to marginalize Muslims through the employment of slanted and biased stereotypes used to describe and "exoticize" members of this religious community and of the larger geographic region of the Middle East, as a whole. While this work does not presuppose the existence of an intentional effort on the part of the American judiciary to promote an agenda designed to marginalize Muslims, it does seek to question the manner in which Muslims as a group have been characterized.

The Self-Image of American Muslims

In addition to considering the manner in which U.S. courts have responded to matters involving Muslim litigants, it is important to explore the evolving self-perception of Islamic communities in the West. An important part of Muslim self-perception is rooted in the expectations of community members concerning their own relationship to the Islamic law system. This relationship will serve as a secondary focus of this analysis. Here, the question concerns the nature of the "Islamic law" that American Muslims believe should prevail in twenty-first century communities situated in Western democracies, like the United States. More particularly, are those classical moral understandings and religious norms routinely referred to as Islamic law, and arising predominantly from the cultural setting of Arabia, relevant to American Muslims?

These are important and controversial questions because they underscore the broad and burgeoning debate between Muslim liberals in the West and those embracing a more traditionalist approach. In a sense, the magnitude of this controversy may be glimpsed through a consideration of the range of positions taken by Muslims on this subject. For example, in a statement deemed controversial or perhaps even heretical by many Islamic traditionalists, at least one leading American Muslim has argued that Islamic law should be shaped broadly by its context. Speaking for a growing progressive Muslim community in the West, Khaled Abou El Fadl has asserted that the strength of the Islamic moral system lies in its adaptability to present circumstances.[22] Abou El Fadl perceives an undue rigidness in the decisions of Muslim jurists in some parts of the world. Thus, the application of Islamic legal decisions arising from contexts quite distinct from those prevailing in the U.S. should not be determinative for Muslims residing in this Western nation. Indeed, it has been argued, American Muslims are obliged by their religious tradition to respect U.S. law and social practice even when such adherence runs contrary to traditional religious expectations.

At the same time, the validity of Islamic law itself has been questioned, as it has come into conflict with broadly accepted Western ethical norms. Abdullahi Ahmed An-Na'im has observed that numerous Islamic law provisions contravene broadly accepted modern notions of universal human rights and, accordingly, the demand that such provisions be implemented in the West must be abandoned.[23] As well, there have been calls for the broad reinterpretation of Islamic law in an effort to incorporate basic values of gender equality.[24] While these may be singled out for special attention here, others in the liberal reformist camp may be viewed as desiring equally broad changes.[25] Such reformers seek to constrain the role of Islamic law in the lives of U.S. Muslims.

Conversely, the concern of traditionalists may well be summed up in the statement of one religious scholar who has observed, "Western-educated intellectual" Muslims have produced religious communities in the U.S. that are "devoid" of respect for or understanding of Islamic law or tradition.[26] Thus, others are pressing for the establishment of a

---

[22] "Conference of Books Revived," *The Minaret* (October 1996): 43-44.

[23] "Shari'a and Basic Human Rights," in *Liberal Islam*, Charles Kurzman, ed. (Oxford: Oxford University Press, 1998).

[24] See Mohommed A. Muqtedar Khan, *American Muslims: Bridging Faith and Freedom* (Beltsville, Md.: Amana Pub., 2002): 90-94.

[25] See generally Azzam Tamimi, "The Origins of Arab Secularism," in *Islam and Secularism in the Middle East*, John Esposito and Azzam Tamimi, eds. (New York: New York University Press, 2000). Tamimi points particularly to the writings of Ali Abdel Raziq and the community of his followers. Ibid., 25.

[26] Muhammad Khalid Masud, "The Obligation to Migrate: The Doctrine of Hijra in Islamic Law," in *Muslim Travelers*, Dale Eickleman and James Piscatori, eds. (Berkeley: University of California Press, 1990): 29-48. See

more traditional Muslim judicial system within the U.S., designed to preserve and promote long-held Islamic moral ideals.[27] And in the absence of a broad public platform for the consideration of claims rooted in Islamic law, systems of private Islamic justice have emerged with imams establishing "Islamic arbitration committees."[28] This work considers some of the ways in which individual Muslim leaders and local communities are attempting to address this collective controversy.

Undoubtedly, this debate will help define the manner in which Muslim communities of the West are shaped in the future and how they relate to secular groups and social institutions within the countries where they reside. As well, this debate may additionally affect the relations of Muslims in the West with their own brethren in the faith living in regions of world where Islam predominates.

Already, some scholars have suggested that American values and ideals have seeped deeply into the Islamic consciousness, influencing the community in many ways. It has been argued, for example, that American culture has served to influence everything from the design of Muslim mosques to worship preferences.[29] Thus, second generation American Muslims have displayed a preference for visiting the mosque on Sunday, rather than at the traditional Friday evening prayer service. This may be referred to as an "Americanization" of Islamic institutions in the U.S. Yet, while these influences have been documented, there has been no broad investigation of the impact of American culture

---

also Ali Asani, "On Pluralism, Intolerance and the Qur'an," *American Scholar* 71, No. 1 (Winter 2002): 52-60.

[27] There are at least three organized groups that appear to desire the establishment of formal *fiqh* councils in the United States. These are the Shari'a Scholars Association of North America, the Muslim Student Association and the Islamic Society of North America. The creation of one or more such councils would provide American Muslims with a venue to seek advice on the resolution of practical issues in a manner consistent with Islamic law principles. Perhaps, these councils will be structured to provide mediation or other more formal dispute resolution processes, as well.

[28] Leonard, *Muslims in the United States*, 99.

[29] Saba Mamood, "Modern Power and the Reconfiguration of Religious Tradition," Interview with Tala Asad, *Stanford Humanities Review* 5, no. 1 (1996), http://www.stanford.edu/group/SHR/5-1/text/asad.html (accessed May 22, 2009).

specifically upon Islamic law. The foundation for such an inquiry is laid here.

Through examination of practical responses by American Muslims to calls for adherence to Islamic law, this work seeks to identify instances where American social and cultural patterns appear to have potentially affected the shape of religious behavior and self-perception among Muslims living in the U.S. Still, this ethical and cultural analysis is not intended to serve as the foundation for a normative examination of the theological implications of insights gained. Indeed, while this work considers shifts in self-perception among Muslims, an investigation of variation in understandings related to the contours of religious belief, itself, is beyond the scope of this analysis.

A View from Abroad

Finally, the consideration of these associated issues prompts at least a limited exploration of the manner in which other Western governments, including European Union member countries and Canada,[30] treat conflicts rooted in Islamic law when they come before their own tribunals. Through this work, the experiences of Muslims functioning within the American social system will be considered alongside those of practitioners of the faith residing in other jurisdictions. Through this comparative analysis, information will be gleaned that may inform the practices of U.S. courts and offer guidance to Muslims residing in this country. This work asks, then, whether, in the response of other countries to such conflicts, there lie seeds of insight that may inform and offer alternative pathways to resolving conflicts as they arise in the U.S.

Ultimately, the issues raised by this work are potentially far more significant for American Muslims than may be ascertained by the consideration of any individual court decision, alone. It is hoped that the collective examination of this set of issues may offer insight into

---

[30] According to recent news reports, the government of the province of Ontario, Canada is considering whether to establish an arbitration system as part of the judiciary that will entertain cases involving civil disputes between Muslims. See "Shari'a Law," Transcript of BBC News Interview with Syed Mumtaz Ali (August 17, 2004), http://news.bbc.co.uk/1/hi/programmes/ breakfast_with_ frost/3574040.stm (accessed August 12, 2007).

the future of the growing community of American-Muslims. This analysis should shed some light upon the future of the evolving self-perception of American-Muslims and the manner in which such Islamic worshippers may relate to sister communities scattered across the globe. Further, these issues may become more important when viewed in light of the potential long-term global influence of the American-Muslim community. For, while this community may be relatively small in terms of its present numbers, its global influence may well be much greater than such numbers would suggest based upon growth trends in the community and its access to Western media and avenues of communication.

Thus, it is expected that the conclusions drawn here may not be relevant merely to the American-Muslim community. Instead, the long-term impact of challenges to Islamic law and changes related its interpretation and the manner in which it is applied may well affect Muslims across the globe and the experience of other religious minority communities in the U.S. in the future. At the very least, the debates hatched within the United States by Muslims on topics related to the employment of Islamic law may prompt some global conversation within the larger Islamic community. In some respects, then, it is expected and hoped that this work will contribute to this conversation.

CHAPTER 1

Orientalisms In Practice

> *While social forces in Europe may alienate Muslims, it is political forces in the United States that repel many. Although the vast majority of American Muslims do not live in economically depressed physical ghettos, many live in a psychological ghetto caused by the lack of acceptance they feel from their neighbors and colleagues, especially in the post-September 11 era. This psychological ghetto may prove the largest challenge in the war on terrorism.*
>
> *Those of the ghetto mentality experience a kind of self-righteous schizophrenia. Outside home and the mosque, they abide by the rules and work for their economic improvement. But elsewhere they fall prey to the extremist recruiters who present no more than a forgery of Islam.*[31]

It is likely that not all Muslims living in the United States would recognize the dire picture painted by Al-Marayati of psychological ghettos and religious estrangement. Still, his dramatic observations serve as a reminder that at least some Muslims living in the West feel alienated from and, perhaps, even ostracized by the culture that

---

[31] Salam Al-Marayati, "America's Muslim Ghettos," *The Washington Post* (August 15, 2005): A15.

surrounds them. To what extent may we find evidence for the marginalization of Muslim culture in the West and, if it exists, who are the culprits?

Following the events of September 11, 2001, it may be argued that those attempting to embrace and balance the often competing identities of Muslim and American are under greater strain than ever before. Yet, while recent events have served to heighten the social pressures felt by American-Muslims, it is worthwhile to recognize that these strains are not entirely new. What is the image of the Muslim in America held by average Americans?[32] How and when was this image cultivated? These are questions of significant import, and they are not easily resolved. Still, in an effort to offer some meaningful response to them, it seems useful to consider the nature of the broader relationship between the Muslim community and the United States and how it has evolved over the course of time.

Images: Traditional and Modern

U.S. Navy Rear Admiral Alfred Theyer Mahan is broadly credited with inventing the term "Middle East." He is said to have coined the term in

---

[32] Public opinion polls would seem to suggest that a significant numer of Americans hold unfavorable opinions of both individual Muslims and Muslim majority nations. A 2007 Pew study indicated that about 43 percent of Americans held positive impressions of Muslims, while 35 percent held unfavorable impressions. The percentages of those holding unfavorable impressions of Muslims was decidedly higher for those over the age of 65, those having no more than a high school education, those who described themselves as "conservative," and those described as Protestant "evangelicals." See "Public Expresses Mixed Views of Islam, Mormonism," from the website of the Pew Forum on Religion and Public Life (Sept. 25, 2007), http://pewforum.org/surveys/religionviews07 (accessed June 5, 2009). At the same time, some 46 percent of Americans were said to have an unfavorable opinion of Muslims countries. See "Poll: Few Americans have Favorable View of the Muslim World," from the website of CNN News (June 2, 2009), http://www.cnn.com/2009/POLITICS/06/02/us.muslims.poll/ (accessed June 2, 2009).

an article which appeared in the *National Review* in 1902.[33] Since that time, the term has generally been understood to refer to a region stretching from Western North Africa, through Egypt, into the Arabian Peninsula and extending north into Syria and even Turkey. And the people of this region tend to be identified as part of the larger global culture of the "Orient."

In his recent volume entitled *Power, Faith and Fantasy: America in the Middle East 1776 to Present*,[34] Michael Oren argues that Western political policy makers and social leaders have historically characterized this region as being:

> …unified by a distinct civilization, typified by unique modes of government, social structure, architecture and dress. Its inhabitants, known to Westerners by an assortment of interchangeable names – Arabs, Levantines, Algerines, Moors and Turks – were presumed to be hostile to foreigners and spoke languages grating to the Western ear.[35]

The most distinctive characteristic of the people of this region is their religion, according to Oren, that being Islam. In the end, he describes Muslim Arabia as an "amorphous primitive civilization" and as the "ultimate other" in the eyes of eighteenth and nineteenth century Americans.[36]

Scholar Robert Irwin has argued that a popularized stereotypical view of Muslims in the United States was purposefully cultivated beginning sometime during the decade of the 1930s. Through an influx of European-educated academic elites, certain ideas associated with the "Orient" began to take root and sprout in America. Among this group of transplanted scholars was Gustave E. von Grunebaum, Hamilton Gibb, Franz Rosenthal, Bernard Lewis and Joseph Schacht.[37] Referring

---

[33] Roger Adelson, *London and the Invention of the Middle East: Money, Power, and War, 1902-1922*, (New Haven: Yale University Press, 1995), 22-23.

[34] (New York: W.W. Norton & Co., 2007).

[35] Ibid., 41.

[36] Ibid., 42.

[37] See Robert Irwin, *Dangerous Knowledge: Orientalism and its Discontents* (New York: Overlook Press, 2006), 245-246.

specifically to the writings of von Grunebaum, Irwin summarizes what he perceives to be a set of central themes that marked the images of Muslims cultivated in such works:

> Islam was a mimetic civilization, compounded of borrowings from other cultures and incapable of independent innovation. Its copycat civilization reached its peak under the Abbasids in the ninth century, but thereafter it was doomed to stagnate, as Muslims were constrained by the intransigence of the Qur'anic revelation and doomed by their religion's fatalism.... In general, he envisaged Islamic civilization as being defined by prohibitions, omissions and absences – no pork, no figurative art, no drama, no objective studying of other cultures and so forth and so on.[38]

If such images are among those that marked the evolving popular impression associated with the Muslim community that has dominated in this country for roughly the past century, the broad question, then, may be the extent to which this portrait has changed in the more recent past. This, of course, is a multifaceted inquiry and one well beyond the scope of a single work, such as this. Still, there are aspects of this inquiry that may be approached reasonably for the purpose of laying a foundation for broader conclusions.

The Birth of "Orientalism"

In some measure, perhaps, the broad examination undertaken here may be recognizable, at least in part, because of the earlier research of the late scholar Edward Said. Since it was first published in 1979, Said's best-known work, *Orientalism,*[39] along with subsequent works that have expanded his original themes,[40] have prompted a re-examination of Western attitudes, impressions and "stereotypes" related to the

[38] Ibid., 246-247.

[39] (New York: Vintage Books, 1978).

[40] Perhaps, the most notable additional works of Said in this regard are *Covering Islam* (New York: Vintage Books, 1997) and *Culture and Imperialism* (New York: Vintage Books, 1994).

predominant religious and social cultures of the Arabian Peninsula, North Africa and the Eastern Mediterranean region.

Said was not without his critics and it must be recognized that many of his individual claims have been effectively countered by subsequent scholars.[41] Still, his broad thesis seems to have provoked a vast array of additional research aimed at reconsidering the image of the Muslim community. At its heart, Said's work claimed that a stereotypical vision of varying Eastern cultures, but most particularly Muslim society, had become firmly rooted in the collective Western psyche, a product, in part, of the scholarship and writings of Western authors. This portrait depicted such "Orientals" as vengeful, suspicious, shallow, irrational, discriminatory, cruel and untrustworthy, according to Said. Moreover, the image was static, taking little account of transformations shaping and re-shaping the identified communities or of the great diversity that marks the varying sub-cultures represented within the vast region colored by such skewed images. As Said observed regarding these images:

> To speak of Orientalism therefore is to speak mainly, although not exclusively, of a British and French cultural enterprise, a project whose dimensions take in such disparate realms as the imagination itself, the whole of India and the Levant, the

---

[41] Perhaps, the most charged and broad assault upon the ideas cultivated in Said's work Orientalism have come in the recent volume by Ibn Warraq, *Defending the West: A Critique of Edward Said's Orientalism* (New York: Prometheus Books, 2007). In the volume, Ibn Warraq criticizes Said's methodology, his logical reasoning and even his ability to read and interpret history accurately. He makes the further charge that Said likely willingly and purposefully misrepresented Western intents and culture. He likewise suggests that the long-term impact of Said's hypothesis has been corrosive in terms of the Western understanding of Islam and the Middle East. See Malcolm H. Kerr, "Review of 'Orientalism'," *International Journal of Middle Eastern Studies*, Vol. 12, No. 4 (1980): 544-47; Jane Miller, *Seductions: Studies in Reading and Culture*, (London: Virago,1990); Reina Lewis, *Gendering Orientalism: Race, Femininity and Representation*, (New York: Routledge, 1995); Bill Ashcroft and Pal Ahluwaila, *Edward Said: The Paradox of Identity*, (London: Routledge, 1999); and Robert Irwin, "Oriental Discourses in Orientalism," *Middle Eastern Lectures*, Vol. 3 (1999): 87-110.

> Biblical texts and the Biblical lands, the spice trade, colonial armies and a long tradition of colonial administrators, a formidable scholarly corpus, innumerable Oriental "experts" and "hands", an Oriental professorate, a complex array of "Oriental" ideas (Oriental despotism, Oriental splendor, cruelty, sensuality), many Eastern sects, philosophies, and wisdoms domesticated for local European use the list can be extended more or less indefinitely.[42]

The myth of the untrustworthy Oriental, would become accepted as a reality in the West, according to Said. In effect, then, Said claimed that the Orientalists, who have made it their duty to study and comment upon the cultures of the Near East, Africa and Asia, have drawn an imaginary line of demarcation between the East and the West. That line highlights the stark contrasts that differentiate these cultures. This exercise in cultural segregation has generated, within the larger Western collective psyche, an image of the Oriental as untrustworthy, irrational and erratic.

For Said, the greatest culprits in this Orientalist campaign to mold and shape broader images of Eastern cultures were Western scholars, political institutions and the media, which have acted with the encouragement of the institutional Christian community. The cultivation of such broad-scale misrepresentations of a large grouping of cultures was possible, according to Said, only because of the political and militaristic dominance of Europe over the Middle East and Asia. Indeed, it is Europeans who become the true target of Said's original thesis, with particular emphasis placed upon the role played by the English and French. Again, as Said argued:

> Unlike the Americans, the French and British--less so the Germans, Russians, Spanish, Portuguese, Italians, and Swiss--have had a long tradition of what I shall be calling Orientalism, a way of coming to terms with the Orient that is based on the Orient's special place in European Western Experience....[43]

---

[42] Said, *Orientalism*, 4.

[43] Ibid., 2.

In noting the role of Christian-oriented religious institutions in this Orientalist campaign, Said further observed:

> This rigorous Christian picture of Islam was intensified in innumerable ways, including during the Middle Ages and early Renaissance a large variety of poetry, learned controversy, and popular superstition. By this time the Near Orient had been all but incorporated in the common world-picture of Latin Christianity as in the *Chanson de Roland* the worship of Saracens is portrayed as embracing Mahomet *and* Apollo. By the middle of the fifteenth century, as R. W. Southern has brilliantly shown, it became apparent to serious European thinkers "that something would have to be done about Islam," which had turned the situation around somewhat by itself arriving militarily in Eastern Europe.[44]

So, if it is present, just how deeply does this Orientalist image reach into the history of Western civilization? The answer to this may well depend upon whom one asks. As is noted above, not every member of the scholarly community is convinced that such biases have been perpetuated on the level implied by Said. Further, there are certainly those who would strongly resist the notion that, if there has been bias, it has been rooted in an intentional campaign against the Muslim community or that any affects of incidental bias are as significant as may be suggested. Still, even among non-Muslim Western scholars, there is a persistent belief that Orientalism is very real and runs rather deep in our collective history. As the Swiss writer Roger Du Pasquier has asserted:

> The West, whether Christian or de-Christianised, has never really known Islam. Ever since they watched it appear on the world stage, Christians never ceased to insult and slander it in order to find justification for waging war on it. It has been subjected to grotesque distortions the traces of which still endure in the European mind. Even today there are many Westerners for whom Islam can be reduced to three ideas: fanaticism, fatalism and polygamy. Of course, there does

---

[44] Ibid., 61.

> exist a more cultivated public whose ideas about Islam are less deformed; there are still precious few who know that the word *Islam* signifies nothing other than 'submission to God'. One symptom of this ignorance is the fact that in the imagination of most Europeans, *Allah* refers to the divinity of the Muslims, not the God of the Christians and Jews; they are all surprised to hear, when one takes the trouble to explain things to them, that '*Allah*' means 'God', and that even Arab Christians know him by no other name.[45]

It is interesting to note that while Said, within the volume *Orientalism*, did not directly identify the United States as a central player in the process of crafting this Orientalist image of subject cultures, certainly it is impossible to discount the deep cultural interaction between the communities of Europe and North America and their influence upon one another. Accordingly, it must be imagined that, in large measure, a significant commonality of perspective exists between these cultures in the modern era. Further, if there is such a biased perception of Muslims among Europeans, then this perspective is certain to have permeated North American consciousness, as well. And, of course, in Said's subsequent volume *Covering Islam*, readers are introduced to the proposition that the North American community is not exempt from his larger criticism.

In one of his most controversial claims, Said argued that, the broad collective effort to divide the Orient from the Occident served to reinforce and expand the globally dominant position of Western culture. In effect, Western society has attempted to cultivate a positive self-portrait precisely by cultivating a list of negative qualities of the "Orient," whether real or imagined, and by distinguishing its own perceived characteristics from them. Thus, whether intentional or not, the efforts of Orientalists to isolate and reduce the image of the Oriental to a set of unalterable traits standing in direct contradiction to those of Western society, in the opinion of Said, served also to diminish the global political and economic positions of the groups falling into this broad definitional category.

While Said may not always ascribe an overt malicious motive to those Westerners whom he believes have worked together to cultivate

[45] *Unveiling Islam* (Cambridge: Islamic Texts Society, 1992), 5-7.

this erroneous and damaging, albeit convenient, caricature of Muslims and Arabs, he does seek to quantify the negative results of such efforts, which amount to a preservation of Western cultural and political dominance.[46] Again, not all scholars accept the conclusions of Said, though even many of his critics acknowledge a peculiarity in the popular depiction of Muslims.

Thus, even many of those who have challenged certain of his conclusions or his methodology have not gone so far as to wholly deny the existence within Western culture of a biased or negative set of stereotypes that affect public perspectives associated with Islam. Robert Irwin, while seeking to expose some of the errors he attributes to Said, devotes significant attention to the rather charged images that he admits have been associated with Arabs and Muslims in the West. While their roots may have sprouted as early as the birth of Islam as a religious institution and its initial encounters with Christendom, such stereotypes coalesced into something that might be termed "Orientalism" as early as the 16th century. As Irwin, Said's critic, writes:

> ...[T]here was nobody one could consider to be a serious Orientalist prior to Guillaume Postel (c. 1510-81), and that Orientalism either begins in the sixteenth century with him or, if not quite so early as that, then no later than the early seventeenth century, when Jacob Golius (1596-1667) and Edward Pococke (1604-91), as well as other not quite so

---

[46] See generally Matthew Olmstead, "Are things Falling Apart? Rethinking the purpose and Function of International Law," 27 *Loyola of Los Angeles International & Comparative Law Review* 401 (Summer 2005), 408, where the author argues: "At its core, Orientalism is about cultural dominance. Through the analysis of texts by various Western authors, Said shows how Western culture has sought over time to represent and dominate its "others" in a way that has allowed it to maintain a superior self-image. In its material manifestation, Said defines Orientalism as "the corporate institution for dealing with the Orient - dealing with it by making statements about it, authorizing views of it, describing it, by teaching it, settling it, ruling over it: in short, Orientalism as a Western style of dominating, restructuring, and having authority over the Orient." Ibid.

learned or industrious figures, published their ground-breaking researches.[47]

In other words, despite even his own critique of Said, Irwin acknowledges the existence of a community of influential Orientalist thinkers in the West. To the degree that damaging stereotypes of Muslim culture prevail in the West, the question raised here is the extent to which these images have been cultivated in North America and, particularly within governmental institutions, including the judiciary.

Orientalism in the 21st Century

What, if any evidence, may be found of continued Orientalist influences at work within the cultural landscape of modern America? In responding to this question, it seems useful to consider voices from inside and outside the Muslim community itself concerning the presence of recognizable biases or Orientalist tendencies at work in the broader American social arena.

This examination may begin in the political sphere. Evidence of an Orientalist-type bias may be found within responses to a range of public and foreign policy issues that have confronted the United States during recent decades, according to scholar Douglas Little. Arguing in a recent volume entitled *American Orientalism: The United States and the Middle East Since 1945*,[48] Little blames Orientalist biases for failings with regard to many major foreign policy endeavors of the past several decades, though the foundations for such disappointments were laid much earlier. As evidence of an early popularized Orientalism taking root in the United States, he turns to, among other sources, Mark Twain who, in his widely-read travel narrative *Innocents Abroad*, described Muslims as "a people by nature and training filthy, brutish, ignorant, unprogressive [and] superstitious."[49]

According to Little, it was suspicion of Egypt, rooted in Orientalist assumptions, that led the U.S. to distance itself from the country during the emergence of the Arab nationalist movement under Gamal Abdel

---

[47] Irwin, *Dangerous Knowledge*, 6-7.

[48] (Chapel Hill: University of North Carolina Press, 2002).

[49] Ibid., 13.

Nasser. This policy of distance provided an opening for the Soviet Union to build significant political alliances in Egypt and the broader region, prompting expansion of the Cold War. It was Orientalist tendencies, as well, that prompted the U.S. to fight revolutionary inclinations in Iran, Iraq and Lybia, by propping up traditional regimes. This, like the policy with regard to Egypt, led the U.S. to lose significant influence within these countries and the larger region, as these regimes were replaced.

Little carries his thesis into the post-September 11 environment, suggesting that it was Orientalist misinterpretations that led the Bush administration to pursue a policy goal of democratizing the Middle East and launching a military campaign in Iraq. He intimates that this policy was destined to fail precisely because it overlooked the broad complexity of the Middle East region. In the end, he argues, despite these political setbacks, Americans have failed to fully internalize the lessons of such experiences and they continue to embrace many Orientalist misimpressions. As he observes:

> Although there is greater appreciation for the complexities of the Muslim world than a generation ago, most Americans still view radical Islam as a cause for instant alarm. Having been fed a steady diet of books, films, and news reports depicting Arabs as demonic anti-Western *others* and Israelis as heroic pro-Western partners and having watched in horror the events of 11 September 2001, the American public understandably fears Osama bin Laden and cheers Aladdin.[50]

Mimicking in some ways the arguments of Little, a recent editorial in the online journal *American Chronicle* argues that it was the work of specific Orientalists, including Bernard Lewis, that laid a foundation for the broader public embrace of military action in Iraq and the cultivation of the idea that America could, in some manner, re-chart the very destiny of the region of the Middle East.[51] The misrepresentations

---

[50] Ibid., 3.

[51] "Preface to Orientalism," *American Chronicle* (November 17, 2007), http://www.americanchronicle.com/articles/viewArticle.asp?articleID=34993 (accessed November 17, 2007).

of this region, the article suggests, are pervasive. As the unnamed commentator suggests:

> Today bookstores in the US are filled with shabby screeds bearing screaming headlines about Islam and terror, Islam exposed, the Arab threat and the Muslim menace, all of them written by political polemicists pretending to have knowledge imparted to them and others by experts who have supposedly penetrated to the heart of these strange Oriental peoples.[52]

The editorial goes on to argue that such sustained misrepresentations lead, ultimately, to an estrangement of societies resulting in undue perceptions of distinction on one side and anger and resentment on the other.

The concern that Orientalist-style misinterpretations of Muslim culture may generate strongly negative reactions is underscored by others. In a recent article from *New Internationalist* magazine, it is argued that stereotype and misrepresentation of Muslim society has helped fuel both "Islamophobia" in the U.S., as well as religious extremism abroad.[53] Noting that such misrepresentations affect not just political radicals, but also become internalized even by well-intentioned members of the public, the article suggests that the breadth of relationships between the U.S. and the Muslim world has been affected. The result has not been merely the cultivation of a skewed picture of Muslims in the West, but also the prompting of reactions by members of the Islamic community that have widened and deepened divisions between the societies. As the author observes:

> But in recent years Orientalism has become an even greater problem. It has become the scapegoat, the shield and sword of Muslims themselves. Among Muslims the existence of Orientalism has become the justification for every sense of grievance, a source of encouragement for nostalgic romanticism about the perfections of Muslim civilization in

---

[52] Ibid.

[53] Merryl Wyn Davies, "Wilful Imaginings: Merryl Wyn Davies Shows how Orientalism Feeds both Islamophobia and Muslim Fundamentalism," *New Internationalist*, no. 345 (May 12, 2002): 22-24.

> history and hence a recruiting agent for a wide variety of Islamic movements. It has generated a sense of exclusivity, of being apart and different within Muslim communities and societies that has no precedent either in Islam as religion or Muslim history.[54]

Orientalist-style misrepresentations of Muslim culture, it is argued, have driven the community to become "reactive" and immersed in an "addiction to a culture of complain and blame," which prompts greater feelings of powerlessness and an increased desires to strike back. Orientalism has turned Muslim culture into the "dark alter ego" of Western civilization. The curiosity, however, is that neither the West nor Muslim society would exist, as we now know them, without the contributions of the other. This latter fact tends to be omitted from the highly charged confrontations between the communities.

In the text of a speech delivered to the annual meeting of the Middle East Studies Association in 1997, years prior to the events of September 11, 2001, a similar sort of concern was expressed by scholar and Fulbright Fellow Abdallah Laroui. Laroui argued that the ideals that undergird both Orientalism and Muslim extremism have much in common in terms of their sources of origin and the processes they employ. Further, these common approaches, he argued, serve to fuel the anxieties of the other.[55]

> Orientalism is Western when it takes the West not as an event, but as an idea preordained in all eternity, complete and final from the beginning. And if it starts from this point, it has to construct its subject-matter as an explicitly, totally different item, reduced to the form it had at its birth. The two assumptions are clearly related; if the West is a fulfilled promise, the non-West has to be unfulfilled since unannounced.[56]

---

[54] Ibid., 23.

[55] "Western Orientalism and Liberal Islam: Mutual Distrust? *Middle East Studies Association Bulletin,* 31, no. 1 (July 1997): 3-10.

[56] Ibid., 6.

The end result of such efforts to differentiate is the fueling of an ongoing polemic debate in which both sides resort to the use of subjective and opportunistic characterizations of one another. And while he suggests that the American academy is better at disguising its efforts than the collective of Muslim extremist thinkers, such polemic qualities can be detected in the works of both communities.

Muslim Voices

In many ways, this analysis has as much to do with perception as reality, to the extent that there is a difference between the two. In that regard, it is important to poll not just the community of scholars, but also Muslims themselves. To what extent do Muslims living in the West perceive that they are the victims of Orientalist characterizations?

If Davies is correct in her assessment that misrepresentations of Muslim culture prompt a strong sense of grievance, one would suspect that the charges of Oriental bias would be broadly aired in the United States by members of the Muslim community. Instead, one finds charges of Oriental bias, but they are not as wide-spread as one might suspect. What are Muslim community members saying?

Though the voices may not be as numerous as might be expected, there is reflected within the Muslim community a detectable sense of anxiety and frustration regarding what is understood to be a popular bias in the West directed at Islam. This perceived bias may be reflected in many places. As Muqtedar Khan, a Muslim scholar living in the United States and Visiting Fellow at the Brookings Institute's Saban Center for Middle East Policy, expressed in an online column:

> There is now in America more room for bigotry and intolerance to thrive. The search for security at any cost has created an environment that is emboldening Islamophobia – a nasty cousin of anti-Semitism – to manifest itself in nearly every sphere of American society. Muslims are feeling discrimination and demonization and experiencing a palpable sense of alienation in schools, universities, in the workplace, and most severely on the information highways – radio, TV, and the internet.
>
> Last week, I noticed a really offensive bumper sticker on a car in front of me. It said, "Kill them all, Let Allah sort

> them out." This was especially shocking to me. I have worked night and day to advance a moderate vision of Islam, provided a scathing criticism of Islamic extremism, and worked to develop common ground for inter-faith and inter-civilizational understanding.[57]

Khan goes on to blame evangelical Christian groups for stoking the fires of bias, citing in particular the words of the Reverends Jerry Falwell, Pat Robertson and Franklin Graham. Still, he does not end his list here, but also turns attention to certain political figures, as well. At the same time, he argues that many Christian groups are warming to the advantages of serious Christian-Muslim dialogue and expressed hope for a stronger inter-relationship between the religious communities.

Though always present, social biases directed at the Muslim community in the West are not always evenly applied, it is argued. Within the broader sphere of what may be termed Oriental bias are both blatant and purposeful mischaracterizations, as well as subtle and unintentional error. Yet, all of these contribute to the same ultimate consequence for Muslims. As has been argued by one Muslim commentator:

> Certainly, not all Western writings on Islam have the same degree of bias. They run the range from willful distortion to simple ignorance and there are even a few that could be classified as sincere efforts by non-Muslims to portray Islam in a positive light. However, even most of these works are plagued by seemingly unintentional errors, however minor, due to the author's lack of Islamic knowledge. In the spirit of fairness, it should be said that even some contemporary books on Islam by Muslim authors suffer from these same shortcomings, usually due to a lack of knowledge, heretical ideas and or depending on non-Muslim sources.[58]

---

[57] "The Public Face of Evangelical Christian Bigotry," Published on the website GlocalEye.org (May 25, 2003), http://www.glocaleye.org/bigotry2.htm (accessed October 16, 2007).

[58] Abû Imân ᶜAbd al-Rahmân Robert Squires, "Orientalism, Misinformation and Islam," Published on the website Islamic-Awareness.org,

Curiously, at least one observer has argued that, while Orientalist bias may be perceived as broadly affecting Muslims across American society, certain community sub-groups face special difficulties stemming from such prejudice.[59] In particular, a specific form of Orientalist bias has affected the black community in the United States. This bias, it is suggested, has led to discrimination and ostracism directed against black Muslims by others within the larger black community. According to this critique, the Arab Muslim community has been portrayed as possessing an anti-black predisposition. In effect, despite their own experience of religious discrimination, Arab Muslims have served to perpetuate racial discrimination against the black community. Thus, by embracing the religious system of the Arab Muslim, a member of the black-American community commits effective "racial apostasy," it is argued. As the author argues:

> Its ultimate aim is to challenge, if not undermine, the propriety of the esteem enjoyed by Islam in the Black-American community by projecting onto the Muslim world a set of imaginings, self-perceptions, resentments, and stereotypes that are far more the product of the black experience in America than they are of any direct relationship with or knowledge of Islam, especially in the Muslim world. By highlighting the purported historical race prejudice of the Muslim world, as well as, in some instances, the alleged responses to this prejudice, the aim is to impugn the propriety of the relationship between Islam and Black-Americans by ultimately calling into question Black-American Muslims' status as authentic, loyal Black-Americans.[60]

In the end, it may be argued that Orientalism has played a significant role in the distortion of popular understandings associated

---

http://www.islamic-awareness.org/Quran/orientalism.html (accessed October 12, 2008).

[59] "Islam and the Black American: Black Orientalists" *Islamica Magazine* 20 (online) http://www.islamicamagazine.com/Issue-14/Islam-&-the-Black-American-Black-Orientalists/Page-3.html (accessed August 20, 2007).

[60] Ibid., 3.

with the nature of Islam and its practitioners. Yet, it may not be the Muslim community alone that is affected by this process. Indeed, it has been asserted that through the process of drawing distinction, the popular identity of the non-Muslim is affected just as is the Muslim. This, at least, is the position argued by one Muslim scholar living in the West.

Muhammad Shamsaddin Megalommatis has argued that an ongoing Orientalist campaign to distinguish Muslims from others living in the West has led to the solidification of deep-seated misunderstandings and apprehensions. These distortions have laid the foundation for the sprouting of the mistrust and fear that have come to dominate the relations between Muslims in the West and their non-Muslims neighbors. Yet, it is the West, alone, that is in a position to rectify this imbalance and conflict. This is because, as Megalomatis asserts, no infrastructure currently exists within the Muslim world that would permit it to examine issues of self-identity objectively. In other words, there does not exist a social infrastructure of sufficient breadth within the Muslims community of the West that is capable of facilitating a community-wide response to such concerns. The weakened state of the Muslim social community is a result, at least in part of the colonial legacy, it is argued. As Megalomatis observes:

> The identification of these two worlds, conventionally called 'Muslims' and 'Westerners', is erroneous; both worlds are equidistant from Truth as regards their identity, nature, character, deeds and pending consequences. The very serious point is however that this issue is not primarily an Identity issue. That is why the attempt of 'Western' rationalists trying to place a kind of equilibrium and symmetry in the approach to the two worlds – that would superficially make the approach appear impartial and just – is not correct, and apparently does not work. The sooner some 'Westerners' realize this, the better for them; and no one should expect the 'altera pars', namely the 'Muslims', to understand that there is

> an Identity issue for them. Preponderantly, this issue is an Existence issue.[61]

In considering this same divide, scholar Andrew Rotter has observed that Orientalist bias, finally, exists as a reflection of Western communal fears. While arguing that Said's observations have affected the manner in which Western diplomats interpret relations between the region they represent and the Muslim community, Rotter notes:

> Even as Said insists that Western scholars take others seriously, his analysis in *Orientalism* reminds us that our others are to a large extent reflections of ourselves. We project onto others our hopes and fears; others become repositories of characteristics we cannot abide in ourselves because they are shameful or revolting. This suggests, ironically, that the new internationalism in diplomatic history must be predicated on a closer examination of who we are, as Westerners and Americans.[62]

Legal Orientalisms

Based upon the work of the authors cited above, it seems that a significant body of both Western Muslim thinkers and U.S. scholars from varying disciplines believe that stereotype and bias, which may be termed "Orientalist" in nature, has broadly affected the position and experience of Muslims living in America. The question that may be asked further is whether specific evidence of such bias can be identified within the American legal system.

In subsequent chapters, this work turns to specific examples drawn from the work of U.S. courts. At present, however, it is worth considering the thoughts on this subject from a Muslim living in the United States. Mohammad Fadel has specifically argued that such bias may be glimpsed within the ostensibly objective U.S. halls of justice.

---

[61] "The Impossibility of Muslims' Integration in Europe," *American Chronicle* (August 13, 2007), http://www.americanchronicle.com/ articles/ view Article.asp?articleID=34993 (accessed September 8, 2007).

[62] "Saidism Without Said: Orientalism and U.S. Diplomatic History," *American Historical Review* 105, no. 4 (October 2000): 1-25, 25.

Armed with a few isolated case examples, including one judgment reported in the *New York Times* in which a woman sought a divorce on the grounds of physical abuse leading the judge to observe that the "Koran… sanctions such physical abuse," Fadel argues that Orientalist bias frequently taints the consideration of matters related to Muslim litigants. As he argues, judges have permitted "exotic stereotypes of the 'otherness' of Islamic law" to lead them to render what he describes as "astonishing results."[63] A perplexed Fadel laments, U.S. judges, when faced with the opportunity to rule on matters related to Islamic law, have tended to either ignore "cavalierly" the Muslim legal system or to interpret it in a manner that is drastically inconsistent with its spirit.

> That Orientalism should continue to flourish in the legal system, however, is profoundly disturbing to me, both on a personal level in terms of my commitments to contributing to the development of Islamic law so that it can play a positive role as constituent element within the global legal system, and on a professional level by evidencing the utter failure of the judge to take the legal principle of comity — a doctrine that lay at the heart of this decision and remains an important and legitimate concept within private international law — seriously when it comes to issues dealing with Islamic law.[64]

In part, Fadel argues that courts, in analyzing Islamic law, have tended to approach it as being fundamentally in opposition to the ideals underpinning U.S. law. As he argues, Islamic law and U.S. law are represented as if they "exist in alternate universes."

Pointing to the case of *National Group for Communications and Computers Ltd. v. Lucent Technologies International Inc.*,[65] in which a contractual arrangement that presumably would have been upheld based upon U.S. law was stricken down based upon a curious

---

[63] Mohammad Fadel, "The German Judge and Legal Orientalism," the website of Muslims for Progressive Values (March 27, 2007), www.progressiveislam.org/german_judge_and_legal_orientalism (accessed September 6, 2007).

[64] Ibid.

[65] 331 F.Supp.2d 290 (Dist. Ct. N.J. 2004).

interpretation of Islamic law, Fadel argues that judges in the U.S. frequently misapply Islamic law in a manner that serves to reinforce negative stereotypes. In effect, then, the erroneous application of Islamic law by U.S. courts has often served to produce results that violate basic notions of justice. In such instances, the underlying commonalities between the systems may be ignored. As Fadel continues:

> Going back to the doctrine of comity and legal orientalism, comity ought to be the ideal antidote for legal orientalism. Comity is grounded in the notion that jurisdictions ought to give effect to the law of other jurisdictions when the interests of that other jurisdiction predominate over the interests of the tribunal's jurisdiction. In short, it is a principle of neighborliness. For comity to work, however, the tribunal applying foreign law must treat the law of the foreign jurisdiction with a spirit of respect, certainly not one of condescension. In fact, judges, when applying the doctrine of comity, are required explicitly to engage in an act of empathy with the laws of the other legal system by taking on, in effect, the role of a judge within that other legal system. Federal courts do this everyday when they exercise diversity jurisdiction in the United States.[66]

This review of sources and arguments related to Orientalism is offered neither to promote nor reject the basic assumptions of Said. Instead, it serves to provide a foundation for the consideration of the particular relationship of Muslims to American courts. It is beyond the scope of this work to attempt to determine the full dimensions of any prevailing Western Orientalism. However, this review does lay a useful beginning point for a specific consideration of the actions of U.S. courts.

---

[66] Fadel, "The German Judge and Legal Orientalism."

CHAPTER 2

The Qadi and Images of Injustice

The qadi's court meets in a long narrow room at the side of the city hall. The qadi, a clerk by his side, sits behind an expansive desk at one end of the room while litigants mill about in a courtyard just beyond the door at the other end. A uniformed aide ushers parties in as their case is called. This aide serves as a translator for Berbers who cannot understand the qadi's Arabic and as a monitor of courtroom order, although his embellishment of the court's inquiries and his patronizing choreography of litigants lends an air of self-aggrandizement to these otherwise modest tasks. The qadi first determines who is who and how, if at all, they are related to one another. His first substantive question is usually the signal for the shouting to begin. The parties begin by talking to the qadi but often end by addressing the aide, the clerk, others crowded into the courtroom, and even the stray anthropologist. The qadi mutters, nods, and questions; the principles sit, stand, shout and cry; the aide tries to quiet people by pinning down their hands, in the certain knowledge that no Moroccan can speak if his hands are not free; and the clerk rushes to finish writing up the last case and find the correct dossier for the present one. Eventually one person gets to tell a more or less coherent story, and women no less

> *than men speak with great verve and style. Most cases are treated very rapidly.*[67]

Who or what is a *qadi*? This, is a more complicated question than might first be suspected. Generally, the temptation may be to describe a *qadi* merely as a Muslim judge, though such a definition seems inadequate and narrow. Lawrence Rosen suggests that the *qadi* plays a far broader social role than many would assume. At least within the context of modern Moroccan society, Rosen sees the *qadi* as filling a multiplicity of duties. The *qadi* acts as a sort of community mediator, seeking to draw parties toward dispute resolution. The *qadi*, likewise, plays the role of communal therapist, giving litigants an opportunity to air their feelings and emotions publicly, as much as their claims. The *qadi* is also a teacher, both of societal norms and religious order. Most importantly, however, the *qadi* is responsible for the assessment of character. As Rosen reflects, "when stories are told of really clever *qadi*s, they often involve the *qadi* trapping one of the parties in a display of his true character."[68] Of course, while all of the direct evidence collected by Rosen to support his observations comes from Morocco, his conclusions are understood to pertain, to a greater or lesser degree, to *qadi*s from across Muslim society.

While Rosen cultivates a useful picture of the *qadi* in practice, it is not true that this court official, historically associated with the implementation of Islamic legal norms, has always been so favorably represented. Especially within the body of American legal materials, the *qadi* has frequently taken on a decidedly more negative image. One may wonder why the *qadi* has fallen victim to what some may describe as character assassination, though the more important inquiry may have to do with the impact of such depictions. Here, the utilization of the figure of the *qadi* by Western courts and secondary legal materials is considered, with the purpose of seeking a greater understanding of the impact of such depictions upon larger impressions associated with Islam itself.

---

[67] This is the description of the operation of a qadi court as interpreted by scholar Lawrence Rosen. It stands as part of a broader analysis of the process of the implementation of Islamic law in modern Morocco. *The Justice of Islam* (Oxford: Oxford University Press, 2000), 11-12.

[68] Ibid., 14.

The *Qadi* of Western Scholarship

While Rosen's broad consideration of the social roles played by the *qadi* provides an insightful beginning point for the consideration of the jurist's place in history, others have sought to characterize the Arab court official more narrowly, though not always consistently. In turning to Western legal and scholarly sources, many images of the *qadi* may be found. Both Ballentines and Black's law dictionaries describe the *qadi* similarly, referring to one holding this position as a "Turkish, Arab or Persian civil magistrate."[69] Interestingly and somewhat surprisingly, this description does not imply a direct association between the *qadi* and the Muslim community. At the same time, it does seek to assign the *qadi* to a particular and narrow cultural context.

In some respects, then, the definitions of Ballentines and Black's law dictionaries appear to lean upon an idealized understanding of the person of the *qadi*, which appears to discount or ignore the connection between this jurist and the religious sphere surrounding him. David Pearl, in his Western *Textbook on Muslim Law*,[70] refers to the *qadi* as a creation of the Umayyad dynasty. The individuals who served as the earliest *qadis*, he observes, were judicial officers of the state appointed by the Governors of individual regions and, quite often, opposed by local community leaders. Many of these individuals, he argues, were "open to the influence" of others and their decisions varied from region to region, based upon local influences and circumstances.[71] As well, they were subject to persuasion in their decision-making capacity by the local political leadership. Thus, in contrast to the image cultivated by Rosen, Pearl offers a rather unflattering assessment of the *qadi*.

Accordingly, when such latter sources, ranging from law dictionaries to the work of Pearl, are combined, a curious picture of the *qadi* emerges. Those playing the role of *qadi* are not always tied definitionally to Islam, but are viewed as civil mediators representing the interests of Middle Eastern or Arab societies. Perhaps, this inclination by Western legal scholars to minimize the role of religion in

---

[69] See *Ballentine's Dictionary of Law*, New York: Thomas Delmer Pub., 2003; *Black's Law Dictionary*, Dallas: West Law School Pub., 2004.

[70] (Oxford: Oxford Univ. Press, 1964).

[71] Ibid., 124.

the work of the *qadi* is influenced by the largely secular nature of the judicial systems of modern Europe and North America. At the same time, while charged with representation of community interests, the judgments of these individuals are described as being inconsistent and open to influence from varying sources, political and social. Thus, while idealists may have imagined these community arbitrators to be representatives of communal justice, it is unclear from the image crafted by these sources that the *qadi*, in practice, served such interests.

Arguably, one of the best-known and most controversial voices of Western scholarship on the topic of Islamic legal institutions is Joseph Schacht. His work, *An Introduction to Islamic Law*,[72] is recognized as one of the more influential volumes available in the West on this topic. Indeed, Schacht's influence is sufficiently broad that some may not be surprised to detect strong parallels between his own works and more recent secondary Western legal resources, which may be found here in the cited descriptions of the *qadi*. At the same time, he argues that the primary role of the *qadi* evolved during the course of the Umayyad dynasty from that of secular administrative oversight to one of enforcer of theological norms. Thus, by the end of the Umayyad dynasty, the *qadi* had become more interested in the preservation and expansion of religious culture than in the administration of some form of civil or secular justice.

In his widely-read volume, *A History of Islamic Law*,[73] N. J. Coulson considered the role of the *qadi* in the establishment of an identifiable system of Islamic law. Coulson observed that there was no ascertainable uniformity within the body of decisions of the early *qadis*. This claimed diversity within the corpus of early *qadi* decisions he attributed, in part, to the "unrestricted power of the individual judge to decide according to his personal opinion."[74] Further, he blamed the lack of a unifying system of binding precedent as exacerbating the troubling lack of continuity within the body of decisions made by the early *qadis*. This generally negative description of the *qadi* is reinforced by, and, in some measure, likely dependant upon, the earlier work of J. N. D Anderson.[75]

---

[72] (Oxford: Oxford University Press, 1964).

[73] (Edinburgh: Edinburgh University Press, 1964).

[74] Ibid., 30.

[75] *Islamic Law in the Modern World* (New York: New York Univ. Press, 1959).

It must be acknowledged that some would desire to dismiss the work of all of these authors. Indeed, it would likely be argued by some that these combined works, when viewed collectively, do little more than reinforce Orientalist stereotypes, which are devoid of substantial historical support. At the same time, it must be additionally recognized that these authors continue to be among the most widely-read and influential resources on the topic of Islamic law available to Western students of law, even into the present.[76] Accordingly, even if the criticisms of these authors are deemed meritorious, it seems highly problematic to merely dismiss such works due to their broad influence.

These same themes are often reflected in secondary sources within the field of law of a more recent vintage. An example is Frank Vogel's 2001 volume, *Islamic Law and Legal Systems*.[77] The text focuses particularly upon the legal system of Saudi Arabia, and in that context describes the social position of the *qadi*. The *qadi*, Vogel suggests, is "not bound by judicial precedent, and the concept of *stare decisis* does not exist." Instead, the *qadi* "must strive for the divine truth for each case that confronts him, without being bound by past opinions, even his own."[78] Again, this description of the *qadi* appears to imply the possibility or probability of wildly erratic decision-making being undertaken by those holding this office. As Vogel emphasizes, decisions addressing particular topics vary not only by region or community, but even within the singular body of work of the individual *qadi*, himself.

The *Qadi* in the Supreme Court

Turning to the body of American jurisprudential reference to the *qadi*, one particular example stands out among the rest. It assumes a position of importance, in part, because it was penned by one of the most prominent U.S. Supreme Court judges of the modern era. In 1949, Justice Felix Frankfurter wrote, in his dissenting opinion in the case

---

[76] See generally, Mohsen Haredy, "Hadith Textual Criticism: A Reconsideration," Published at Islamonline.net (May 4, 2005), http://www.islamionline.net/english/HadithAndItsSciences/HadithStudies/2005/05/01.shtml#2 (accessed February 2, 2008).

[77] Ibid., at section 143:2-4.

[78] Ibid.

Terminiello v. City of Chicago,[79] "We do not sit like a *kadi*[80] under a tree dispensing justice according to considerations of individual expediency." For its time, the curious stereotypes implied by this statement may not be deemed surprising. Still, the statement carries an undeniable bias. Though the statement, on its own, may not have generated significant controversy, what makes it particularly interesting, challenging, and subject to some criticism, today, is the extended life that it has received through its later adoption by subsequent courts.

Taken on its own merits, the brief phrase seems to suggest many things about the *qadi*, as well as the society served by this communal arbitrator. Like Coulson and Andersen, Frankfurter seemed comfortable with the notion that the *qadi* was not motivated by concerns of equal treatment or continuity of result. Moreover, the image of such a figure sitting under a tree appears to imply an inherent lack of erudition and sophistication, as well as the absence of an institutional structure capable of restricting one's ability to exercise unbridled or excessively broad discretion in his decisions.

These immediate impressions prompt a further inquiry. Indeed, it could be asked, what sort of community would allow itself to be guided by such a figure? The answer by implication is that only a community that is rash, inconsistent in its own judgment, uneducated and unsophisticated would find such a system acceptable. As has been observed regarding the employment of the image of the *qadi* by the U.S. judiciary, "U.S. judges have offhandedly used the term *qadi* justice to symbolize a total denial of the law, namely, unprincipled, expedient and arbitrary lawmaking."[81]

It has been suggested by some, including justices of the Supreme Court of Rhode Island,[82] that Frankfurter may have effectively borrowed his description of the *qadi* from the work of the German thinker and social commentator Max Weber. It was in his work *Law in*

---

[79] 337 U.S. 1, 11, 93 L. Ed. 1131, 69 S. Ct. 894 (1949).

[80] The term *qadi* is Arabic in origin and is transliterated into English in varying forms, which may include *qadi*, *kadi* and *cadi*.

[81] John Makdisi, "Legal Logic and Equity in Islamic Law," *The American Journal of Comparative Law* 33, no. 1 (Winter, 1985): 63-92.

[82] See Credit Union Central Falls v. Groff, 871 A.2d 364 (2005), and footnote 27 and accompanying text, below.

Ecomony and Society[83] that Weber coined the term "*qadi* justice," which he described as being the product of a "legal system oriented not upon fixed rules of a formally rational law, but ethical, religious, political, or otherwise expediential postulates of a substantively irrational law."[84] Whether Frankfurter actually relied specifically upon Weber as his source is unclear. Yet, it does seem clear that his own statement appears consistent with the thesis and perspective of Weber.

Weber's reference to the *qadi* was in support of his broader thesis that legal systems throughout the globe tended to be characterized by either an arbitrary approach to decision-making or a logical process rooted in precedent. The arbitrary legal systems were, according to Weber, "irrational" in that they produced decisions based almost exclusively upon such factors as the peculiar circumstances of the parties and the whims of the judge. Meanwhile, they resisted the employment of a consistent body of precedent. As such, these tribunals represented the "archetype of non-Western legal systems,"[85] and the body of judgments they have produced serves as an exemplar of an "ideal type of substantively irrational law."[86]

Underlying Weber's consideration of legal systems was a perceived link between the types of economic and social systems cultivated by individual cultures and the forms of religious practice that tended to predominate within these societies. Thus, the Protestant faith, with its heightened emphasis upon values of thrift, hard work and prudence, was deemed to be compatible with capitalism and other highly rational social institutions. Islam, meanwhile, with its rooting in charismatic leadership, was considered to be less inclined toward such rational economic or social systems. The legal systems crafted by members of these cultures served as evidence of the rationality or irrationality of the larger systems, themselves, according to Weber. Whether Weber saw a causal link between the rise of religious order in a society and the establishment of rational social institutions is subject

---

[83] (Stanford: Stanford University Press, 2005, reprint).

[84] Pierre Bourdieu, "The Force of Law: Toward a Sociology of the Juridical Field," 38 *Hastings Law Journal* 38 (1987): 805-830, 825 n.33.

[85] Heim Gerber, *State, Society and Law in Islam: Ottoman Law in Comparative Perspective* (New York: State Univ. of New York Press, 1994), 11.

[86] Vogel, *Islamic Law and Legal Systems*, 28-29.

to debate, however. Bryan Turner has argued that Weber himself affirmatively denied intending to imply such a causal relationship.[87]

Of course, any such causal relationship has been strongly denied by some within the Muslim community. Pointing to the great trading systems cultivated during the periods of the Abbasid and Ottoman empires, it is argued that the actual experience of the Muslim movement has evidenced the flawed nature of Weber's thesis.[88] As well, it may be argued that Weber failed to recognize the highly developed commercial systems that have been the product of urban environments within the larger Muslim society throughout its history, beginning in Mecca.[89]

The chief representative of what Weber saw as an irrational legal system cultivated within Muslim society was the institution of the *qadi*. As has been argued regarding Weber's characterization of the *qadi*:

> In the case of substantive, irrational law, law makers do not follow general principles, but judge each case according to purely arbitrary factors. The paradigmatic case of such law, in Weber's view, was that of the *qadi* who judge each case on personal, particularistic grounds. The law resulting from *qadi* decisions lacks generality and stability.[90]

In the present context, then, it may be observed that Weber relied upon the *qadi* to evidence the existence of erratic and irrational decision-making within Muslim societies, in much the same way as does Frankfurter.

---

[87] "Islam, Capitalism and the Weber Thesis," *The British Journal of Sociology* 25, no. 2 (June, 1974): 230-243, 231.

[88] Mustafa Akyol, "Islamocapitalism: Islam & the Free Market," Turkish Daily News (June 19, 2006), http://www.turkishdailynews.com.tr/ /article.php?enewsid=66511 (accessed February 18, 2008).

[89] Syed Anwar Hussain, "Max Weber's Sociology of Islam: A Critique," *Bangledesh e-Journal of Sociology* 1, no. 1 (January 2004), http://www.bangladeshsociology.org/Max_Weber-Anwar_Hosain,_PDF.pdf (accessed February 12, 2008).

[90] Turner, "Islam, Capitalism and the Weber Thesis," 235-236.

The Adoption of *Terminiello*

Whether dependent upon the work of Weber or not, the fateful phrase employed by Frankfurter attributing irrational judgment to the *qadi*, meanwhile, has come to be adopted as a legal term of art by many American courts.[91] Justice Frankfurter's words have been employed by a number of Federal and State courts in the U.S. during the decades since it was first articulated, and continues to be used for the purpose of speaking to the legitimate role of the system of American courts. In particular, the phrase has been used as a reminder of the importance of the imposition of limitations upon the scope of power exercised by U.S. courts. The limitations generally implied relate to the extent of the authority of U.S. appellate courts to review the decisions of lower courts. As the phrase is typically employed, the *qadi* is pointed to as an exemplar of unbridled discretion, of the type that should be avoided within the confines of a "just" legal system. In other words, the unrestrained *qadi* effectively stands in opposition to the ideal self-description of the U.S. judicial system, in which courts are understood to exert reasonable discretion in their administration of justice.

The Frankfurter dictum has subsequently been adopted by numerous American courts throughout the ensuing decades since it was first articulated.[92] Recently, it has been employed by the Rhode Island Supreme Court in the 2005 case of *Credit Union Central Falls v. Lawrence S. Groff.*[93] In the case, the high court employed language from the *Terminiello* dissent as it considered the appropriate boundaries of the appellate review process. In the matter, the defendant Lawrence Groff, an attorney, was accused of having misappropriated more than $200,000 of the funds of his client Credit Union Central Falls. Upon discovering the apparent misappropriation, the credit union attempted to freeze and attach funds in Groff's personal bank account.

---

[91] See generally Stewart v. Thorpe Holding Co. Profit Sharing Plan, 207 F.3d 1143 (9th Cir. 2000); Hillcrest Foods, Inc. v. United Food & Commercial Workers Union, Local Union No. 576, 753 F. Supp. 1541 (Dist. Ct. Kansas 1990); Olivieri v. Ward, 801 F.2d 602 (2nd Cir. 1986); New Alliance Party v. Dinkins, 743 F. Supp. 1055 (So. Dist. N.Y. 1990); Espy v. Espy, 192 Cal. App. 3d 1444; 238 Cal. Rptr. 182 (1987).

[92] See note 91, above.

[93] 871 A.2d 364 (2005).

Subsequently, a second client of Groff's, Doris Riendeau, likewise determined that certain funds that were part of an estate settlement had been wrongfully withheld from her by Groff. She, in turn, sought to intervene in the attachment procedure initiated by the credit union and stake a personal claim against Groff's available assets, as well. She also sought a protective order designed to ensure that the credit union did not disburse the funds at issue. Ultimately, the court was faced with the dilemma of determining the validity of Riendeau's claim against Groff's assets, a claim which the Credit Union Central Falls argued was not valid. The trial court ruled against Riendeau. Yet, upon appeal, the issue of which of the parties had a rightful claim to the funds was revisited, and it is this review that provided the context for the introduction of the *Terminiello* dictum.

On appeal, the credit union claimed that Riendeau's interest in the attached funds was moot because she had other avenues of recourse preserved for her. The court ultimately disagreed, recognizing Riendeau's claim as being both valid and important. It did so, however, only after acknowledging that the court would not entertain "moot, abstract, academic or hypothetical questions."[94] In making this point, the Supreme Court turned to Justice Frankfurter's phrase to illustrate the challenges associated with excessive judicial authority.[95] To admit a moot claim would have been to act as erratically as the *qadi*, according to the court, and such an action would have jeopardized the very integrity of the institution, itself. This case, meanwhile, does not stand alone in its employment of the image of the *qadi* as an archetype of injustice. Thus, it is important that other references to the personality of the *qadi* by U.S. courts designed to cultivate images of injustice be examined.

---

[94] Ibid., 368.

[95] Ibid. The court also cites *Sullivan v. Chafee,* 703 A.2d 748, 753 (R.I. 1997) for the same proposition. In a footnote, the court goes on to refer to Max Weber's term "kadi justice," and, in so doing, observes that such systems are not rooted in "formally rational law," but, instead, in "expediential postulates" derived from subjective thought. Ibid., 369.

Systems in Opposition

A common trait within the body of decisions that have adopted the *Terminiello* language is the perpetuation of a vision of an ideal justice system poised against its inferior opposite. Thus, in such decisions, the system of legal enforcement employed by the *qadi* typically stands in stark opposition to that imposed by U.S. courts. Within this context, the *qadi* courts are depicted as being synonymous with a spirit of injustice, which is, itself, inherently incompatible with the foundational ideas that support the U.S. judicial system.

For the U.S. District Court for New Jersey, the *qadi* is depicted as the enforcer of legal norms that are radically distinct from, and incompatible with Western notions of justice. In particular, in the case of *National Group for Communications and Computer Technologies v. Lucent Technologies International*,[96] the court faced a question of comparative law. In the matter, the court was asked to determine the appropriate national law to apply to the interpretation of a contract. One party sought to have a specified contractual provision interpreted according to the law of Saudi Arabia, a system based in part upon principles of Islamic law, while the other party sought to have the provision interpreted pursuant to U.S. law. In resolving the matter, the court expressed significant concern regarding the extent to which contractual arrangements would receive full and fair protection under the law of certain Arab states. The court went on to voice its fear that the judicial systems of the nations of the Middle Eastern region, including that of Saudi Arabia, tended to interpret contracts and other business agreements in a highly inconsistent manner. As the court observed in this regard:

> In English law the sanctity of contract means that the promise endures despite the normal vicissitudes of fortune. It is right that the promise should be kept 'for better or for worse', 'through thick and thin', because this in line with the popular belief that tenacity of purpose to some degree controls events and that the human will determines the future. The promise must dominate the circumstances.

---

[96] 331 F. Supp. 2d 290 (New Jersey Dist. 2004).

> For Islam, as it serves to inform the legal systems of many Middle Eastern states, precisely the converse is true. Circumstances dominate the promise. Future circumstances are neither predictable nor controllable but lie entirely in the hands of the Almighty ... If the tide of affairs turns then the promise naturally floats out with it.[97]

The court also seemed interested in differentiating the legal system employed in Saudi Arabia, specifically, from that of the U.S. In this regard, the court essentially described these systems as being in diametric opposition to one another. Of course, Said and others have argued that Orientalist-style stereotypes tend to promote such dualistic understandings. Perhaps, then, the present case serves to lend evidence to such assertions. As the court interpreted the nature of the Saudi legal system, it concluded:

> The legal system in Saudi Arabia is fundamentally different from that of the United States. Western conceptions of the role that law plays in society, the legal process, and methods of legal interpretation, often mistakenly assumed to be universal in nature, are in many ways poles apart from those concepts in Islamic countries such as Saudi Arabia. The difficulties in understanding Islamic law are multiplied by the fact that there is a paucity of literature specifically targeted at those who, like this Court, are steeped in other legal mindsets and seek guidance as to Islamic law's interpretation.
>
> ....
>
> Generally speaking, the Saudi Arabian legal structure is highly traditional and judges strictly apply classical Islamic law. In contrast to other Islamic countries that have adapted religious tenets to meet modern demands, in Saudi Arabia, Shari'a remains free of compromising reforms.[98]

It is not just the legal system of Saudi Arabia that is strongly critiqued by this court. Thus, not unlike Frankfurter's often-used dissenting language, this opinion appears to paint the picture of a judicial system,

---

[97] Ibid., 296.
[98] Ibid., 294-295.

employing *qadis,* that is wildly erratic, subject to whim, and unappreciative of the economic importance of a stable contractual and business environment. As the court further asserted:

> When a Saudi Arabian judge, known as a "qadi," attempts to resolve disputes, his decision must be in accordance with the Shari'a. Therefore, he will turn to the aforementioned Qur'an, the Sunnah, and fiqh to guide his legal determination. Saudi Arabian judges are not bound by judicial precedent (in fact, Saudi Arabian judicial opinions are not published) and the concept of stare decisis does not exist.[99]

The *qadi*, then, is associated with a form of judicial exercise that for many U.S. courts appears to be inherently incompatible with even basic notions of justice.

In the case of *Miller Brewing Co. v. Brewery Workers Local No. 9 AFL-CIO*, the United States Court of Appeals for the Seventh Circuit similarly compared inherently flawed and overzealous interpretations of collective bargaining agreements by arbitrators with the type of justice that might be afforded by a *qadi*.[100] In the matter, a former union employee of a Schlitz brewing facility sought to be included among a group of new hires being retained by a Miller Brewing Company plant in the same locality. In his claim, the former Schlitz employee relied upon a provision of his union contract which guaranteed "preferential treatment" in the hiring of brewery employees to union members who had been previously laid-off. The union contract applied to all unionized brewery facilities in the defined region. Ultimately, upon review of the union contract, an arbitrator agreed with the claim of the former Schlitz employee that he had a contractual right to be hired, and Miller appealed the decision.

The Court of Appeals was faced with the decision of whether the arbitrator had exceeded the limits of his authority in reaching this conclusion, by venturing beyond the terms of the contract, itself, as it sought a fair interpretation of the binding agreement. While the court found that the arbitrator had not exceeded the limits of his authority in this instance, the justices went on to characterize such excesses, when

---

[99] Ibid., 295.

[100] 739 F.2d 1159 (1984).

they do occur, as being akin to "*qadi* justice." As the court commented, "[o]ur function is complete when we are satisfied that the arbitrator was not dispensing *qadi* justice."[101]

Authority without Limitation

While the *qadi* may frequently be depicted as acting in an arbitrary or capricious manner, unlike the reasoned processes employed by U.S. courts, the figure is also associated with unbridled authority. In other words, any reasoned system of justice is one that places constraints upon its actors. The very ability of one to act without limitation appears to contradict any useful notion of justice. Though many Muslim scholars and historians may seek to argue that the scope of a *qadi's* authority is constrained by considerable institutional limitations, the stereotype of the unbridled decision-maker has served the useful function of underscoring broader assumptions made concerning the nature of Islamic law. It is such a vision that underlies the Frankfurter dictum, as well as the interpretations of other U.S. courts.

As an example, in the case of *Dexter v. State Bar of Idaho*, the Idaho Supreme Court compared a law license review process, characterized as "nonaccountable," "unconstrained by formal standards" and "ignorant of research" within its field of review, to the functioning of a *qadi* court.[102] In the matter, the plaintiff, Dexter, applied to take the Idaho Bar examination, with the intention of being licensed to practice law in the state. Upon receipt of Dexter's application, the Idaho State Board of Commissioners, the body charged with reviewing such applications, denied Dexter's application on the grounds that he was unsuited to practice law in the state. Dexter, subsequently, challenged the decision, complaining that the Board's determination was not supported by any specific findings of fact related to his personal suitability to practice law in the state and that, in the absence of such a factual determination, he was deprived the ability to remedy any specific failings.

Ultimately, the Court, on appeal, determined that, while the Board had the authority to deny such an application, any denial must be supported by factual findings identifying the specific personal or

---

[101] Ibid., 1204.

[102] 116 Idaho 790; 780 P.2d 112 (Idaho 1989).

professional failings of the applicant. The failure to support an administrative denial of such an application with appropriate factual findings was tantamount to "*qadi* justice" according to the court. Curiously, in support of its own determination in the matter, the court turned to Max Weber as an ally. As the court stated in a supportive footnote to its decision:

> The current administration of moral character criteria is, in effect, a form of Kadi justice with a procedural overlay. (Fn. *See M. Weber, Bureaucracy*, in From Max Weber: Essays In Sociology 196, 216-21).[103]

The court went on to describe the process employed by the Idaho Board in reviewing Dexter's application to take the bar examination as "empirically dubious" and stated, further, that such a process would, "yield intrusive, inconsistent, and idiosyncratic decision-making."[104] Of course, the specific phraseology used by the court here is significant in that it largely mirrors what Said claimed to be the types of negative presumptions cultivated by Orientalists in an effort to define and describe Muslim, Arab and other communities of the East.

As well, in a Texas case where the oversight work of a state Commissioner of banking was viewed as being in contradiction of both state and federal banking laws, such activity was compared to the boundless judgment of the *qadi*.[105] In the matter, a savings and loan association made application to the office of the Savings and Loan Commissioner of Texas to relocate its facilities to a new location within the same county. The application for relocation was approved by the Commissioner over the objections of other banking institutions located in the area of the planned relocation of the savings and loan association. In approving the application, the Commissioner required no finding of fact that there was a "need" for the services to be provided by the savings and loan association in the new area, this despite the fact that federal regulations demanded such a finding. In the end, upon review of the Commissioner's actions, the court expressed dismay regarding

---

[103] Ibid., 11.

[104] Ibid.

[105] First Federal Savings and Loan Assoc. v. Vandygriff, 639 S.W.2d 492 (Tex. Ct. App. 1982).

the approval of the relocation, suggesting that such an exercise of power was, in effect, "undisciplined and arbitrary."[106] The court went on to chastise the Savings and Loan Commissioner for acting in "Oriental fashion," by effectively acting as if he were a *qadi* "sitting under a tree" and dispensing justice in accord with personal interests, rather than broader notions of justice.

The *Qadi* in History

It must be acknowledged that these varying images of the *qadi* and the *shari'a* system being employed by U.S. courts are not particularly flattering. Indeed, these images appear to stand in direct opposition to the vibrant self-image of free and just Western democratic judicial systems. Yet, however unflattering, is this portrait of the system of law employed by Muslim societies and its overseer, the *qadi*, acceptable as a truism? Is it possible, one may argue, to defend such images, as in a libel action, based merely upon the claim of truth?

Much recent scholarship has argued against the truthfulness of these claims. In a 1999 article, John Makdisi argued that the role of the *qadi* was in many ways actually similar to the role played by the English judge.[107] Both approached the matters before them as impartial arbitrators, and both allowed the parties to, in part, orchestrate the presentation of their respective claims through the use of specific evidentiary standards. The *qadi* was not unbridled in his discretion, but was bound by the contours of the evidence presented. Yet, there is still one glaring difference between the Western judge and the *qadi*, according to Makdisi. The *qadi* court is not subject to the imposition of the sort of highly technical evidentiary rules that are open to manipulation and misuse by parties. At the end of the day, Makdisi suggests that a truly just and reasonable verdict may be more likely to be produced within the context of a *qadi* court than within a Western court.

Focusing particularly upon the *qadi* courts of the Ottoman Empire, Walid Iqbal has argued similarly that this judicial institution was unusually well positioned to deliver judicious, informed and well-

---

[106] Ibid., at p. 21.

[107] "The Islamic Origins of the Common Law," *77 N.C.Law Rev. 1635* (June 1999).

reasoned decisions.[108] As Iqbal observes regarding Islamic judicial officials:

> [T]he independence of the *kadi* was beyond question. While the central or imperial authority appointed and removed *kadis*, set administrative limits to jurisdictions, and regularly corresponded with *kadis*, it never interfered in the judicial functions of the *kadi's* office.

Iqbal goes on to note the emphasis placed by *qadi* courts upon reconciliation between parties to a dispute, rather than "strict enforcement" of judgments. Often, matters in dispute were settled through a sort of mediation that tends to mirror Western-styled alternative dispute resolution systems. As well, the *qadi* courts were "uncomplicated," relying upon few intricate procedural processes, which, according to Iqbal, may serve to impede justice. As Iqbal asserts, the *qadi* courts "were aimed at ascertaining the truth and dispensing justice through minimal involvement in procedural intricacies."[109]

And while it could be argued that Iqbal and Makdisi are biased and, accordingly, unreliable due to their personal ties to the Muslim community specifically, similar sorts of claims can be gleaned from the works of Heim Gerber,[110] who argued that the *qadi* decisions of the Ottoman empire were remarkably consistent, or Rosen, who has similarly argued that, within the body of studied *qadi* decisions, there exists a perceptible regularity. As Rosen concludes:

> [R]egularity lies not in the development of a body of doctrine which is consistent with other elements of that doctrinal corpus itself, but rather in the fit between the judge and the

---

[108] "Dialogue and the Practice of Law Spiritual Values: Glimpses into the Islamic Tradition," *Fordham Urban Law Journal* 28 (April, 2001): 1035-1045.

[109] Ibid., 1037-1038.

[110] *State, Society and Law in Islam: Ottoman Law in Comparative Perspective* (Albany: State Univ. of New York Press, 1994).

> cultural concepts and social relations to which they are inextricably tied.[111]

The Unbridled *Qadi*

It should be recognized that not all scholars would wholly agree with the characterizations of the *qadi* and the system of Islamic law that may be gleaned from these sources. In a recent volume, Middle Eastern scholar Sami Zubaida has painted a less flattering picture of the *qadi*.[112]

As Zubaida suggests, the autonomy of the *qadi* is not technically absolute. The *qadi* is subject to the appointment of the local ruler. As well, the judgments of the *qadi* are constrained by the prescriptions of the *shari'a*. Yet, it is the practical constraints upon the authority of the *qadi* that may be the most troublesome. As Zubaida suggests, the *qadi* was historically subject to the "patronage and favor of the princes" for his appointment. Accordingly, it is argued that such appointive powers may have exerted significant influence upon the judgment of the *qadi*. The notion that political influence may have affected the judgments of the *qadi* is reinforced by the recognition of the fact that many local political groups, including merchants unions and craft guilds, often were given the authority to appoint their own *qadis*.[113]

Still, within the *qadi*'s courtroom, the judicial operative functions with significant autonomy. As Zubaida observes, the *qadi* has few constraints upon the manner in which he conducts his office and upon his judgment. As Zubaida states with regard to the *qadi*'s practice:

> Qadi courts are presided over by a solitary judge who pronounces judgment on his sole authority. There are no judicial tribunals in Islam, no assembly of judges and no juries. The qadi may consult with a mufti on points of law, or may employ experts, such as those on succession law, or those with special knowledge of buildings or women's bodies. The judgment, however, emanates from one single authority.[114]

---

[111] *The Anthropology of Justice* (Cambridge: Cambridge University Press, 1989), 18.

[112] *Law and Power in the Islamic World* (London: I.B. Tauris, 2003).

[113] Ibid., 44.

[114] Ibid.

Zubaida likewise raises interesting questions regarding the payment of *qadis* and evidence of potential corruption among the jurists. Ideally, the *qadi* was not supposed to profit from the exercise of his duty. Instead, the duties were seen as a function performed in service to God. In practice, meanwhile, this ideal was often compromised. During the Abbasid and Umayyad dynasties, *qadis* were paid stipends for their service and, likewise, received "grants and gifts" from rulers pleased with their service.[115] In addition to these sums, the practice of charging litigants for services provided became widespread and, at the same time, the *qadi* would frequently assess fees for providing non-judicial functions in the community.

As Zubaida suggests, however, all of these varying forms of remuneration may have paled in comparison to that generated by the *qadi* office through corrupt activity. As anecdotal evidence for this proposition, Zubaida points to the writings of the 8th century *qadi* appointed to serve in the territory that is now the modern city of Bagdad, Iraq, Yaqub ibn Ibrahim al-Ansari, generally known as Abu Yusuf. Interpreting the records of Aub Yusuf, Zubaida observes:

> As early as the second century of Islam, we find Abu Yusuf…, advising the caliph to be careful as to whom he entrusts the funds of the orphans and the strangers, for most qadis are not to be so trusted, and that they and their auxiliaries do not hesitate to despoil the weak of their goods and rights of inheritance.[116]

Zubaida also points to the "farming" or selling of judicial appointments as an additional observable form of corruption in the qadi system, prompting the payment of "gifts, bribes, extortion and embezzlement."[117] By the fourth century of the development of the Islamic community, Zubaida suggests that corruption associated with the office of the *qadi* "was no longer incidental but systematic."

[115] Ibid., 47.

[116] Ibid., 48.

[117] Ibid., 49.

Justice for the *Qadi*

So what may be made of the ongoing use by the American judiciary of the *qadi* as a symbol of erratic, unrestrained and corrupt leadership? What are its effects upon historical and popular understandings associated with the development of Islam? Moreover, to what extent does the academic tug-of-war regarding the personality of the *qadi* serve to perpetuate this struggle?

It cannot be denied that the *qadi* has been construed to be reflective of perceived differences between Western notions of justice and characteristics attributed to the system of Islamic law. Though the archetypal *qadi* has been introduced in varying contexts, it is, perhaps, the *Terminiello* dissent that has given it such broad reach in the United States. Following this decision, the *qadi* has been seen as epitomizing such social ills as the illegitimate exercise of power by a governmental institutions, the employment of processes that are chaotic and subject to whim, and the exercise of authority without limitation. Further, it must be observed, that whatever is said of the *qadi* influences the prevailing image of Islam and Muslim practitioners. The attributes associated with the *qadi* necessarily color popular impressions of the larger society which gave the figure birth – the Muslim community. Thus, by implication, it seems that the presumed injustice attributed to the *qadi*, through images employed by U.S. courts, provides the foundation for similar assumptions to be made with regard to aspects of the broader Muslim community.

As Said and his supporters have asserted, the legacy of Orientalism is the continued painting of the Muslim world with broad and negative stereotypes, including such traits as injustice. While it may not have been an intentional result, it seems clear that the impact of the language first expressed by Frankfurter, and later adopted by numerous other courts, has been to reinforce such stereotypes. In some senses, then, such language may sanction non-Muslims, particularly those with limited exposure to Islamic society, to embrace such stereotypes. For Muslims themselves, the impact of such aspersions may be felt, at least in part, through the discriminatory responses of others directed toward them individually and their culture as a whole.

Of course, this analysis should not be taken as an assertion that all courts and judges in the U.S. have adopted these or similar Arab or Muslim stereotypes within the bodies of their relevant decisions. Indeed, while there are a number of instances in which the figure of the *qadi* has been employed by U.S. courts precisely for the purpose of criticizing some form of unbridled discretion, these cases, as a whole, constitute a very small proportion of the vast number of recorded state and federal decisions. Still, they seem sufficiently prevalent to generate some legitimate interest in their ultimate impact upon both legal and social thought.

Meanwhile, it is worthwhile to ask whether evidence sustains the observations made by Frankfurter and adopted by latter courts. Based upon the work of scholars, it may be observed that the actual legacy of the *qadi* is rather ambivalent. While justices have employed the image of the *qadi* to exemplify excesses in the exercise of authority, the actual record of the *qadi* appears rather mixed, based upon available scholarship. One can find evidence of their playing a positive historical role. Yet, at the same time, evidence of the corruption of some within the ranks of the *qadi* seems likely. Still, does this evidence point to a social institution that has functioned historically in such a manner that it must be seen as reflecting ideas that are in direct opposition to the very notion of justice itself? This claim would appear to be a rather large stretch.

Indeed, one may question whether any judicial system is entirely exempt from the claim that its tribunal have been used to perpetuate unjust practices at times. For evidence of this proposition, one may need to look no further than the records of proceedings by American courts relative to matters involving racial minorities during the early part of the nineteenth century. Especially in the South and West, decisions by such bodies may be characterized as often erratic and subject to corrupt influence. Still, these instances have not served to color the entirety of the U.S. judicial system with the taint of injustice. A question of importance, then, is whether there is evidence present that should reasonably serve to distinguish the record of the *qadi* from Western courts broadly, leading to the conclusion that the former is wholly unjust. Again, the mixed scholarship does not appear to fully support such a conclusion.

Further, it is useful to question the necessity of the utilization of such imagery by the U.S. judicial system, in the first instance. In other words, does the image of the *qadi*, as cultivated by the courts cited here and others, serve a necessary role in the process of judicial analysis? Upon reflection, the answer to this question must be negative. The *qadi*, it may be argued, has become a sort of defenseless straw man, within the context of these and other judicial decisions, serving almost exclusively to symbolize the dangers associated with the exercise of unbridled power. Yet, these dangers might be better depicted through the use of contemporary, local examples. Indeed, while the Frankfurter language is sensational, it is unclear that most readers would find the imagery of the *qadi* fully accessible.

The question moving forward, then, may be whether such images will persist and, if so, how these will impact the impressions of Muslims and non-Muslims toward one another. In the end, we should question the impact of the employment by the courts of any such stereotypes. Whether we choose to label them "Orientalist" descriptions or not, and regardless of our impressions of the broad thesis of Said, it appears difficult to deny that at least a portion of the American judiciary has associated a peculiarly Muslim institution, the *qadi*, with many negative characterizations. Further, the full social impact of these characterizations cannot be fully known.

CHAPTER 3

Terrorism and Jihad

Two West Bank Christian churches were hit by firebombs early Saturday, and a group claiming responsibility said it was protesting Pope Benedict XVI's remarks about Islam.

Pakistan's legislature unanimously condemned Pope Benedict XVI. Lebanon's top Shiite cleric demanded an apology. And in Turkey, the ruling party likened the pontiff to Hitler and Mussolini and accused him of reviving the mentality of the Crusades.

Across the Islamic world Friday, Benedict's remarks on Islam and jihad in a speech in Germany unleashed a torrent of rage that many fear could burst into violent protests like those that followed publication of caricatures of the Prophet Muhammad.

By citing an obscure medieval text that characterizes some of the teachings of Islam's founder as "evil and inhuman,"

> *Benedict inflamed Muslim passions and aggravated fears of a new outbreak of anti-Western protests.*[118]

Many within the global Muslim community erupted in anger following Pope Benedict's reference to *jihad* in 2006. This was not the first such episode. Numerous large-scale protests by Muslims were staged across Europe earlier in the same year following the publication of political cartoons in a Danish newspaper that were claimed to belittle the Islamic faith system. The year before, in 2005, dramatic and violent protests by Muslims in France led to the declaration of a state of emergency. The protests were in response to claims that police were over-zealous in their pursuit of a pair of teen-age Muslim crime suspects. And in March, 2009, Muslim protesters critical of the war effort in Iraq disrupted a parade in Luton, England, honoring veterans of the conflict.[119] These represent only a few examples of the many and sometimes violent responses by Muslims living in the West to situations deemed unfair or insulting to either individual practitioners of Islam or the faith system, itself. What do each of these situations have in common? Some would say very little. Still others would argue that they each stem from misunderstandings of the Muslim community rooted in Western bias. The question here is whether such bias may be detected within the body of decisions made by the U.S. judiciary.

The terms *jihad* and terrorism have become pervasive in the media in the West. These twin terms possess the ability to strike fear into the hearts of Americans. They have become the substance of screaming newspaper headlines and, increasingly, have been employed by Hollywood as symbols of ultimate evil. Still, it is worthwhile to ask how the terms are understood by the broader public within the United States and to what extent these terms, as they are now understood, provide accurate estimations of Muslim intent. In addition, how has the U.S. judiciary responded to the increasingly frequent invocation of

---

118 "Pope's Remarks Enrage Muslims: Violent Protests Erupt as Islamic World Condemns Pontiff's Comments," Associated Press News Service (September 16, 2006).

119 "Muslim Protest Arrests over Army Homecoming," from the Times of London Online (March 11, 2009), http://www.timesonline.co.uk/tol /news/uk/article5884941.ece (accessed June 10, 2009).

these terms? It is this latter inquiry that lies at the heart of the discussion in this chapter.

The Battle Over *Jihad*

In many ways, the term *jihad* has come to define an entire religious culture for some skeptical outsiders, particularly in the U.S. At the same time, it is worthwhile to ask whether the assumptions and presumptions associated with this term by many non-Muslims are constructive or valid. Here. The utilization of the term *jihad* within and by U.S. courts is considered, with focus upon the question of whether the use of the term by U.S. courts has served to exacerbate or bridge divisions separating Muslims and non-Muslims within North America.

Defining Jihad

Few, if any, Arabic terms are as recognizable in the West as the word *jihad.* Most members of the public would likely be able to articulate some definition of the term and many, perhaps, associate it with particular current events or news media images. Still, while individuals may be able to articulate some definition of the term, it is unclear whether such perceptions bear commonality to the Muslims community's own understandings of the term. Indeed, any attempt to directly translate or succinctly define this single word is a complex endeavor, as is evidenced by the many attempts by scholars who have strained to undertake this very task.

On a basic etymological level, *jihad* may be identified as a verbal noun stemming from the Arabic root *jahada.* This root is generally understood to connote extreme exertion or striving within the scope of a response to some external or internal threat or challenge. *Jihad*, then, may be said to imply the physical act of such striving. Yet, this dictionary definition, alone, may not be sufficient to convey the true spirit of the term, especially as it has come to be understood within the setting of the Muslim faith.

In order to capture the true spirit of this term, it seems essential to consider the nature of the object against which one may be striving when one undertakes *jihad.* Meanwhile, it is this question of the appropriate object of such striving that seems to underscore the heart of what may be labeled as the primary controversy surrounding this term for Muslims.

Many commentators have attempted to make the argument that, within the Muslim community, *jihad* is equated with violent conflict sanctioned by the Muslim faith and carried out against non-Muslims. In effect, the term *jihad* is described as a sort of "holy war." While proponents of such a position call upon the works of a number of Muslim Qur'anic commentators, both ancient and modern, to support their understanding. perhaps, none of them is more closely associated with this perspective than Sayyid Qutb.

It is one of Qutb's most influential writings, *Ma'alim fi-l-Tariq* (popularly translated in the U.S. as "Milestones" or "Signposts"),[120] which provides the most explicit statement of the author's own understanding of the nature of *jihad*. In particular, in the fourth chapter of the volume, a section entitled "*Jihad*," Qutb interprets the Qur'an to call Muslims to declare "war… against those from among the 'People of the Book' (generally understood to be Christians and Jews) who declare open enmity [toward Islam]."[121] He appears, then, to be effectively equating the notion of *jihad* precisely with the idea of violent confrontation between Muslims and Non-Muslims in an effort to secure the position of Islam.[122]

---

[120] (New Delhi: India Book Service, 2005). The volume was first published in Arabic in Egypt in 1964.

[121] Ibid., 115.

[122] In the volume, Qutb argues for the interpretation of the Qur'an as a progressive revelation, such that those verses last revealed obviate verses previously revealed which are in conflict. It is the last revealed verses, he argues, that have called Muslims to such a violent engagement. Thus, he writes:

> Thus for thirteen years after the beginning of his Messengership, he called people to God through preaching, without fighting or Jizyah, and was commanded to restrain himself and to practice patience and forbearance. Then he was commanded to migrate, and later permission was given to fight. Then he was commanded to fight those who fought him, and to restrain himself from those who did not make war with him. Later he was commanded to fight the polytheists until God's religion was fully established. Ibid., 94-95.

It is undoubtedly clear that Qutb found a constituency for his charged writings and philosophy among Egypt's disenfranchised. He is often credited with inspiring significant anti-government sentiment in Egypt during the decade of the 1960s. Since then, his works have served to undergird the positions of many who have promoted a violent response aimed at secular institutions across the globe. Still, it must be acknowledged that the publication of the writings of Qutb and the dissemination of his philosophy are relatively recent events, following centuries of evolution of Muslim thought. Thus, it is important to look beyond the writings of Qutb in testing his philosophy.

Commenting upon the debate concerning the true meaning of *jihad*, scholar David Cook has argued that the term is adequately understood only as implicating an aggressive and violent engagement. Seeking to support his thesis through the writings of key classical Muslim thinkers and jurists, Cook argues, "'Warfare with spiritual significance' is the primary and root meaning of the term (*jihad*) as it has been defined by classical Muslim jurists and legal scholars…."[123] He goes on to argue, citing the *Encyclopedia of Islam*,[124] a Western scholarly resource, that his asserted definition of the term has become the "standard" accepted definition for the preponderance of global Muslims.

Such interpretations of *jihad*, linking it necessarily with violent and potentially aggressive action, appear to be tied to particular depictions of the nature of the world promulgated by Muslim thinkers. Thus, many classical jurists divided the world into two primary realms. *Dar al-Islam* ("house of Islam") referred to that territory in which Islamic law prevailed. Meanwhile, *Dar al-harb* ("house of war") referred to regions not under Muslim rule or occupation. It is argued that this framework is the product of the third century of the development of the Muslim community and, accordingly, arises at about the same time that the very term *jihad* attains a codified status and the Muslim Empire reaches its broadest geographical reach.[125] Meanwhile, it is clear that these terms do not appear in the Qur'an and it may be argued that there has been controversy surrounding them from their earliest origins.

---

123 *Understanding Jihad* (Berkeley: University of California Press, 2005), 2.

124 Clifford E. Bosworth, ed. (London: Brill Aacdemic Pub., 2004).

125 Emmanuel Sivan, "The Holy War Tradition in Islam," *Orbis* 42, no. 2 (Spring 1998): 171-94.

Qutb and other Muslim thinkers have used the terms *dar al-Islam* and *dar al-harb* precisely for the purpose of inciting individuals to violent "*jihad*." These terms have been employed to promote a worldview in which the globe is understood to be divided between regions hospitable to Islam and those which are in conflict with it. This worldview assumes a perpetual state of engagement until the entirety of the globe is under the governance of an essentially pro-Islamic governance system. The tool designed to guide the global community toward this desired ideal state is *jihad*.

It may be observed, however, that even in the earliest period of development of the philosophies associated with these terms, there was not unanimity regarding their interpretation. Some within the early Muslim community questioned the accuracy of the strongly dualistic worldview, arguing for the existence of yet a third category of lands, designated *dar al-sulh* ("house of peace"). Those lands falling into this third category were understood to be non-Muslim territories. Yet, these territories would have peaceful relations with their Muslim neighbors.[126] In effect then, according to proponents of this alternative perspective, non-Muslim countries did not need to be classified as enemy territories by necessity.

At the same time, even within the scope of that original strongly dualistic worldview, which divided the globe into spheres which are hospitable to Islam and those which constitute enemy territory, significant limitations on the sorts of actions that might be undertaken were gleaned from sacred texts and applied by some to the conduct of holy warfare. Thus, as one observer has argued:

> These texts also require notice to the adversary before an attack, require that a Muslim army must seek peace if its opponent does, and forbid committing aggression against others and suicide.[127]

---

[126] Manoucher Parvin and Maurie Sommer, "Dar al-Islam: The Evolution of Muslim Territoriality and Its Implications for Conflict Resolution in the Middle East," *International Journal of Middle East Studies* 11, no. 1 (February 1980): 1-21, 4. This is a position that arises out of the Shafi'i sect. Ibid.

[127] Michael Knapp, "The Concept and Practice of Jihad in Islam," *Parameters* 33, no. 1 (2003): 82-96.

And whatever the predominant interpretation of *dar al-Islam* and *dar al-harb* was within the body of Islamic classical literature and regardless of the relationship these concepts bore to *jihad*, it may be argued that they are rooted in the peculiar circumstances of an historical period long passed. Thus, for some, such terms have ceased to be relevant to modern conversations related to the nature of Islam and the relationship of the faith to surrounding communities.[128]

Accordingly, while Cook and others are not alone in arguing that the natural and dominant understanding of *jihad* is one that sees this term as implying the necessity of violent conflict, it may be likewise observed that significant classical evidence is available to argue for a much less strident interpretation of the term.

Jihad in the Qur'an

Both the Qur'an and many traditional Quranic commentaries utilize some variation of the Arabic verb *jahada*. In the Qur'an, there are some 32 verses that employ variations of this term.[129] Many of these appear rather innocuous, such as verse 25:52, which may be translated, in part, as, "Then do not follow the unbelievers, and strive against them with a great striving." Another such verse is 29:69, which states, "And those who strive for us, we will guide them in our way; and Allah is with the doers of good." In general terms, each of these passages appears to point toward some sort of desired alignment of the Muslim faithful with a particular life course and against elements that are, in some way, opposed to this course. At the same time, there seems to be no clear implication of the necessity of an aggressive or violent resistance aimed at non-Muslims. Indeed, in his volume *Jihad: From Qur'an to bin Laden*,[130] Richard Bonney argues that of the Qur'anic verses utilizing some version of the Arabic verb *jahada*, only about four employ derivations of the word that seem to imply some "warlike"

---

[128] See Heiko Henkel, "Rethinking the dar al-harb: Social Change and Changing Perceptions of the West in Turkish Islam," *Journal of Ethnic and Migration Studies* 30, no. 5 (September 2004): 961-78.

[129] These Quranic verses include: 2:218; 3:142; 4:95; 5:35; 5:54; 8:72; 8:74-75; 9:16; 9:19-20; 9:44; 9:73; 9:81; 9:86; 9:88; 16:110; 22:78; 25:52; 29:6; 29:8; 29:69; 31:15; 47:31; 49:15; 60:1; 61:11; and 66:9.

[130] (London: Palgrave MacMillan, 2004).

or violent intent. Many others, he would argue, appear not to implicate any particular sort of violent or aggressive behavior.[131]

The differences in the emphases displayed in these varying verses necessarily prompt consideration of the Muslim doctrine of the progressive nature of the revelation of the Qur'an.[132] According to this interpretive principle, where one finds a direct conflict in Quranic materials, latter revealed verses obviate or abrogate former ones. In other words, in the event of an irreconcilable internal conflict in the text, the latest revelation in time serves to overcome the earlier contradicting revelations. This system of abrogation, though controversial even among the broad global community of Muslims, is rooted in the basic notion that segments of the Qur'an were revealed only as the fledgling Islamic community gathered around the Prophet Muhammad was ready to receive them.

Looking to a variety of early sources, Scholar Reuven Firestone has sought to trace the evolution of the doctrine of *jihad* within the Qur'anic text. Particularly, Firestone outlines the manner in which the early Muslim community sought to reconcile apparently conflicting Qur'anic texts related to *jihad* by applying the doctrine of abrogation.[133] In that traditional interpretation of *jihad* as an evolving Qur'anic doctrine, the earliest revealed verses encourage a spirit of "nonconfrontation." In other words, such verses are marked by their passive nature. In a second period of the evolving revelation, defensive fighting was specifically authorized by the Quranic text. In the third evolutionary stage, aggressive attacks upon those opposed to Islam appear to have been permitted, but only within certain defined strictures. Finally, in the last stage of the evolving revelation, Muslims were called unconditionally to fight unbelievers.

Among the verses falling into the final category identified by Firestone is the infamous "sword verse" (Sura 9:5), which calls upon the Muslim faithful to "kill the idolaters wherever you find them...."[134]

---

131 Ibid., 28.

132 This idea of progressive revelation is typically referenced in Arabic by the term *nask*, often translated into English as abrogation.

133 *Jihad: The Origin of Muslim Holy War*, Oxford: Oxford Univ. Press, 1999, at pp. 50-65.

134 A more traditional translation, from Abdullah Yusuf Ali, read, "...fight and slay the Pagans wherever ye find them..."

The verses assigned to each of the defined periods articulated by Firestone, except for the last, then, are understood by some Muslims to have been abrogated by the revelations that followed them. It is also worthwhile to note that none of the verses that appear to serve as direct calls to aggressive and violent engagement, including Sura 9:5, actually employ the term *jihad* specifically. Instead, they are associated with the term by latter Qur'anic commentators.

Both Firestone and Bonney have questioned the traditional application of the theory of the progressive revelation of the Qur'an. Bonney has argued that the application of the theory of abrogation to those Qur'anic verses having to do with any sort of aggressive engagement may violate the broader intent of the Qur'an. Thus, only a "holistic" reading of the Qur'an may provide the most accurate interpretation of the text. A holistic engagement of the text would not result in the dismissal of any individual Qur'anic passages, but would, instead, point to the existence of varying logical positions on the subject of when, where and whether violent engagement is permissible based upon Qur'anic dictate. In his re-examination of the doctrine of abrogation, Firestone argues for the existence of four separate schools of thought regarding the necessity or permissibility of the use of violence by the Muslim community. Thus, instead of a consistent and methodical movement from Qur'anic verses rejecting violence to those serving as a call to aggressive violence, Firestone suggests that there were multiple positions being expressed regarding the nature of *jihadist* action during much of the early formative period of the establishment of the Islamic religious movement. Instead of a transition from one to the next, under this view such groups engaged in a doctrinal battle that continued for some time. In the end, while those embracing the most strident position regarding the use of violent means may have won this internal doctrinal battle, there was not a smooth transition and supporters of alternative positions on this question may have persisted in their positions for decades.[135]

The historical analysis of Bonney and Firestone may derive support from the writings of the Qur'anic interpreter and scholar M. Amir Ali, who divides the concept of *jihad* into twelve effective stages

---

[135] Ibid., 67-91.

of engagement, all rooted in the notion of struggle.[136] According to Ali, while the possible utilization of violent engagement cannot be completely withdrawn from the collection of potential *jihadist* tools, such engagement must be used exclusively for the preservation of the Muslim faith and community and may not be called upon in an effort to preserve mere political or nationalistic interests.

Defensive Jihad

Ali is not alone in interpreting the term *jihad* as condoning a multiplicity of avenues of religious action, including, but not limited to, the employment of aggressive or violent measures. Muslim scholar A.G. Noorani[137] has argued that the term *jihad* may imply, at least in part, the potential engagement of an individual or group in some form of violent confrontation, but it is only a particular type of warfare that would be permissible in keeping with the spirit of this term. Specifically, while violence may be a necessary tool in the arsenal of those seeking to protect the larger Muslim community, this tool is to be employed only for defensive purposes and in the face of some identifiable threat. In support of this position, he turns to both the *Qur'an* and the noted 19th century Quranic commentator Maulvi Chiragh Ali.[138] Within the pages of the Qur'an, Noorani argues, the

---

[136] M. Amir Ali, "Jihad Explained," published on the website of the Institute of Islamic Information and Education, www.themodernreligion.com/jihad/jihad-explained.html (accessed April 6, 2007). Ali creates a sort of hierarchical approach in which the first sense of jihad is understood as "recognizing the Creator and loving him most." He continues with "resisting pressure of parents, peers and society," "staying on the straight path," "striving for righteous deeds," "having courage and steadfastness to convey the message of Islam," "defending Islam and the community," "helping allied people who may not be Muslim," "defense through pre-emptive strikes," "gaining the freedom to inform, educate and convey the message of Islam," "freeing people from tyranny," and "removing tyranny, treachery, bigotry and ignorance and replacing them with justice and equity." In support of his thesis, Ali relies upon verses from the Qur'an and various hadith. Ibid.

[137] *Islam and Jihad: Prejudice Versus Reality* (London: Zed Books, 2002).

[138] Moulavi Cheragh Ali, *A Critical Exposition of the Popular Jihad: Showing that all the Wars of Mohammad were Defensive, and the Aggressive War, or*

concept of *jihad* is always tied to the notion of "oppression" and the struggle against it. As he states, "the Qur'an is replete with references to the protection of the oppressed and to forbearance from aggression."[139] Leaning on the earlier work of Ali, Noorani cites a relevant string of verses from the Qur'an, in an effort to underscore the cumulative weight of the scriptural text, and to highlight the importance of reading particular Quranic passages in context. The string of verses he cites begins with Sura 2:190, which is translated as:

> And fight for the cause of Allah against those who fight against you, *but commit not the injustice of attacking them first*; verily Allah loves not the unjust. (emphasis added)

The importance of this passage lies, in part, in its emphasis upon the defensive quality of *jihad*. It is likewise important, however, that this verse be read in context, due to its relationship by proximity to a latter Qur'anic verse that is often relied upon to ascribe an offensive quality or character to *jihad* - verse 2:189. This latter verse may be translated as:

> And do battle against them until there be no more persecution and the only worship be that of Allah; but if they desist, let there be no hostility, except against wrong-doers.

This verse is often highlighted as one providing scriptural authority to the Muslim community to engage in an offensive campaign of violence. Noorani, however, suggests that such an interpretation of this verse is possible only if it is read in isolation. Looking again to Chiragh Ali, Noorani argues that 2:191 must be read alongside the companion verses of 2:188-190.[140] When such a contextual reading is undertaken, the

---

Compulsory Conversion, is not allowed in the Koran (Calcutta, India 1885, reprinted Karachi, Pakistan, 1977).

[139] *Islam and Jihad*, 55-56.

[140] A popular traditional translation of these verses by Abdullah Yusef Ali reads:

> 2:190 Fight in the cause of Allah those who fight you, but do not transgress limits; for Allah loveth not the transgressors. 2:191 And

defensive nature of *jihad* becomes unmistakable, according to Noorani. Indeed, it is only a contextual examination of such verses in the Qur'an that affords readers true insight into the spirit of this scriptural tradition, he suggests.

Political Jihad

Cheragh Ali, meanwhile, further argues that the very association of the term *jihad* with "fighting against an enemy" is a purely post-Qur'anic invention. Indeed, he argues that both Muslim and Christian commentators of the period of the life of Muhammad and the development of Qur'anic texts interpreted the term *jihad* to refer to a personal or religious struggle, but not a military or violent campaign.[141] The association of the word *jihad* with such a campaign is, according to Cheragh Ali, one aspect of what he refers to as a period of "corruption of the Arabic language," which evolved from the political upheaval of the first and second centuries following the death of Muhammad.[142]

This argument seems to gain some partial support in the more recent work of scholar Michael Bonner.[143] Bonner argues that the purposeful cultivation of definitional understandings of the term *jihad* implicating aggressive warfare may have been directly tied to the efforts of latter rulers of the early Islamic Empire to support their political and militaristic endeavors. Treatises and legal writings of the

---

slay them wherever ye catch them, and turn them out from where they have turned you out; for tumult and oppression are worse than slaughter; but fight not at the sacred mosque, unless they fight you there; but if they fight you, slay them. Such is the reward of those who suppress faith. 2:192 But if they cease, Allah is oft-forgiving, Most Merciful. 2:193 And fight them on until there is no more tumult or oppression, and there prevail justice and faith in Allah; but if they cease, let there be no hostility except those who practice oppression.

[141] Moulavi Cheraqh Ali, *A Critical Exposition of the Popular Jihad* (New Delhi: Global Media, 2003), 167-168.
[142] Ibid.
[143] Michael Bonner, *Jihad in Islamic History: Doctrines and Practices* (Princeton: Princeton Univ. Press, 2006).

period, he argues, were often commissioned by such political elites with the purpose of lending religious support to political or nationalistic campaigns. The linkage between aggressive warfare and the term *jihad* seems to have been cemented by the end of the 8th century of the Common Era, he claims.[144]

Greater Jihad

While an intentional link clearly appears to have been drawn by certain early Muslims between the term *jihad* and the idea of militaristic conflict, the precise moment at which this association is cultivated is not as apparent. Accordingly, it may be asked what other definitional options were available to early Muslims. What other understandings may have been associated early with the term *jihad*?

A number of commentators have argued for the existence of an early dual understanding of the nature of *jihad*. Both Firestone and Noorani distinguish between concepts of "Greater Jihad" and "Lesser Jihad" as they evolved through the early centuries of Islamic development. The Greater *Jihad* is defined as the personal struggle of individuals to live in accord with the moral and ethical commands of the Islamic system. In some senses, then, this Greater *Jihad* is the internal struggle to align oneself and one's own self interests with Qur'anic dictate. The Lesser Jihad, meanwhile, is associated with struggles involving any sort of external threat, including militaristic endeavors. Firestone notes that there may be many types of *jihad* that one may recognize and most of these, he asserts, are not rooted in any sort of violent behavior. In particular, he cites the "*jihad* of the heart," which he describes as an internal struggle against one's own sinful inclinations, and the "*jihad* of the tongue," which he describes as speaking on behalf of the positive or good forces within the world.[145] Still, Firestone associates the origins of the concept of Greater *Jihad*, in general, with the narrow group of early Muslim mystics, predominantly.

Arguing against the notion of an early cultivation of the idea of Greater *Jihad*, David Cook, meanwhile, has placed the beginning point for the development of this concept as being the publication of Al-

---

[144] Ibid., 7-8.

[145] *Jihad: The Origins of Muslim Holy War*, 16-17.

Ghazali's work *Ihya 'ulum al din* in the early part of the 12th century.[146] In effect, then, he dismisses the notion that the concept of Greater Jihad had rooting in the earliest stages of the development of the Muslim community. Instead, the dualistic understanding, often referred to by modern Muslim apologists, he would reason, is a product of a rather late discourse.

Though the specified labels of "greater" and "lesser" which were applied to categories of *jihad* may be assigned to a rather late period, others, such as Noorani, disagree with Cook's conclusions. Such authors assert the existence of numerous Qur'anic passages that appear to tie the term *jihad* to language of a pacifist nature. These passages, they would assert, provide evidence of the existence of a dualistic interpretation of *jihad* dating from the very origins of the Quranic narrative, irrespective of the existence of specified descriptive labels assigned to such positions.

In the end, it may be argued that there are numerous ways of understanding the term *jihad* that may be extracted from Qur'anic language and the writings of early and late Muslim commentators. Without question, some have come to understand *jihad* as a term referring specifically to some form of violent engagement. Still, whether such an engagement may be aggressive or must be defensive in nature is subject to some debate. As well, there seems to be strong sentiment that any such violent engagement must have a religious purpose. Others, meanwhile, may argue that the term *jihad* is subject to a multiplicity of meanings. These include the purposeful distinction made between the categories referred to as "Greater Jihad," understood as some personal struggle against internal tendencies to live and act in ways that are inconsistent with divine intent, and "Lesser Jihad," which includes any sort of violent campaign, but may also include any sort of effort to support the larger community or to act as an agent for "justice."

Of course, the purpose of this lengthy overview is not to arrive at conclusions related to the larger scholarly and religious debate concerning the appropriate manner to define *jihad*, but, instead, to provide a limited introduction to the complexities associated with the very task of defining this term. Such background is necessary to begin

---

[146] *Jihad: From Qur'an to bin Laden*, 37.

a detailed consideration of the utilization of the term *jihad* by U.S. courts and the implications that may stem from this usage.

Jihad in the Courtroom

In the past couple of decades, the term *jihad* has made its way, increasingly, into the opinions of American jurists. Many of the cases in which the term has been employed involve matters related to state terrorism. There exists a smattering of other types of cases in which the term has been employed, as well. The key question to be asked here, as was the case with the earlier consideration of the utilization of the term *qadi*, is whether these references by courts invoke reasoned interpretations of the term *jihad* or whether they seem steeped in stereotype and designed to inflame. Further, it may be asked, what, if any, implications for the broader Muslim community in the U.S. may be seen as stemming from these references?

One particularly useful case in the consideration of such inquiries is the matter of *U.S. v. Khan*.[147] This matter was initiated by a 32-count indictment, charging Masoud Khan and other defendants with various crimes, including conspiring to "levy war against the United States" and providing material support to organizations identified as being involved in terrorist activities aimed at the United States, including support of al Qaeda and the Taliban. Factually, prosecutors claimed that the named defendants in the matter were engaged in a common conspiracy aimed at planning and preparing to use militaristic or terrorist tactics against the United States and certain of its allies abroad. Among the specific actions of concern utilized as evidence of the conspiracy was a visit to what is described as a terrorist training camp in Pakistan made by several of the defendants.

For present purposes, this matter is of some relevance because of the descriptive terminology employed by the court in outlining and considering the charges leveled against the named defendants. In particular, the court appears to routinely associate the term *jihad* with terrorism, itself. For example, in describing the allegations asserted in this matter, the court observes that the defendants were said to have been engaged in activities that constituted "preparation for violent *jihad* overseas against nations with whom the United States was at peace and

[147] 309 F. Supp. 2d 789 (Eastern Dist. Vir. 2004).

providing material support to terrorist organizations."[148] The court goes on to reiterate the prosecutorial claim that some of the co-conspirators attended a "terrorist and *jihad* training camp." The court further asserts the factual claim that the defendants attended this camp with the intent to "fight" for the Taliban and Al-Qaeda.[149]

In its own findings of fact, the court observes that the practical circumstances alleged to have taken place were generally not in dispute. However, the entirety of the case turned on the interpretation of those factual circumstances. In particular, much of the case centered upon the interpretation of the visit by Khan and other defendants to the camp in Pakistan, alleged to have been a Taliban training facility, and the periodic organization of paintball games by Khan and others in the U.S., which were characterized by the prosecution as being training exercises in preparation for future armed conflict. Khan and other defendants in this case argued that both the camp and the paintball activities were purely recreational.

This matter serves as a particularly interesting case study precisely because the court, while liberally utilizing the term *jihad* throughout its decision, acknowledges the complexity of any attempt to define the term adequately. As the court observes, "Jihad literally means a struggle, which may range from exercising self-discipline, such as controlling one's appetite, to violent combat against perceived enemies of Islam."[150] Later, in a footnote, the court discusses the idea of "dying in a state of *jihad*," and acknowledges that such a death need not be necessarily tied to violence or combat. Instead, as the court observes, to die in a state of *jihad* may involve a death occurring while one is engaged in any sort of religious or spiritual struggle.[151]

Despite these acknowledgements, the court seems to persist in drawing what would appear to be an unnecessary and gratuitous linkage between the term *jihad* and violent engagements of a terrorist nature. The court speaks of the apparent interest by the defendants in

---

[148] Ibid., 796.

[149] Ibid., 802.

[150] Ibid., 803.

[151] Ibid., n. 5, at p. 806. Referring to a defense expert witness called in the case, the court observes, "to die shaheed means to die in a state of jihad, which does not necessarily mean combat because jihad includes all struggles, not just violent ones." Ibid.

the war in Chechnya, noting that the group established a paintball website, which they used to distribute information about the war. In describing the website, the court states that it "was used to disseminate information about *jihad*." The court describes tapes depicting the conflict in Chechnya and witnessed by defendant Al-Hamdi, as "videotapes about *jihad*."[152] And one defendant in the matter is described as being turned away from service in Chechnya because he lacked "*jihad* experience."[153] In describing another defendant, the court observed that the individual identified himself as a moderate Muslim who "does not subscribe to terrorism." In an apparent effort to negate this claim, the court went on to argue that his varying activities appeared to be "training for *jihad*."[154]

Meanwhile, the acknowledged testimony of certain defendants seems to suggest that an apparent mental distinction was being made by these individuals between the nature of the term *jihad* and terrorism, even while the court sought to merge the two concepts. These differing definitional approaches created some confusion. As the court reasoned, one particular defendant responded negatively when he was asked if he had attended a "*jihad* training" in Pakistan, and this negative response was characterized by prosecutors as a lie. The defendant, however, understood the exchange quite differently. According to the defendant, the interrogator asked him if he had attended a "terrorist" camp and he observed that the camp he attended was not for the purpose of training terrorists.[155] Thus, whether the statement made by the defendant was true or false seemed to hinge on the precise definition of *jihad* recognized by an individual. Numerous other instances of the use of the term *jihad* may be observed scattered throughout the court's

---

[152] Ibid., 807.

[153] Ibid., 808.

[154] Ibid., 816.

[155] Ibid. As the court further observed, "Lastly, if going to the LET camp was innocent, Chapman would have had no reason to lie to FBI agents in July 2003 when they asked him if he had ever received jihad training or been to LET when he was in Pakistan. Chapman answered no to both questions, and falsely told SA Christopher Mamula that he had gone to Islamabad to go hiking. Chapman explained at trial that the agents did not ask him about attending an LET camp, but asked about a terrorist camp, and Chapman did not consider the LET camp to be "terrorist." Ibid., 817.

opinion. In general, the word *jihad* appears to be called upon by the court as a sort of term of art designed to refer to activities that might otherwise be described as violent, combative or of a terrorist nature.

While the term *jihad* makes repeated appearance within the court's analysis, it is not clear that the invocation of this term serves any meaningful purpose in the attempt to evidence the specific crimes alleged. In the first and one of the most significant counts alleged in the original indictment against the defendants, the claim of conspiracy, much of the court's attention is focused upon whether the group conspired to violate the Federal Neutrality Act.[156] As the court outlined the elements that must be proven in order to support such a claim, the key activity required is the organization of a "military expedition" against a foreign state with whom the U.S. is "at peace." On its face, it seems clear that no finding of engagement in a "*jihad*" is necessary in order to prove these elements. Indeed, in its discussion of whether there was sufficient evidence present to prove such a conspiracy to violate the Neutrality Act, the court never referred to *jihad* conceptually, nor did it employ the term in describing the activities of the defendants relevant to this charge. Further charges leveled against the defendants claiming members of the group conspired to "overthrow, put down or destroy by force the Government," conspired to provide material support to Al-Qaeda, and conspired to support the Taliban were similarly disconnected from the term *jihad*.[157]

Again, within its discussion of whether the defendants engaged in such criminal acts, the court never refers to the activity of *jihad*. It does discuss the Pakistani training camps and the apparent connection between these camps and such groups as Al-Qaeda, but no discussion of *jihad*, per se, was apparently deemed necessary to resolve the question of whether these defendants committed the specified crimes.

In general, then, this opinion is noteworthy precisely because of the repeated invocation of the term *jihad* by the court during its consideration of the facts associated with this matter and the notable absence of significant reference to the term by the court within its analysis of the elements of the charged crimes and its consideration of the sufficiency of the evidence to establish the guilt of the defendants of such charges. Significantly, while many of the crimes alleged in this

---

156 *18 U.S.C. § 960.*

157 U.S. v. Khan, 820-827.

matter hinge upon claims of the commission of violent or terrorist activities, or the support of such actions, none of the counts seek proof of a religious motivation for these endeavors. It may be reasonable, then, to question the necessity of invoking such a religious term within a judicial decision examining such a controversial and prominent criminal matter. Further, it seems important to question the larger social impact of such a utilization of religious language.

At least within the United States, there appears to be a significant portion of the populace with little or no understanding of the Muslim faith. The totality of the knowledge such Americans possess regarding the Muslim faith, its history, and its ritual practices, may be summed up frequently in a few isolated phrases and anecdotal observations. For such individuals, the purposeful linkage between Islamic religious terms and terrorism by a vital and public arm of the government may serve as a determinative event in the shaping of private impressions regarding the Muslim community and its members.

It is interesting to note that in the appellate reconsideration of this case, the United States Court of Appeals for the Fourth Circuit[158] invests little effort in seeking to better define the nature of *jihad*, turning, instead, to a copy of Webster's Dictionary as its source of understanding. From that popular resource, the court accepts the rather stilted definition of *jihad* as being "holy war undertaken by Muslims as a sacred duty."[159] Accordingly, it found little fault in the use by the lower court of such terminology.

While the matter of *U.S. v. Khan* is useful as a beginning point in such a discussion, this case does not stand alone. A similarly useful matter may be the appellate decision in the case of *U.S. v. Abdel Rahman.*[160] In this opinion, even while recognizing the potential definitional breadth of the word *jihad* as a term implying "struggle," the court, nonetheless, repeatedly refers to the alleged violent conspiracy lying at the heart of the case as a "*jihad*," and to the group of alleged conspirators as the "*jihad* organization."[161] The charges against the defendants in this matter stemmed from the 1993 plot that

---

[158] U.S. v. Kahn, 206 U.S.App. LEXIS 22791 (Decided September 1, 2006).

[159] Citing *Webster's Unabridged Dictionary* 1029 (2nd Ed. 2001).

[160] 189 F.2d 88 (2nd Cir. 1999).

[161] Ibid., 104.

resulted in the bombing of the World Trade Center towers in New York City.

In introducing the matter, the court observed that, according to prosecutors, Rahman, a blind Islamic cleric, was responsible for gathering a conspiratorial group whose purpose was to engage in "*jihad*." The court further noted that Rahman and others alleged to have been involved in the conspiracy believed that "*jihad*" against the United States and Egypt was authorized based upon Quranic texts.[162] Indeed, the court observed that Rahman encouraged the constitution of a "*jihad* army." Again, this matter seems to highlight the question of the appropriateness of the use of religious terminology to describe criminal endeavors within the confines of court decisions.

This decision may be of particular importance in addressing the present question precisely because defendant Rahman attempted to assert that heightened protection should be afforded to his actions because they were of a religious nature. In other words, Rahman attempted to invoke religion into the discussion of the claims made against him. Meanwhile, the court seems to have specifically rejected the relevance of religious questions in assessing the merits of the case. In explaining the primary charges made against Rahman and others concerning the alleged seditious conspiracy against the United States, the court noted that such a plot is formed by the conspiring of two or more individuals to "levy war" against the U.S.[163] There is no requirement that the alleged conspiracy be rooted in some sort of

---

[162] Ibid.

[163] Ibid., 111. The provision in question was *18 U.S.C. § 2384*. The statute provides:

> If two or more persons in any State or Territory, or in any place subject to the jurisdiction of the United States, conspire to overthrow, put down or to destroy by force the Government of the United States, or to levy war against them, or to oppose by force the authority thereof, or by force to prevent, hinder or delay the execution of any law of the United States, or by force to seize, take, or possess any property of the United States contrary to the authority thereof, they shall each be fined under this title or imprisoned not more than twenty years, or both. *18 U.S.C. § 2384*

religious activity. Indeed, in speaking to the actions of Rahman, individually, the court specifically rejected the notion that the cleric's religious predilections had any impact upon the assessment of his guilt or innocence related to this criminal charge.

As the court observed in the matter, "freedom of speech and of religion do not extend so far as to bar prosecution of one who uses a public speech or a religious ministry to commit crimes."[164] While acknowledging that religious speech is among the types of speech most ardently protected by the First Amendment of the Constitution, the court went on to hold, "one is not immunized from prosecution for such speech-based offenses merely because one commits them through the medium of political speech or religious preaching."[165] Still, the court felt comfortable in employing decidedly religious terminology within its own assessment of the matter.

It is also interesting to note that the court, meanwhile, sustained the lower trial court's decision to exclude expert testimony from a Rahman witness that was aimed, in part, at clarifying the nature of the term *jihad.* In particular, the expert was to claim that *jihad* is commonly understood within the modern Muslim community as referring to the effort to "combat oppression."[166] The court asserted that such proof would not overcome the criminality of Rahman's actions, merely because they were "justified...within the framework of Islamic law."[167] The court speculated that the inclusion of such testimony would have likely led to confusion on the part of jurors. As the court stated:

> The question whether such acts on his part would have been condoned or forbidden by Islamic law could lead to an evidentiary dispute about Islamic law that would have little likelihood of illuminating whether he committed the forbidden acts of terrorism.[168]

---

[164] U.S. v. Rahman, 117.

[165] Ibid.

[166] Ibid., 135. Among the claims to be made by the expert witness was the assertion that, "Jihad [had its] origins in Islam after Prophet Mohammed began preaching in the 7th Century . . . . Jihad is cast in the mold of a legal doctrine . . . . Jihad has come to mean . . . the combating of oppression . . . ." Ibid.

[167] Ibid., 136.

[168] Ibid.

The language of the court is, at best, curious in that it seems to emphasize what it perceives as the inherent irrelevance of religiously-oriented ideas in the determination of the matter, even while it seems interested in utilizing religious language for descriptive purposes.

Again, the text of this decision seems to raise the question of the utility of invoking religious language within the confines of such a legal determination. In general, the activities alleged to have been undertaken by the defendants in the matter appear easily describable without resort to the use of a term like *jihad*. Again, in the assessment of culpability of the varying defendants, the court's analysis was not dependent at all upon the use of this term. At the same time, since the term *jihad* is peculiar to the Muslim religious faith, the invocation of the term within the framework of such an opinion may be viewed as being likely to contribute to broader societal misunderstandings of the religious community and its adherents.

Jihad in Other Cases

The apparent use of the term *jihad* as a short-hand descriptive device to refer to violent, combative or terrorist activities may be witnessed in a number of other court decisions. In each instance, it is questionable whether the utilization of such peculiarly religious terminology is necessary or even useful in the broader effort to render a decision upon the specific criminal charges leveled in these matters. For example, in the recent case of *U.S. v. Sabri Benkahla*,[169] the defendant was charged, in part, with falsely denying his participation in a combat training camp in Afghanistan or Pakistan during 1999. This case proves interesting due to the continued reference by the court to the camp as a "*jihad* camp" and to the training received there as "*jihad* training." Ultimately, the central question in the case related to whether the defendant had received combat-related training, an issue that does not appear to be dependent upon a finding of religious motivation or orientation.

In certain other instances, it seems, prosecutors appear to have found it advantageous to attempt to draw a specific linkage between the acts of Muslim defendants and the charged term *jihad*. An example

---

[169] U.S. Dist. LEXIS 71458 (Eastern Dist. Va. 2006).

may be the recent case of *U.S. v. Muhamad Mubayyid.*[170] In this case, individual defendants were charged with making false statements on an application to form a non-profit corporation under U.S. and state law. The alleged falsehoods and omissions of information were said to have been made with the intent of disguising the true purpose of the organization, which was alleged to be the support of terrorist activities abroad. Prosecutors in the matter sought to draw a direct linkage between the sorts of efforts that were said to have been supported by the non-profit corporation and the term *jihad.* Significantly, prosecutors defined *jihad* as "violent, religiously-based military conflict overseas."[171]

Still, not all courts have overlooked the complex nature of the term *jihad.* In the concurring opinion in the U.S. Supreme Court case of *Clay v. United States,*[172] involving a claim by the defendant that he conscientiously objected to participation in war, Justice Douglas observed:

> War is not the exclusive type of *jihad*; there is action by the believer's heart, by his tongue, by his hands, as well as by the sword. As respects the military aspects it is written:
>
> "The *jihad,* in other words, is a sanction against polytheism and must be suffered by all non-Muslims who reject Islam, or, in the case of the dhimmis (Scripturaries), refuse to pay the poll tax. The *jihad,* therefore, may be defined as the litigation between Islam and polytheism; it is also a form of punishment to be inflicted upon Islam's enemies and the renegades from the faith. Thus in Islam, as in Western Christendom, the *jihad* is the *bellum justum."* The *jihad* is the Moslem's counterpart of the "just" war as it has been known in the West....[173]

This observation by the court seems to emphasize the potential breadth of the varied ways in which the term *jihad* may be understood by members of the Muslim community. The recognition of such breadth

---

170 U.S. Dist. LEXIS 16556 (Mass. Dist. Ct. 2007).

171 Ibid., 4.

172 403 U.S. 698, 91 S.Ct. 2068 (1971).

173 Ibid., 2075, citing *War and Peace in the Law of Islam*, 56.

in meaning, perhaps, should serve to prompt caution in the employment of the term.

An Emphasis upon Terror

Perhaps, it is not solely the link made between *jihad* and terrorism that is of significance in regard to the portrayal of Islam in U.S. courts. In certain cases, there may be a more direct connection drawn between Islam, itself, and terrorist activity, and such an association has the potential of being quite powerful.

The explosive influence such an association may carry was underscored by a 2007 news report concerning polling advice provided to congressional Republican lawmakers. According to the report, partisan lawmakers were encouraged to draw an intentional link in speeches between Islam and "terrorism," while avoiding the employment of terms such as "radical" or "extremist" when speaking about the religious faith.[174] These latter terms did not, apparently, offer the same potential for generating popular fear and anxiety, as did the term terrorism. As the article reported:

> One adviser, who was part of two closed-door briefings by the consultants to GOP congressional members and aides over the past two weeks, said most Americans polled are not threatened by "Muslims" and that the words "extremist" and "radical" conjure up an image of people who make threats but don't follow through with them. "People believe terrorists act, so we should be using that instead of extremist or radicals. Calling the threat 'an Islamic terrorist' or 'al Qaeda' works better than 'Muslim radical,'" said the consultant.[175]

This charged verbal linkage of Islam and terrorism has not been confined to the world of politics. The phrases "Islamic terrorism" or "Islamic terrorist" have made their way frequently, since 2001, into

---

[174]Paul Bedard, "GOP Urged to Cite "Islamic Terrorists," *U.S. News and World Report* (September 27, 2007), http://www.usnews.com/blogs/news-desk/2007/09/27/gop-urged-to-cite-islamic-terrorists.html (accessed September 29, 2007).

[175] Ibid.

court opinions on a range of issues. An example may be seen in the 2007 dissenting opinion in a matter in which charges were leveled against the U.S. corporation Exxon concerning alleged abuses committed by its security personnel working in Indonesia.[176] While the question of the religious identification of those involved in the matter was not at issue, the dissent sought repeatedly to emphasize the role played by the country of Indonesia in the U.S. war against "radical Islamic terrorist organizations." As the court observes:

> The fourth largest nation in the world (and the largest Muslim nation), Indonesia has been a key partner of the United States since September 11, 2001, in the ongoing war against al Qaeda and related radical *Islamic terrorist* organizations.[177] (emphasis added)

In a host of cases related to petitions by immigrants seeking asylum in the United States, the term "Islamic terrorism" served some role, though it was not always clear that such terminology was necessary or accurate in its description of existing circumstances. In a 2005 case, a Chinese immigrant, fleeing his immediate former home in Jakarta, Indonesia, sought refuge in the United States, based primarily upon grounds of ethnic discrimination.[178] In each of the substantive grounds alleged in the matter, the asylum seeker indicated his belief that he had been physically threatened while in Indonesia, due to his ethnic Chinese heritage. Later, in the court's factual findings, certain of the asylum seeker's assailants are termed "Islamic terrorists."[179] While the asylum seeker claimed Christianity as his personal faith, this purposeful linkage of the apparently terroristic acts of his assailants with a specifically Muslim identification seems a curious characterization, especially given the predominant emphasis in this case upon ethnicity, rather than religion.

This matter does not stand alone. In a 2004 case, an immigrant from Pakistan, seeking asylum for political retribution, was curiously

---

[176] John Doe v. Exxon Mobil Corporation, 473 F.3d 345 (D.C. Cir Ct. App., 2007).

[177] Ibid., 358.

[178] Fen Lie Tjhen v. Ascroft, 123 Fed. Appx. 520 (3rd Cir. Ct. App, 2005).

[179] Ibid., 522.

described as having been assaulted by "plain clothed police and/or Islamic terrorists."[180] His claim was rooted in his assertion that as a member of the minority "left-leaning Pakistan People's Party," he came under threat in his local home. This threat eventually led to his imprisonment and the extraction of an 80,000 rupee payment. The horrendous nature of the incident is obvious. Still, the characterization of the asylum seeker's assailants through the use of religious identity seems curious. Again, whether this individual's assailants were Muslim was not known and was a fact that was apparently not relevant to the larger set of issues addressed. Still, the court felt it worthwhile to draw a purposeful linkage between terrorist activity and the Islamic faith. It would be interesting to consider whether the same sort of description would have been applied had the individual's assailants been Christian or Buddhist.

Similarly, in a matter involving an Algerian seeking asylum in the United States, the term "Islamic terrorists" was used to describe what appeared to be threatening political players.[181] In the matter, a former Algerian general claimed he was threatened in his native land, after retiring from the military, for failing to provide assistance to a militant political organization. There was no assertion of religious bias made by the claimant. Other similar matters out of the immigration realm may be cited.[182]

In a case outside the immigration realm that bears a resemblance to those cited, an individual sought an economic recovery from the government of Iran for damages and distress resulting from an incident in which he was held captive or hostage in Lebanon.[183] The individual, an official with the American University in Beirut, was claimed to have been taken hostage by Hizbollah and held under torturous

---

[180] Syed Zufiqar Ul Hassan v. Ashcroft, 116 Fed. Appx. 348 (3rd Cir. Ct. App, 2004).

[181] Abdel Moumene Malki v. Ashcroft, 74 Fed. Appx. 655 (7th Cir. Ct. App, 2003).

[182] See Nagay Lotfy Saleh v. Gonzales, 172 Fed. Appx. 471 (3rd Cir. Ct. App., 2005); Jayshree Christian v. U.S. Dept. of Justice, 155 Fed. Appx. 29 (2nd Cir. Ct. App., 2005); and Aruta v. Immigration and Naturalization Service, 80 F.3d 1389 (9th Cir. Ct. App., 2006).

[183] Cicippio-Puelo v. Islamic Republic of Iran, 353 F.3d 1024 (D.C. Ct. App. 2004).

circumstances for apparently political purposes. His claim in this matter was aimed at the government of Iran, who, it was said, supported and used the Hizbollah organization to secure political ends. Yet, the court sought to identify the individual's captors specifically as "Islamic terrorists," placing an undeniably religious overtone upon a matter that appears to be best described as political.

Despite the use of the phrase "Islamic terrorism" in court decisions, at least a couple of courts have, themselves, acknowledged the potency of such terminology. The first came within the context of a libel suit. In the matter, certain individuals associated with a non-profit corporation were accused of supporting activity termed "Islamic terrorism." In response to the charge, the trial court judge who heard the matter observed:

> The court finds that the specific posting on the internet of victim names, home addresses, coupled with repeated inflammatory rhetoric connecting them with concepts like *Islamic terrorism* and racism are a violation of the anti-harassment order issued April 19, 2001....[184]

In the second matter, a Muslim litigant sought to have a judge removed from a case due to what he perceived to be bias on behalf of the jurist.[185] Ultimately, the court disagreed with the claim of bias. However, the court, likewise, seemed to acknowledge the potential for harm that might flow from the linkage of Islam with such terms as "terrorism." As the court observed, after examining in detail the precise words uttered by the judge in question:

> These words in no way show any form of bias against Muslims in general or Defendant, in particular, nor do they draw any association between Defendant, Iraq, *terrorism*, or *Muslims*. The admonitions address pragmatic concerns that even peaceful demonstrations might temporarily block traffic and access to the courthouse.[186] (emphasis added)

---

[184] Trummel v. Mitchell, 131 P.3d 305 (Wash. Sup. Ct., 2006), 317.

[185] U.S. v. Potts, 2007 U.S. Dist. LEXIS 65316 (East. Dist. Penn., 2007).

[186] Ibid.

Courts, Jihad and Terrorism

The term *jihad* is subject to the same potential for misuse as the intentional linking of Islam with some form of "terror." Due to media coverage of events ranging from the overthrow of the Shah of Iran to the more recent military campaigns of the United States in Iraq, the term *jihad* appears linked inextricably to the idea of violence, at least in terms of popular impressions. At the same time, the term cannot be disassociated from the religious tradition with which the term is associated – Islam. Thus, when employed, the term *jihad* seems capable of, if not likely to imply that Islam is necessarily a religion that is inherently violent or unduly subject to the adoption of violent means. A similar conclusion seems to be the most probable one to be drawn from any effort designed to link Islam with the terms "terror" or "terrorism."

Following the events of September 11, 2001, if not before, it may be observed that the popular image of Islam in the West has become mired in concerns regarding personal security and terrorism. Whatever one makes of these broad societal concerns and impressions, it seems worthwhile to ask to what extent the judiciary may have played a role, willingly or unintentionally, in the perpetuation of popular mistrust and anxiety directed at the Muslim community.

Language of the type employed by the courts implicated in this analysis seems capable of serving the role of perpetuating bias. Still, one may ask, does the employment of the terminology in question serve a vital or useful role? In the examples presented here, the necessity of the utilization of the descriptive terms *jihad* or Islamic terrorism may, indeed, be often subject to question. In considering the specific uses of these terms, it seems arguable that narrower and more specific terms may have often yielded greater precision within the scope of the judicial analysis. At the same time, these scattered opinions seem to raise precisely the question of the implications of the employment of such terms. Does the invocation of terms such as *jihad* or Islamic terrorism in the context of official governmental documents and records serve to perpetuate popular stereotypes of Muslims or Islamic society? Moreover, what may be the impact of such actions upon the self-image of Muslims living in the United States? These, it seems, are important social inquiries.

At the end of the day, while this work does not offer quantifiable analysis of the psychological impact upon Muslims individually or as a community stemming from these characterizations, it does presuppose that the effect of these associations can only be negative. The coupling of a religion with connotations that promote fear and anxiety must lead to the cultivation of negative impressions of the target social group. Perhaps, the inevitable consequence of such negative impressions must be the encouragement of discrimination and ostracism. While words such as *jihad* and terrorism are a part of our vocabulary and, as such, are to be used, the question begged here is one of appropriate use. The consequence of using such terminology to subtly perpetuate a form of quiet discrimination is problematic. Thus, it may be argued, an informed employment of such terms is desirable. If court officials are to employ such terms, it seems important that they be better informed of the complex meanings associated with them and reminded of their potential for long-term discriminatory effect.

CHAPTER 4

Child Custody and American Muslims

Since September 11, some American Muslims say an anti-Muslim backlash has put them at risk of losing their children. Why? Because since then, more than a dozen Muslim parents nationwide have been sued for custody of their children by non-Muslim ex-spouses and grandparents who don't want the children reared by the Muslim parent, according to the Council on American-Islamic Relations, a Washington-based advocacy group.

That compares with two such lawsuits reported in the year leading up to the terrorist attacks. Most of the cases are scattered across the South and Midwest. At least five are in Texas, the most in any state.

....

But Will Harrell, executive director of the American Civil Liberty Union's Texas chapter, said many family judges are the product of an evangelical Christian movement dominating the state's school board and family courtrooms in recent elections. "All those people who compared Muhammad to terrorists are the same people who dominate the political agenda and whose policy is being reflected," Harrell said.

> *"They happen to be in the position to perpetuate the bigotry."*[187]

It is unclear exactly how many current U.S. residents claim allegiance to the Muslim faith. Estimates of the numbers of Muslims living in America vary widely, from about 1.2 million[188] to as many as 7 million.[189] However, most scholars seem to agree with the basic proposition that there exists a Muslim community in the United States of significant size, which is expanding at a rate faster than that of most other ethnic or religious communities. It may be argued that the presence of this apparently growing community is being felt throughout modern American society. As this community expands, its members will increasingly be confronted by situations necessitating an engagement with governmental institutions, including the judiciary.

Thus, it seems important to consider the relationship between the Muslim litigant and the U.S. courtroom. Of particular concern may be those matters involving the claim of rights or interests rooted in Islamic law and the reactions of U.S. courts to such claims. Through the examination of a series of cases from the narrow field of the law of personal status, this chapter and the next investigate the implications for Muslims and the larger society that extend from the interactions between the courts and Islamic faithful.

In part, this examination focuses attention upon the reasonable expectations that Muslims may possess based upon their brief history of involvement with U.S. courts. As well, this examination focuses upon the extent to which Western cultural or Judeo-Christian religious biases may affect court rulings aimed at the resolution of claims involving Muslim litigants within the American judicial system. The precise issue considered here, then, is whether claims of right made

---

[187] Manya Brachear, "Torn between Cross and Crescent," *Beliefnet.com* (Feb., 14, 2003) http://www.beliefnet.com/story/119/story_11987.html (November 12, 2007), re-printed with permission from *The Dallas Morning News*.

[188] See Tom W. Smith, "Estimating the Muslim Population in the United States," Study for the American Jewish Committee (March 3, 2006), www.ajc.org (accessed January 5, 2007).

[189] Ihsan Bagby, Paul Perl, and Bryan T. Froehle, "The Mosque in America: A National Portrait," *Report of the Mosque Study Project*, Council of American-Islamic Relations (April 2001).

pursuant to Islamic law and presented in U.S. courts receive equitable and consistent treatment and whether cultural or religious presumptions may negatively affect the response made to such claims. Further, it may be asked, what are the consequences for litigants, themselves, of the decisions of U.S. courts related to such claims of right?

Stakes in the Battle

The individual and social costs of judgments affecting the personal status of Muslim litigants can be high, indeed. As one Muslim commentator notes, marriages established pursuant to Islamic law are particularly vulnerable in American courts. Thus, a couple that marries pursuant to Islamic law requirements, but fails to follow even technical civil marriage requirements in a given state, may find their union declared void, a circumstance that can create profound economic consequences for both the couple and the larger community. As well, where males enter into polygamous marital relationships before entering the U.S., courts may refuse to extend marital right to the second, third or fourth wives. Accordingly, claims for economic support and inheritance rights can be broadly impacted. In some instances, women may be left with limited or uncertain means of support.[190]

In an effort to illustrate the social costs that may extend from a court's failure to recognize the legal actions of another jurisdiction, the experience of one Muslim woman was detailed in a recent speech. In an address before the United Nations Fourth World Conference on Women in Huairou, China, the story of Fatima, an immigrant to the United States was related.[191] According to the case study, Fatima married a man, Omar, outside of the U.S. pursuant to Islamic law and immigrated to the U.S. following their union. Fatima was Omar's second wife. The couple lived together and had children, but

---

[190] Shaheen Ahmad, "American, Ambitious and Muslim," website Islam for Today, http://www.islmafortoday.com/americanambitious.htm (accessed March 8, 2008).

[191] Samer Hathout, "Challenges and Opportunities Facing American Muslim Women," Speech before the Non-Governmental Organization Forum of the United Nations Fourth World Conference on Women, Huairou, China (September 7, 1995).

eventually, Omar refused to provide any further support to Fatima or their children. Ultimately, Fatima challenged Omar's refusal to provide support in a U.S. court. Through the litigation, the marriage of Omar and Fatima was deemed to be void by the U.S. court, due to the existence of the prior marriage. Fatima was left without visible means of support. As the situation was described:

> Omar shirked his responsibilities under Islamic law – didn't give her (Fatima) anything, didn't give their children anything, even though he assured her before the marriage that he would. And Fatima could not do anything under U.S. law because they weren't legally married. Fatima was able to get no financial support from Omar because there was no legal institution compelling Omar to comply with Islamic law.[192]

As this case study suggests, the failure of U.S. courts to recognize rights established pursuant to Islamic law can result in the imposition of significant personal hardship upon individual Muslims. At the same time, it may create a great deal of uncertainty.

The consequences and uncertainties may follow Muslims even beyond American shores. Thus, legal actions and decisions of U.S. courts that contradict principles of Islamic law may create significant complications for Muslims when and if they take up residence in other jurisdictions. In particular, for those who are temporary immigrants or who maintain familial ties in countries that impose some form of Islamic law, decisions rendered in U.S. courts may, themselves, be subject to being voided once individuals return to their home jurisdictions.

Definitional Considerations

Initially, this inquiry demands that the basic legal regime governing such issues be briefly considered and that, where necessary, certain terms be defined, at least as they relate to the present exploration. Generally, the matters considered here, and in the following chapter, are rooted in claims relating to the establishment of marriages, the dissolution of marriages, the right to custody of children and ownership

---

[192] Ibid.

of marital property. Issues related to the validity and dissolution of marriages generally are to be resolved in accord with the laws of the state or jurisdiction that originally sanctioned the legal union. Of course, in those instances where the event in controversy took place in a foreign jurisdiction, specific questions may arise as to the appropriate law to be applied and whether judgments rendered under the foreign system will be recognized. Issues related to the validity of marriages and divorces will be entertained in greater detail in the subsequent chapter.

The legal regime that typically governs child custody cases brought in U.S. state courts, where one of the litigants claims rights under the law of another country or territory, begins with the Hague Convention on Civil Aspects of International Child Abduction ("Hague Convention").[193] Broadly, the purpose of the Hague Convention is to provide civil remedies designed to encourage the return of any child wrongfully taken out of his or her country of residence and to facilitate cooperation between signatory countries on such efforts. The Hague Convention is problematic, however, in that countries must voluntarily submit to its terms. While the United States has adopted the Hague Convention, very few majority Muslim states have, likewise, agreed to adhere to the strictures of this international regime.

In addition to this treaty-based legal framework, standards for the determination of the appropriateness of child custody arrangements are generally influenced by the terms contained in two model codes. The Uniform Child Custody Jurisdiction Act ("UCCJA") has been adopted, with occasional modification, in every state of the union. The supplemental Uniform Child Custody Jurisdiction and Enforcement Act ("UCCJEA") was designed to clarify its predecessor, the UCCJA, and has been adopted in whole or in part by the majority of states.[194] Together, these legal systems were intended to bring into harmony the laws of the states as they relate to issues concerning the award of child custody. Each of these legal systems, then, becomes important to the

---

[193] Hague Convention on the Civil Aspects of International Child Abduction, Oct. 25, 1980, art. 5, 99 U.S.T. 11 (codified as 42 U.S.C. §§ 11601-11610 (2001)).

[194] See Monica Henderson, "U.S. State Court Review of Islamic Law Custody Decrees – When are Islamic Custody Decrees in the Child's Best Interest?" *Brandeis Journ. Family Law* 36 (Summer 1997/98):423-448.

consideration of child custody matters brought in American courts, where at least one party to the proceeding claims citizenship or residence in almost any country other than the United States.

An additional term of particular importance for purposes of the present inquiry is "Islamic law." As was observed in the introductory chapter, there are significant differences of opinion as to whether there exists a recognizable and unified transnational system of Islamic law and, if so, what obligations and right such a system may impose upon its participants. Inquiries into the nature and scope of Islamic Law, generally, are beyond the limitations of this work and, thus, for the present purposes, the term "Islamic law" will be used to relate to any legal system that recognizes as primary sources of legal authority the *Qur'an* and the Muslim *Sunnah*, whether it be a private system of law or a system established and enforced by a particular political jurisdiction. Still, certain basic ideas and principles extending from this broad system of religious law may be articulated.

Legal Principles Affecting Child Custody Matters

In general, decisions of foreign states related to child custody are entitled to *comity*. According to the doctrine of comity, a legal standard that is incorporated into the UCCJA and the UCCJEA, the decision of a foreign court is broadly entitled to recognition and enforcement.[195] An exception to the doctrine of comity may be applied, according to the UCCJA, when the decision of the foreign court offends "the public policy" of the enforcing state, based upon either substantive or procedural grounds. Where such a violation of public policy is identified, the foreign judgment may be nullified or ignored by the U.S. court. The exception to the doctrine of comity under terms of the UCCJEA offers a standard that is a bit more demanding, allowing a foreign judgment to be overruled if it "violates fundamental principles of human rights."[196]

---

[195] See Lara Cardin, "The Hague Convention on the Civil Aspects of International Child Abduction as Applied to Non-Signatory Nations: Getting to Square One," *Houston J. Int'l L.* 20 (1997): 141-175, 170.

[196] Uniform Child Custody Jurisdiction and Enforcement Act, § 105 (c) (1997), available at http://www.law.upenn.edu/bll/ulc/uccjea/ final1997act.htm (accessed March 16, 2007).

Broadly speaking, the public policy of a state is deemed to have been violated in any instance where a foreign custody award is reasoned to contradict the basic standards employed by the state for the award of visitation and guardianship rights. In general, U.S. states employ the standard of "best interests" of the minor child in resolving issues related to the award of custody. This standard, however, may itself be seen as inherently problematic, especially when it is utilized to resolve litigated controversies involving one or more parties who claim rights or interests rooted in Islamic law or awarded by judicial bodies of majority Muslim countries.

In its application, many would argue the "best interests" standard frequently invokes subjective measures, potentially including cultural or even religious considerations. Recognizing the potential risks associated with such subjective enforcement of a legal regime, the Hague Convention, itself, abandons the utilization of the "best interests" standard in order to promote greater consistency of judgments in the field of cross-border child custody matters.[197] Of course, as noted above, the Hague Convention offers limited assistance in situations where a litigant in a U.S. court is claiming custody rights stemming from a foreign judgment of a majority Muslim country. Again, this is true precisely because few of these majority Muslim nations have opted to participate in the international regulatory regime outlined in the Hague Convention.

Child Custody under Shari'a

In majority Muslim countries, it is often true that child custody decisions are based upon the system of Islamic law. The standard utilized for making custody-related decisions, according to Islamic law, has been described by at least one commentator as a "religiously-based best interests test."[198] Yet, because Islamic law reflects the religiously

---

[197] Dorothy C. Daigle, "Due Process Rights of Parents and Children in International Child Abductions: An Examination of the Hague Convention and Its Exceptions," *Vanderbilt Journal of Transnat'l Law* 26, no. 4 (1993):865-894, 869-870.

[198] See Danielle Andrews, "Non-Muslim Mothers v. Egyptian Muslim Fathers: The Conflict between Religion and Law in International Child Custody

motivated standards and ideals understood by many to be foundational to the Muslim faith, custody decisions emerging from this system are often deemed inconsistent with the expectations of jurists in the U.S. The prospect for conflict is particularly high when a custody battle pits a non-Muslim mother against a Muslim father in an American state court.

It is, perhaps, worth noting certain essential principles arising from the *Shari'a* system related to the topic of child custody. In general, it may be observed that preference is given in custody determinations made pursuant to Islamic Law to the mother to act as physical custodian of infants and young children. As Jamal Nasir has observed in his widely-read overview of Islamic law,[199] "[w]hether the mother is separated or living with her husband, she has the first claim to the custody of her infant…." This observation is said to encapsulate the general requirements of Islamic law for the Sunni tradition. The Shia tradition, he asserts, accepts the same basic premise, though the two traditions disagree to some degree in terms of the detailed application of this principle.

Further, while the mother is preferred as a custodian of young children, the mother's family is generally preferred as alternate physical custodian, if she is unable to care for the child. Even beyond the person of the mother, the maternal preference is reflected in the order of those eligible to be granted custody in the absence of the mother. For example, if the mother is unavailable, due to death or incapacity, the right of custody passes next to the maternal grandmother, followed by the paternal grandmother, the sister of the mother and maternal aunts.[200]

In general terms, this maternal preference for physical custody extends until the child has reached a specific age. Following the child's maturation to this specified age, the custodial preference will generally shift to the father. Broadly, the age at which the maternal preference ends is between seven and nine years of age for male children and between nine and eleven for female children. Pointing to Saudi Arabia as an exemplar, the U.S. Department of State has described the nation's

---

Disputes and Abductions," *Suffolk Transnat't Law Review* 23 (Summer 2000):595-630, 609.

[199] Jamal J. Nasir, *The Islamic Law of Personal Status* 2 (2nd ed. 1990), 156-57.

[200] Ibid.

recognized system of preferences under Islamic law related to the custody of children, pointing specifically to the favoritism given to the maintenance of the Muslim personality of the household, noting:

> Normally, under Shari'a law, a mother can maintain custody of her male children until the age of nine, and female children until age seven. In practice the courts favor keeping children within a strict Islamic environment. Shari'a court judges have broad discretion in custody cases and often make exceptions to these general guidelines.
>
> Even when a mother who is residing in Saudi Arabia is granted physical custody of children, the father maintains legal custody and has the right to determine where the children live and travel. In many cases, the father has been able to assume legal custody of children against the wishes of the mother when she is unable or unwilling to meet certain conditions set by law for her to maintain her custodial rights. For example, if the mother moves to another country, the father is entitled to have custody. A court can sever a mother's custody if it determines that the mother is incapable of safeguarding the child or of bringing the child up in accordance with the appropriate religious standards. The mother can lose custody by re-marrying a non-Muslim, or by residing in a home with non-relatives. Shari'a law allows custody of children to be awarded to the closest male relative of a Saudi father in the case of death or imprisonment of the father, even if the Saudi father has made clear his wish that the children's mother have full custody.[201]

As the State Department advisory points out, even while the mother is preferred under the system of Islamic law as the appropriate physical custodian for young children, the father is typically granted legal custodianship of minor children.

---

[201] "International Parental Child Abduction: Saudi Arabia," Official website of the U.S. Department of State (November 22, 2007), http://travel.state.gov /family/abduction/country/country_517.html, (accessed February 22, 2008).

Following the period of the early development of children, the award of custodial rights becomes more complex under Islamic law. As Nasir points out, the varying Sunni schools offer inconsistent guidance as to what specifically would happen to children once they cross age-related thresholds. Broadly, there is a preference extended to the father to direct the maintenance and education of the child who has reached the age of the completion of the period of the maternal custody preference, though this paternal preference my be upset by the child's own contradictory desires or a determination that continued maintenance by the mother is preferred.[202]

Thus, of the four primary Sunni schools, the Hanbalis are identified as placing the greatest emphasis upon the precise desires of the children involved, themselves. Under the Hanbali system, a maternal preference for custody should be extended until the child in question reaches the age of seven, at which point, the child should be allowed to choose which parent he or she prefers to act as custodial guardian.[203] The Maliki school, meanwhile, is said to prefer maternal physical custody for male children until the time of puberty and for female children until the time of marriage, while preserving the right of the father to oversee education of the children, throughout. Other variations may be seen in the Shafi'i and Hanafi schools.[204] An example of a variant system of custodial preference may be witnessed in a Tunisian act cited by Nasir, which provides in relevant part:

> The ward shall live with the [mother] until the age of seven years for the boy and nine for the girl, after which age the ward shall be handed over to its father if he so requests, unless the judge shall rule it fittest to keep the ward with the [mother]…."[205]

---

[202] *The Islamic Law of Personal Status*, 167-68.

[203] Ibid., 167, citing Badran Abdul Ainain, *Huquq ul Awlad-fish-Shariat-il-Islamiyya wal Wanoon* (Alexandria, 1981), 87.

[204] The Shafii school is said to prefer maternal custody until the child reached the "age of discretion," after which the father assumes the responsibility of educating the child and may also maintain the child. Hanafis similarly are said to prefer maternal custody until the child has achieved a "degree of independence," defined as being able to feed, clothe and cleanse himself. Ibid.

[205] Ibid., 168, citing Tunisia Art. 67.

Nasir further observes that most modern Arab jurisdictions follow the basic Sunni system of preference. Such preference for the Sunni system may be witnessed in specific legislative enactments from Lebanon, Syria and Jordan and other countries. Focusing particularly upon the interpretation of Islamic Law under the Indian judicial system, Asaf Fyzee has, likewise, recognized the existence of a maternal preference for the physical custody of young children, while further noting that the issue of custody must be differentiated from issues related to guardianship of such children.[206] Citing the Indian Privy Council in the case of *Imambandi v. Mutsaddi*, Fyzee highlights the established maternal preference for physical custody of young children "up to a certain age and according to the sex of the child," but the father, as he further observes, continues to be recognized as the "natural guardian" of the child even throughout this period.[207] As Nasir also notes, the Shia legal system recognizes that the guardianship of the child of a broken marriage is held jointly by the father and grandfather.[208]

Fyzee goes on to observe that even while the maternal parent may be awarded physical custody, the father must be provided access to the child in question, in the form of visitation, during the tenure of the custody. Meanwhile, if the mother remarries, she may loose her custody rights over the children in question, though such a determination may hinge upon a decision regarding the "suitability" of the new environment.[209]

A Court Divided

The complexity of issues associated with the award of child custody may be witnessed within the body of judicial decisions focused upon this topic. These issues are made even more complex by the introduction of a foreign legal regime.

Still, the hallmark of a transparent judicial system is consistency and reliability. The question that may be asked, here, is whether such

---

[206] *Outlines of Muhammadan Law*, Fourth Ed. (New Delhi: Oxford University Press, 1974).

[207] Ibid., 198-99.

[208] *The Law of Islamic Personal Status*, 184.

[209] *Outlines of Muhammadan Law*, 199.

matters have been addressed in a consistent manner by U.S. courts especially in situations where at least one of the litigants is Muslim. In terms of claims filed in the U.S. by Muslims for the custody of children born to marriages that end in separation, such consistency may often appear elusive.

Referring to U.S. judicial decisions relating to child custody claims of Muslim litigants, some courts have reached the conclusion that prior awards made by courts of other international jurisdictions, applying doctrines of Islamic law, should be entitled to comity precisely because they reflect the "best interests" of the minors involved and are, thus, consistent with public policy. Other U.S. courts, meanwhile, have seized upon certain presumptions arising from Islamic legal regimes, especially those relating to maternal and paternal preference, and identified these as arbitrary. Accordingly, these systems have been recognized as being inconsistent with the judicial standard of "best interests" of the child, as a matter of law.

It is, perhaps, a recent appellate case from Louisiana that serves as an ideal point of beginning for the consideration of the differing and often conflicting judgments arising from this line of judicial opinions. In *Amin v. Bakhaty*,[210] the Louisiana Supreme Court was confronted with the question of the appropriate division of custodial rights between the Egyptian mother and father of a nine-year-old boy. The curious circumstances of the case arose as an Egyptian physician ("Dr. Bakhaty") established a medical practice in New Jersey, leaving his wife ("Ms. Amin") to reside in the home of her father in Egypt, with the couple's minor son. Dr. Bakhaty returned periodically to Egypt to visit his wife and son, but maintained a residence in New Jersey and claimed dual citizenship in the U.S. and in his native country.

Approximately six years after the birth of the couple's son, Ms. Amin left Egypt and traveled to the U.S. She brought with her the couple's son and, eventually, settled in Baton Rouge, Louisiana, where her sister resided. In the meantime, upon learning of Ms. Amin's travel to the U.S., Dr. Bakhaty brought criminal charges against his wife in Egypt. The charges accused Ms. Amin of removing a minor from Egypt without the permission of a custodial parent, and Ms. Amin was convicted of the charges by a court in her native country. In January

---

[210] 798 So.2d 75 (Louisiana Sup. Ct. 2001); see also the Louisiana Court of Appeals decision in the matter at 812 So. 2d 12 (La. App. 2001).

1998, only weeks after arriving in Louisiana, Ms. Amin initiated a divorce action against her husband. The day following the filling of Ms. Amin's action, Dr. Bakhaty obtained a certificate from an Egyptian court granting him a divorce.[211] Based upon the actions of the Egyptian court and Egyptian law related to the custody of minors, Dr. Bakahty sought a civil warrant from a Louisiana court seeking the removal of the child from Ms. Amin and the assertion of custody.

While the acrimony expressed between Dr. Bakhaty and his wife may seem rather extraordinary, it is the apparent animosity between the Louisiana courts and the Egyptian legal system that makes this case significant. Ultimately, the Louisiana Supreme Court was confronted with the precise question of whether it would recognize the custody claim regarding the couple's son made by Dr. Bakhaty pursuant to Egyptian law and rooted in Islamic legal principles. In accord with Egyptian law, Dr. Bakhaty held guardianship rights over the child. Such rights aligned with the broader paternal preference for guardianship under Islamic law.

In the original hearing in the matter, the Louisiana trial court ruled that the paternal preferences related to custody built into the Islamic legal structure were inconsistent with the U.S. legal standard of "best interests" of the minor. Ultimately, the Louisiana Supreme Court agreed with the reasoning of the trial court, calling into question the value as precedent of any such decision based upon principles of Islamic law. As the court observed, the very recognition of a custody decision rooted in such a system of preference would "differ" inherently from broader public policy interests of the state of Louisiana.

In its original decision dismissing Dr. Bakhaty's claim of right rooted in Islamic law, the trial court offered language that might be described as reflective of apparent suspicion of or even bias against the Egyptian legal system and its Islamic foundation, when it stated:

> At the outset, it should be noted that Egypt follows Islamic family law. Egyptian family law is "gender biased," as it provides protection to certain people based solely on gender. A husband and wife do not have equal rights.... When there is a minor child born of a marriage, Egyptian law provides that

---

[211] This certificate was issued on January 8, 1998. Ibid., 78.

> the father has the absolute right to…the physical custody of the minor child.[212]

This statement refers to the preference, rooted in Islamic law, for maternal physical custody of children under a specified age, generally, about the age of seven for boys and nine for girls, and the subsequent paternal preference for physical custody of minors of more advanced ages.

Ultimately, the court recognized its authority to accommodate the Egyptian legal standard related to custody based upon the doctrine of comity. Yet, it agreed with the trial court that the social interests in extending comity in this situation were outweighed by a broader desire to protect the "best interests" of the child. And, in this matter, the best interests of the child were expressed not in an award of custody to Dr. Bakhaty, but to the child's mother, instead.

In effect, the message of the court in *Amin* appears to be that, because of the gender-based preference built into the Islamic law of child custody, decisions relying upon such standards should be deemed questionable as a matter of law. As the court observed:

> In this case, the trial court declined to recognize Egypt as a "state" for purposes of determining jurisdiction based on the fundamental differences between Egypt's child custody laws and Louisiana's child custody laws. In Louisiana, custody in all cases will be determined by a court in the best interest of the child. The trial court found that custody laws in Egypt follow strict guidelines, irrespective of the best interest of the child.[213]

Indeed, based upon the language of the court, the strong implication appears to be that any such preference-based system would be inherently inconsistent with the well-established Western standard of "best interests" of the minor. It is, then, the very breadth of this decision that makes it interesting. In affirming the reasoning of the trial court, the message of the Louisiana Supreme Court, here, appears to be that, an entire foreign legal regime on issues related to child custody, as

---

[212] Ibid., 16.

[213] Ibid., 85.

a matter of law, is deemed incompatible with the standards imposed by U.S. courts.

Curiously, the court reaches this conclusion without any obvious consideration of the broad outcomes obtained in matters in which judicial bodies have applied such Islamic legal standards. It also is not apparent that the court sought information related to the practical steps employed in the implementation of such Islamic legal standards by Egyptian and other relevant judicial institutions, as it reached its conclusions; nor did it examine factors taken into account by courts applying such standards or possible exceptions generally considered.

The curious limitation of the court's analysis is made more peculiar by the fact that the court goes so far as to recognize a deep split among U.S. tribunals in terms of their willingness to accept custody decisions rendered pursuant to Islamic law. It attempts to sidestep this rift by arguing that, ultimately, it is the standard of "best interests" of the minor that has been upheld in each of these cases, whether Islamic law custodial standards were accepted or rejected by U.S. courts,[214] though it may be argued that the court's analysis is strained.

The court in *Amin* is not alone in rendering such a decision. Similar reasoning can be witnessed in the Kentucky case of *Al-Ali v. Al-Saba*.[215] In this case, a Kuwaiti husband living in the U.S. obtained a custody order regarding his two minor children from a Jordanian court applying Islamic law. When the custody order was challenged in a Kentucky trial court, it was invalidated. The Kentucky Court of Appeals upheld this lower court decision, indicating its disagreement with the Jordanian adherence to Islamic law and making the curious observation that tribunals of this Middle Eastern country "predetermine custody...based upon factors not related to the best interests of the child."[216]

---

[214] Ibid., 84. The court observed, related to this division among U.S. courts, that "a general principle pervaded" the entire group of decisions. The general principle was that even a foreign decision in which Islamic legal standards were applied may be upheld if it is determined that the judgment is rendered in the "best interests" of the child. Ibid.

[215] No. 93-CA-2297-MR, slip op. (Ky Ct. App. March 10 1995).

[216] Ibid., 3.

If these decisions appear to suggest a broad suspicion of Islamic law, such anxiety may appear elsewhere, as well. In the recent case of *Garg v. Garg*,[217] a matter involving a custody dispute rendered pursuant to Hindu religious law, the trial court judge is quoted as offering this rather remarkable statement regarding countries employing Islamic law:

> In other words, we are not going to have much reciprocity with Islamic countries because Maryland says there is no preference for a parent where Islamic law says there is. So we are not going to honor them. We know doggone well they will not honor us.[218]

The wholesale dismissal of custody orders generated by foreign courts applying Islamic law, as a matter of law, is a result that appears inconsistent with the decisions of certain other American judicial bodies. In the recent case of *Abouzahr v. Matera-Abouzahr*,[219] the Superior Court of New Jersey was petitioned to review a joint custody award made by a *Shari'a* court in Lebanon. That custody order provided liberal visitation rights to the Lebanese father, including the right to transport the children to Lebanon.

The American mother of the child at issue sought to restrict the father's visitation rights following the terrorist attacks on the U.S. on September 11, 2001, and, in particular, she challenged the fact that the order had been issued by a foreign court following Islamic law. Ultimately, the New Jersey court rejected the mother's petition, reasoning that the mere fact that the original custody order had been issued pursuant to Islamic law was not sufficient to deny comity to the decision. The court went on to note the importance of the exposure of the children to their father's home, extended family and religious customs.

In an often cited California decision, *In re Marriage of Malak*,[220] the state's Court of Appeals was likewise faced with the question of whether to extend comity to a decision rendered by a *Shari'a* court in

---

[217] 163 Md. App. 546, 881 A.2d 1180 (2005).
[218] Ibid., 1188.
[219] 361 N.J. Super. 135, 824 A.2d 268 (2003).
[220] 182 Cal. App. 3d 1018, 227 Cal. Rptr. 841 (1986).

Lebanon, which had awarded custody to the resident father. The *Shari'a* court's custody award was rooted in the same gender-based presumptions of the type witnessed in *Amin v. Bakhaty*. Still, the California court granted comity to the Lebanese custody award based upon its observation that the "best interests" of the children were contemplated by the decision, irrespective of any preferences. While observing that there are no universally recognized objective standards for the determination of the best interests of a child, the California court noted that a number of important factors had been taken into account by the Lebanese judicial body. These included the examination of "human, educational, social, psychological, material and moral factors," that seem to lie at the foundation of any reasoned inquiry into the "best interests" of a child.[221]

Similarly, in *Hosnain v. Malik*,[222] the Maryland Court of Special Appeals determined that an award of custody to a father by a Pakistani court applying Islamic law was, likewise, entitled to comity upon its challenge. Again, despite a stated preference for custody to reside with the father for older children, the Maryland court reasoned that Pakistani justices had engaged in a broad consideration of circumstances related to the well-being of the children involved. Thus, the decision rendered by the court was not inconsistent with Maryland public policy or with the standard of "best interests" of the child.

In another Maryland case, the state's appellate court addressed specifically the paternal preference under Islamic law.[223] The matter related to a contest between two Pakistani natives over the custody of their minor daughter. In the matter, the wife relocated to the United States on a student visa, taking with her the couple's daughter. Eventually, a divorce was sought by the husband in a Pakistani court and he was awarded custody of the daughter. When confronted with the issue of whether the Pakistani decision should be recognized, despite its rooting in a system that extends a paternal guardianship preference, the court stated:

> On the record before us, we cannot determine whether Pakistani law lacks conformity with Maryland law. We can,

---

[221] Ibid., 846.

[222] 108 Md. App. 284, 671 A.2d 988 (Maryland Court Spec. App. 1996).

[223] Malik v. Malik, 638 A.2d 1184 (Maryland Court Spec. App. 1994).

> however, resolve the narrow issue of whether the Pakistani order should be denied comity because there is a paternal preference in Pakistani law. If the only difference between the custody laws of Maryland and Pakistan is that Pakistani courts apply a paternal preference the way Maryland courts once applied the maternal preference, the Pakistani order is entitled to comity. A custody decree of a sister state whose custody law contains a preference for one parent over another would be entitled to comity, provided, of course, that the sister state's custody law applies the best interest of the child standard. For example, although Maryland has abolished a maternal preference, FL § 5-203, McAndrew v. McAndrew, 39 Md.App. 1, 8-9, 382 A.2d 1081 (1978), four states (Alabama, Florida, Mississippi, and Tennessee) still maintain the maternal preference doctrine in some form. A Maryland court would not refuse to enforce an award of custody made by a court of competent jurisdiction in any of those states. A Maryland court should not, therefore, refuse to enforce a Pakistani custody order merely because a paternal preference is found in that country's law.[224]

In contrast to other decisions, then the Maryland court appears to have found no particular incompatibility between the paternal custody preferences recognized under Islamic law and the implementation of the "best interests" of the child standard in such matters.

From Comity to Community

While the courts seem split on the issue of whether to recognize or extend comity to custody-related decisions arising from courts imposing variants of Islamic law, it is insightful to consider, in detail, the concerns U.S. courts have cited regarding this foreign legal system. In this regard, the case of *Samman v. Samman*,[225] provides an interesting case study. The case involved a couple, married and later divorced pursuant to Islamic religious law. The matter came before the Michigan Court of Appeals as the wife sought review of the child

---

[224] Ibid., 535.

[225] Slip Op. No. 249877; Lexis 3089 (Mich. Ct. App., Nov. 9, 2004).

custody arrangement made as part of that original divorce decree issued in accordance with Islamic law. That original arrangement provided for joint custody of the couple's minor son. It may be presumed, though this is not specified within the text of the decision, that the body rendering the original divorce and custody award sought to preserve rights to be held by the father and to encourage his involvement in the raising of the minor child. Such a move would be in keeping with the general preference for paternal guardianship of older children under Islamic law.

Upon review, the Michigan court rejected the original joint custody order issued pursuant to Islamic law and awarded sole custody of the minor child to the mother. Of relevance to the present inquiry, however, is the process by which the court reached its decision.

In an attempt to ascertain the appropriate division of custodial rights among the parents, the trial court in the matter had employed the standard of "best interests" of the child. This effort resulted in a determination by the lower court that the father was unsuitable for custody due to the perceived "instability" of his household and the "impermanence" of his family unit, factors which were apparently not of sufficient concern in the original custody decision, based upon Islamic law, to deny him custodial rights.[226] The appellate court affirmed the decision of the trial court to deny Mr. Samman custodial rights, even while acknowledging that the trial court found "the parties equal" in terms of the majority of the factors considered in making its best interests determination. Yet, on one factor, Mr. Samman was perceived as falling below court expectations.

After noting that the wife had remained in the marital home following the separation of the couple, Mr. Samman's living arrangements were described by the court as unstable due, in part, to "cramped quarters" resulting from the fact that he had moved into the home of his brother. As the court observed, "Defendant testified that he slept on the couch and his brother and sister-in-law slept on a mattress in the dining room."[227] The court described the crowded conditions as "unsuitable." As well, along with other concerns, the permanence of the husband's family unit was questioned by the court, in part, due apparently to the combination of his household with that of

---

[226] Ibid., 11.

[227] Ibid.

his brother. While it is unclear whether these factors, alone, would have been sufficient for the court to have reached the same verdict, the mere fact that these issues were raised appears significant.

It is, likewise, important to consider the breadth of the decision, itself. In this matter, the court was not asked to name the mother as the primary custodian, but, instead to re-write a joint custody arrangement so that the father was excluded entirely from the custodial rights and responsibilities.

The question that seems to be begged by this decision is whether such factors as cramped living quarters and the combination of households are, on their own, indicative of conditions that may be reasonably presumed to work to the disinterest of a child. It is clear that, by the second-half of the 20th century, increased levels of personal wealth in North America and Europe had prompted a reconsideration of economic expectations. Changing circumstances made it possible for individuals to provide themselves and their families larger and more comfortable living spaces, along with other conveniences. These enhanced physical living conditions have certainly brought with them certain social advantages. Still, it is not clear that these changes have been universally positive. It may be argued that with the expansion of living areas has come increased familial distance. As well, it may be argued that the increased accessibility of varying "creature comforts" is an extravagance, often reinforcing individualistic emphases, to the neglect of communal interests.

The purpose of this consideration is not to propose a return to an "idyllic" pre-modern circumstance. Instead, the point here is that certain economic and environmental criteria may be poorly conceived as "objective" indicators of circumstances within which children are likely to falter or be inadequately protected. As well, in assessing such standards, it seems important to take into account the cultural presuppositions of those being assessed.

Indeed, in pointing to issues of space and the combination of households as criteria upon which a judgment could be derived regarding the best interests of a child, some may complain that the court placed undue concern upon economic circumstance. In other words, did the court place primacy upon a material calculus and an emphasis on the sustenance of a self-reliant "nuclear family" structure, to the exclusion of other concerns that may be equally valued by members of individual cultures? In particular, it seems worthy of noting that the living circumstances described in the opinion, while apparently deemed inferior in comparison to that of most modern Europeans and North Americans, are likely not different from those experienced in most households throughout the globe and many even in the U.S.

At the same time, the decision in the matter appears to suggest that the court may have failed to consider the priority that appears to be strongly cultivated within the system of Islamic law given to the preservation of extended family and communal units. Such a priority seems to rise above purely economic concerns in such systems. Thus, even while conditions may have been cramped, it is unclear that accommodations secured with extended family would be viewed in an entirely negative fashion by a traditional court imposing principles of Islamic law. Indeed, it may even be asked whether such an arrangement might offer certain positive benefits.

The issue prompted by the examination of this court decision is really one of definition and priority. It is difficult to ascertain whether any of the individual circumstances identified by the court might have been determinative, on their own, in this matter. Still, the entertainment of a more communal perspective, of the type often associated with traditional Muslim values, may have affected the path of analysis adopted by the court in this matter and altered the final outcome. The question may be, ultimately, whether a broader knowledge of the Islamic faith and Islamic law might have led this court to a different final determination in this matter.

Of Comity

These often conflicting judicial decisions concerning the custody of minors raise important questions for examination from a religious, as well as, a legal perspective. In part, these questions relate to the reasonable expectations one may possess regarding claims of right in the area of minor custody. Indeed, whatever one may say about the treatment by U.S. courts of child custody orders entered by foreign judicial bodies imposing some form of Islamic law, the sheer unevenness of this group of decisions must be recognized. One may point to cases in which, as a matter of law, child custody orders rooted in the presumptions cultivated by Islamic law have been dismissed by U.S. courts. In other situations, comparable courts have sought to enforce such arrangements. What, then, one may ask, can a Muslim living in the U.S. and seeking the enforcement of rights granted by foreign courts expect?

The transparent and consistent enforcement of social rights is the hallmark of a functioning judiciary. In general, this is a description that may be applied to U.S. courts as concerns most issues. However, in the case of Muslim litigants, particularly with regard to issues related to foreign child custody orders, it is not as clear that such transparent and consistent enforcement of rights is broadly experienced.

As well, it may be asked whether individual decisions in the field of child custody appear to evidence a tendency by state courts to place primacy upon standards deeply rooted in Western cultural or Judeo-Christian religious traditions, to the exclusion of social and religious emphases arising from other cultural contexts, especially those strongly associated with the Muslim community. The answers to such inquiries appear dependent upon a reasoned consideration of the origins and development of ethical and legal thought in the U.S. and in those countries that claim some primary allegiance to Islam.

Woven deeply into the very fabric of the American cultural perspective is an emphasis upon individual rights and personal responsibility. This emphasis may be witnessed within the expressed language of the founding American social contract, the Constitution, which itself guarantees individuals "certain inalienable rights." Some scholars, such as Max Weber, have attempted to link the rise of such a spirit of individualism in Western society to the emergent Protestant Christian community of the 16th century, and the philosophical understandings expressed by leaders of the Reformation, including Martin Luther. Of course, there were significant cultural factors at play in the drive of Western society toward the broad embrace of fundamental individual rights and freedoms. And, regardless of its origins, this foundational social framework, centered upon the individual, was eventually associated with Christian religious thought. It was, likewise, incorporated into the legal and bureaucratic structures of the United States.

In the area of the law of child custody, we may arguably glimpse this ethical framework at play within the scope of decisions cited here. The *Samman v. Samman* decision may be read as evoking a rather strong disinterest in communal considerations and priorities and a similarly fervent interest in reinforcing individual responsibility and the preservation of a nuclear family ideal. In *Amin v. Bakhaty*, we may identify a parallel emphasis upon individual rights and responsibilities to the broad exclusion of communal considerations.

At the same time, this peculiarly Western emphasis upon individual rights may often appear inconsistent with certain basic emphases that arise from the institution of Islamic law and from Muslim ethical norms. Within many Muslim societies, primacy often appears to be afforded to communal rights and interests, as against individual considerations. We see this at play within the Islamic law's system of preference related to child custody matters, wherein traditional social or communal structures and relationships are strongly reinforced. In general, it may be said that mothers are preferred as physical custodians of young children, under Islamic law, because they are understood to be the most adept at providing the nurture required by those in an early state of development. Male parents are preferred as physical custodians for older children under this system precisely because the father is understood as the one most capable of providing instruction in skill and social development and religious formation. Thus, both parents are deemed vital to the task of child rearing and the system seeks to encourage their mutual participation, though the system anticipates that each parent tends to be more influential at different stages in the development of children. Yet, the system of preference does not end with the parental figures. The system extends to grandparents, uncles, aunts and others. It is the entire communal network of relatives that is thought to play a role of importance in the rearing of a child. These traditional formulations, then, are broadly reinforced by the Muslim social perspective.

While these gender-related preferences, stemming from Islamic law and associated with child custody, receive significant attention by U.S. courts, in most Muslim countries they are not absolutely determinative. A variety of factors beyond gender-related preferences are typically considered in making custody determinations by judicial bodies enforcing Islamic legal standards, including the parent's age, sanity, and capability to protect the child's physical health and moral instruction.[228] Thus, this gender-based preference is one of a variety of factors considered. Still, this gender-based system of preference, rooted in notions of communal order, appears to stand in contrast to Western social ideals of individual rights and responsibilities.

---

[228] Jamal J. Nasir, *The Islamic Law of Personal Status* 2 (2nd ed. 1990), 178.

As concerns matters in which U.S. courts are confronted with the task of reviewing child custody determinations made by other bodies seeking to implement or enforce some version of Islamic law, the real question becomes one of how best to respond. Should the existence of a religiously justified, gender-based mode of preference under Islamic law be deemed, on its face, to provide grounds sufficient to justify the nullification by U.S. courts of all child custody orders rendered in accord with this system? Certainly, this seems to be a position close to the one taken by the court in *Amin v. Bakhaty*. Both practically and legally, however, this result seems problematic. From a practical vantage point, it must be observed that the failure of U.S. courts to recognize or, at least, seriously consider the decisions of their foreign counterparts may lead potential litigants to bypass the American judiciary, seeking preferable outcomes elsewhere. One potential outcome of such forum shopping may be the encouragement of parents to abduct and unlawfully remove minor children to other, more favorable jurisdictions. Ethically, there are serious issues related to the equality of treatment of Muslim litigants stemming from such judicial decisions, as well.

On the other hand, it may be asked, what is at stake if U.S. courts are open to the possibility of enforcing foreign custody orders rooted in Islamic law? What is the consequence of the enforcement of custody orders like the one witnessed in *Hosnain v. Malak*? It may be argued that, while the rejection of foreign custody decisions by U.S. courts are typically justified on the grounds of the need to protect the "best interests" of the minors involved, what is truly being protected in such matters may often merely be cultural or religious preferences, more than identifiable interests of the children involved. Thomas Foley, in his recent article on child custody preferences under Islamic Law, seems to offer just such an understanding, when he observes:

> The custody decisions in Islamic culture, although based on a gender presumption, may provide sufficient consideration of the best interests of the child to meet the substantive thresholds of § 23 and § 105 (of the UCCJA) to warrant the extension of comity. The existence of the gender presumption does not render the Islamic institutions dissimilar in nature or in violation of fundamental principles of human rights because

> there is consideration for both the parent's fitness and the conditions of the child's upbringing.[229]

Scholarship from within the fields of Islamic studies, religious studies and comparative studies may aid in prompting the sort of self-examination necessary to address these concerns meaningfully. Such scholarship may encourage cross-disciplinary engagement and the increased application of academic resources from the fields of Islamic and religious studies to the task of educating U.S. jurists on topics related to Islamic law. Indeed, it is through the lens of child custody litigation that we may glimpse one example of the important practical value of cross-disciplinary engagement.

---

229 "Extending Comity to Foreign Decrees in International Custody Disputes between Parents in the United States and Islamic Nations," *Family Court Review* 41 (April 2003): 257-275, 265.

CHAPTER 5

Marriage, Divorce and the American Muslim

[T]he distance between the Catholic and civil marriage remains great, mainly because of the question of divorce. A marriage which is a sacrament must not be dissolved since it would then be turned into an agreement. Likewise, an absolutely indissoluble marriage would completely lose its character of being a contract by becoming a holy thing which no positivist is ready to accept.

Islamic marriage united these two types of marriage. From the European point of view, Islamic marriage is both a religious and civil marriage. It is at the same time a contractual and a ceremonial religious act. It is performed by a "clergyman" and a government official, but both in one person. An Islamic marriage can be dissolved because it is a contract, but divorce is only allowable for permissible reasons. Prophet Muhammad considered it "the most hated of all permissible things" – which is an expression of religious and moral thinking.... Marriage, as it is in Islam, is a solution aiming to answer the problem of how to reconcile one's spiritual desires and one' physical needs; of how to save chastity without rejecting love, and of how to put in order the sexual love of an animal which can become a man but not an angel. This aim is in its essence Islamic.

Muslim marriage is comparable with justice. They are ideas of a coarser structure which nevertheless will provide more purity and righteousness than their Christian equivalents: chastity and universal love.[230]

While the institution of marriage in both the Christian and Muslim contexts represents the joining of individuals in a relational arrangement marked by mutual rights and obligations, there are certain definitional distinctions that are of some significance. As Muslim communities in the historically Christian West have grown, these distinctions have provided a foundation for the development of much unease and anxiety.

In order to make sense of these points of conflict, it is important to consider the fundamental understandings associated with the Muslim concept of marriage, as it is cultivated within the larger system of Islamic law. How do Muslims define marriage? What constitutes a valid marriage? Under what circumstances may a Muslim marital arrangement be dissolved? With these questions considered, it will be appropriate to explore the interactions between the U.S. judicial system and Muslim litigants airing claims related to the establishment or dissolution of marriages.

The Muslim Marital Contract

As the excerpt above reflects, based upon the classical Muslim interpretation, marriage is a contractual arrangement, with the basic strictures that bind parties to the arrangement being rooted in the larger religious system. Thus, the establishment of a Muslim marriage contract stems from the twin pillars of "offer" and "acceptance." The offer and acceptance are to be entered into by the principals and their proxies or families.[231] The marriage contract is to be effectuated through the explicit statement of words displaying the intent to be

[230] Alija Ali Izetbegovic, *Islam Between East and West* (Plainfield, Ind.: American Trust Pub., 1999), 264-265.

[231] Ibid., 42.

bound by such an arrangement. Some Muslim communities will require that these words be uttered in Arabic.[232] As Nasir notes, this is understood as a civil contract and there is no sacramental value placed upon it.[233] In that sense, then, marriage in the Muslim context stands in some contrast to associations made by the Christian community with this institution.

In the Christian context, the bond of matrimony is often recognized precisely as a sacramental expression, and, in that sense, is understood to be quite different than a mere legal contract.[234] As a sacrament, marriage stands as an expression of the grace bestowed upon humankind by the divine. Thus it is far more than a mere contractual arrangement. It is, instead, an expression of divine love, cemented through divine sanction. Of course, in general, Protestant denominations do not recognize marriage as a sacrament in formal terms. Still even in these branches of the Christian world, marriages are conducted in churches and the ceremonies tend to emphasize divine consecration of the union. The Muslim interpretation of the institution of marriage tends to be more pragmatic.

In order for the marriage contract to be valid in the Muslim context, it is important that certain conditions be met. Each party to the marriage must possess the legal capacity to enter into the arrangement. As well, each party must have attained the minimum age designated for one to enter into such an arrangement. There is significant variation in thought within the many Muslim sub-communities as to what the appropriate minimum age should be for one to enter into this contractual arrangement, though it is often aligned with the age at which one is deemed to be of majority for other legal purposes. Still, not all majority Muslim states tie the general age of majority to the

---

[232] Ibid. The followers of Imam Al Shafii observe that a marriage may be solemnized only in the Arabic language. Ibid.

[233] Ibid., 38. In other examples, the minimum age for one to enter into a marriage contract in Morocco is 18 for males and 15 for females and, in Jordan, the age is 16 for males and 15 for females. Ibid., 44.

[234] The sacramental status of marriage is evidenced in the Council of Trent, canon i, Sess. XXIV: "If any one shall say that matrimony is not truly and properly one of the Seven Sacraments of the Evangelical Law, instituted by Christ our Lord, but was invented in the Church by men, and does not confer grace, let him be anathema."

minimum age for marriage. For example, in Egypt, the age of majority is 21 according to the civil law system, but one is eligible to enter into a valid marriage contract at the age of 16 for females and the age of 18 for males.[235] As well, the parties entering into the marital arrangement must have sufficient mental capacity to be appreciative of the nature of the agreement.

In general, a marriage contract is deemed valid and enforceable until the time that it is dissolved through some recognized process. Portions of the larger Shia community, based upon Quranic language,[236] additionally recognize the possibility of forming a temporary or *muta* marriage. Such a marriage is one established for a proscribed period, which could be a day, a week, a month, a year or more, and which automatically terminates at the end of the designated period. In order to be valid, the term must be established and specified at the commencement of the marriage contract and a dower must be stated. Children born to such a temporary marriage are considered legitimate and entitled to all inheritance rights.[237]

Among the generally observed impediments to marriage under Islamic law principles are prohibitions based upon proximity of kinship. Thus, males are barred from establishing a lawful marital arrangement with their mother, grandmother, daughters, granddaughters, sisters, siblings' daughters, and both maternal and paternal aunts. A marriage may also be impeded due to the existence of a valid present marriage. This is particularly true for women, who may not be married to more than one individual at any given time. Both the Sunni and Shia communities agree that men may have up to four wives at any one time, so long as they are able to adequately maintain each of them. Meanwhile, as Nasir notes, not all jurisdictions that have imposed some form of Islamic law allow for such multiple marriages.[238]

The contractual arrangement is preceded by a betrothal (*khutba*), in which the prospective husband communicates to the prospective spouse and her family his present status, including factors affecting his

---

[235] Ibid., 43.

[236] See Sura 4, verse 24.

[237] *The Islamic Law of Personal Status*, 54.

[238] Ibid., 60-61.

personal character, and the effective terms intended to be included in the marital contract.[239]

The Dissolution of a Marriage

In general, there are several grounds upon which a divorce may be obtained pursuant to Islamic Law. The first and, perhaps, most controversial within Western courtrooms is the divorce by *talaq*. The term *talaq* may be broadly translated to mean "repudiation," and, as Fyzee notes, it suggests a repudiation of the wife specifically by her husband.[240] According to the doctrine of *talaq*, a Muslim husband "may divorce his wife whenever he so desires without assigning any cause."[241] The husband may terminate the marriage by the uttering of a specified formula, or by authorizing an agent to make the statement on his behalf, presuming certain fundamental conditions have been met.[242] Such a *talaq* divorce may be made unconditionally or subject to certain conditions to be specified by the one offering the *talaq* formulation. As well, certain Sunni schools would allow for a deferred *talaq* divorce, designed to take effect at some specified future date.[243] In general, in order to facilitate such a divorce, the husband or his agent must employ specified language, which typically includes the utilization of a form of the word *talaq* or, according to certain schools, a specified Arabic phrase.[244]

---

[239] Ibid., 39.

[240] *Outlines of Muhammadan Law*, 150.

[241] Ibid.

[242] Generally, in order for the husband's dismissal of his wife to be valid according to the doctrine of talaq to be effective, the following conditions must be met: 1) the dismissing husband must not be a minor; 2) the dismissing husband or agent must not be "insane"; 3) the person uttering the dismissal must not be in a state of intoxication; 4) the person uttering the dismissal must not be acting under coercion; 5) the person uttering the dismissal must not be in a state of rage such that he or she would appear to have lost "discretion"; 6) the person uttering the dismissal must not do so in a state of sleep or fainting. See *The Islamic Law of Personal Status*, 104-05.

[243] Ibid., 107-08.

[244] Ibid., 106. For example, the Shia Ithna-Ashari community demands the utilization of specific language, stating "you are repudiated." Ibid.

While this pattern of divorce is often identified as a right held exclusively by the husband, in some jurisdictions, according to the doctrine of *talaq-e tafwid*, a privilege may be afforded the wife to dissolve the marriage through the same or a similar procedure. According to the doctrine of *talaq-e tafwid,* the husband may effectively delegate his own right to pronounce the dissolution of the marriage through *talaq* language to his wife by agreement. The agreement would typically be established as part of the marital arrangement. In India, for example, the reservation of such a right to the wife through an antenuptial agreement has been held to be valid.[245]

In addition to *talaq* as a method for the dissolution of a marriage, such termination may be effected by agreement of the spouses. This form, generally referred to as a *khula* divorce, stems from Qur'anic dictate and rests upon the notion that the wife must offer some consideration in exchange for her freedom.[246] While the consideration paid may often be in the form of an economic incentive, such consideration may consist of virtually any contribution including the agreement to care for and maintain the couple's children following the divorce.

This form of divorce requires that the parties each have legal capacity to enter into such an arrangement. Interestingly, since the wife's contribution toward such an arrangement is considered compensation, while the husband's act is understood to be in the nature of making an oath or promise, the revocability of the arrangement differs for the spousal parties. Traditionally, the wife is understood to be capable of withdrawing her offer up until the time it is formally accepted by the husband. Meanwhile, the husband may not withdraw his offer once it is offered because such a withdrawal would be tantamount to the revocation of a personal oath, once it is made.[247]

These methods for dissolving a marriage depend upon action of individual parties to the marital arrangement. In addition to these, a divorce may be effectuated by a court or other judicial body. In

---

245 *Outlines of Muhammadan Law*, 159.

246 *The Islamic Law of Personal Status*, 111. This form of divorce derives from an interpretation of the Quranic verse 2:229, which provides, in relevant part, "And if ye fear that they (the married couple) may not be able to keep the limits of God, it is no sin for either of them if the woman ransoms herself."

247 *The Islamic Law of Personal Status*, 112.

general, such a divorce must be based upon specific enumerated grounds. The grounds acceptable for substantiating such a divorce may vary from community to community. Potential grounds for such a divorce may include:

(a) injury or discord (generally referring to physical injury to the wife);
(b) a defect on the part of the husband (This refers to some physical defect, ranging from impotence to terminal disease. Communities vary in their opinions as to what constitutes such a qualifying defect and whether the defect of the wife should, likewise, serve as grounds for such a divorce.);
(c) failure to pay maintenance (This refers to the failure of the husband to adequately maintain the wife economically and the positions of the individual communities vary significantly.); and
(d) absence or imprisonment of the husband (The qualifying time of absence may range from six months to three years, depending upon the community and jurisdiction.)[248]

The ability of courts to effectuate the termination of a divorce on such grounds is not universally accepted. In some communities, the grounds upon which a court may base a divorce are extremely narrow. Thus, for the Shia Ithna-Ashari community, such a divorce by the court will be allowed only in the event of the impotence of the husband. At the same time the Lebanese Shia recognize no grounds upon which a divorce may be effectuated by the court.[249] In general, among Sunni

---

[248] Ibid., 115-27. Under its Dissolution of Marriages Act of 1939, the government of India sought to codify the basic requirements of the Sharia related to divorce by a court and made available such a procedure upon the following grounds: (1) missing husband; (2) the failure of the husband to maintain the wife; (3) imprisonment of the husband; (4) failure of the husband to perform marital obligations; (5) impotence; (6) insanity, leprosy, or venereal disease; (7) if the wife is under 18 and the marriage has not been consummated; (8) cruelty; and (9) any other ground recognized under the Sharia law. *Outlines of* Law of *Muhammadan Law*, 168-77.

[249] Ibid., 114.

groups, courts are afforded a broader ability to terminate marriages than is the case in Shia communities.

In addition to these forms of divorce, one's personal choice of religion may play an important role in the maintenance of a marriage relationship pursuant to Islamic Law. Strictly, if either the wife or husband abandons the Muslim religion during the period of the marriage, that union will be dissolved automatically.[250] As well, the embrace of Islam by either the husband or wife may have a similar effect upon the marital institution, according to some Muslim communities, presuming that the party is not joined in the decision by the other spouse. Thus, in India, if a husband converts from a religion other than Judaism or Christianity[251] to Islam, he cannot lawfully retain his wife, unless she agrees to convert, as well. At the same time, however, the embrace of Islam by a wife will not result in the same sort of automatic dissolution of a marriage.[252]

Muslim Marriages in U.S. Courts

The issue of whether to recognize marriages established pursuant to "Islamic law" or divorces effectuated pursuant to Muslim religious order is one that has confronted and challenged U.S. courts. The results of cases focused upon the legitimacy of Muslim marriages have been largely mixed, often turning on particular local circumstance. They lead one to question, as was the case with child custody-related decisions, the extent to which Muslims may have a reasonably secure expectation regarding the manner in which claims of right may be considered and treated by U.S. courts. As well, the case decisions shed some light upon the impressions held by U.S. court officials regarding Islamic religious institutions.

Certain of the case decisions related to the validity of marriages solemnized pursuant to Islamic law have reflected an apparent judicial hesitancy to recognize Muslim marriages, particularly when general secular criteria have not been met. One of the most interesting cases in

---

[250] *The Islamic Personal Status*, 129.

[251] Jews and Christians are considered *kitabiyya* faiths or part of the group of religious traditions referred to in the Qur'an as the "people of the Book," and are accorded special accommodation in certain regards.

[252] *Outlines of Muhammadan Law*, 178-85.

this line is the California decision of *In re Vryonis*.[253] In the matter, a female Muslim had entered into a relationship with a Greek Orthodox man. After the relationship had commenced, the female party suggested that she could not continue unless the couple was married, due to her understanding of personal religious obligations stemming from her practice of Islam. Accordingly, in March 1982, a private marriage ceremony was arranged by the woman, in which both parties participated. The woman argued that the marriage ceremony was consistent with all requirements of Muslim religious law. Meanwhile, no attempt was apparently made by the woman to determine whether the ceremony met California state law requirements related to the establishment of a valid marriage.

In one of the most curious aspects of this case, the couple did not publicly disclose their marriage to anyone and they continued to maintain separate residences following the ceremony. In addition, the couple filed separate tax returns, claiming "single" status, while the putative husband repeatedly refused to have the marriage solemnized at a mosque.[254] By the fall of 1984, the relationship between the two appeared to have soured and the husband announced his intention to marry another individual. The woman, then, filed a suit seeking dissolution of the marriage and support from the man. The man claimed, in his defense, that no valid marital relationship had ever been established by the couple.

Upon review of the matter, the court sought to determine whether a marriage had been established, binding the couple to certain rights and responsibilities. The key inquiry, according to the court, was whether the woman who sought to have the marriage recognized had a "good faith" belief that this legal relationship had been established by the actions undertaken by the pair. And, it was in the consideration of this question that the court took a curious position.

The lower court had reasoned that the woman did have a good faith belief that a marriage had been established based upon compliance with Muslim religious law, alone. On appeal, meanwhile, the court concluded that the appropriate standard to be employed was not one that was based upon the good faith belief that a marriage had been established through any available process. Instead, in order to establish

---

[253] 202 Cal. App. 3d 712; 248 Cal. Rptr. 807 (Cal. Ct. App. 1988).
[254] Ibid., 715.

the existence of such a marriage, one must point to a good faith belief that a marriage had been established specifically under California law, irrespective of any efforts made to comply with religious law or any other legal system.[255] And here, the court concluded, no reasonable attempt was made by the couple to meet requirements of California law related to the establishment of a valid marriage. The court reached this decision even while acknowledging that the woman appeared to have no knowledge of state requirements applied to the marital process.

In the end, the court here appeared largely disinterested in the woman's effort to invoke Muslim religious law. Indeed, the court failed to examine the requirements necessary for the establishment of a valid marriage under Islamic law or whether any such requirements had been met. In other words, the acts undertaken pursuant to Islamic law were deemed to be effectively irrelevant to the determination of the issues raised within the larger proceeding.

In considering this decision, it is worth contrasting it with a Tennessee appellate court decision issued just a few years later. In *Aghili v. Saadatnejadi*,[256] the court was faced with the task of determining the validity of a short-lived marriage constituted pursuant to Islamic law. In the case, Mr. Aghili and Ms. Saadatnejadi were married by a Nashville Muslim religious leader in a local ceremony conducted in 1994. The couple ended their relationship less than one-month later and Mr. Aghili argued that a valid marriage had never arisen.

Both Mr. Aghili and Ms. Saadatnejadi were Americans of Iranian decent. The couple was engaged in Iran, but Mr. Aghili negotiated a marriage contract with the father of Ms. Saadatnejadi in the U.S. The terms of this contract demanded that Mr. Aghili pay Ms. Saadatnejadi the sum of 1,400 Iranian gold coins as a dower and agree not to take another wife, if the couple moved to any location that legally permitted one to have multiple wives.[257] The couple was subsequently married by

---

[255] Ibid., 721.

[256] 958 S.W.2d 784 (Tenn. Ct. App. 1997).

[257] Ibid., 787. In considering the question of the qualifications of the Muslim official, Mr. Aghili cited *Tenn. Code Ann. § 36-3-301(a)*, which provides, in part, that "all regular ministers of the gospel of every denomination, and Jewish rabbis, more than eighteen (18) years of age, having the care of souls. . . may solemnize the rite of matrimony."

a Muslim official at a private home near Nashville and a certificate was filed with the local Mosque recognizing the establishment of the marital relationship. No Tennessee marriage license was completed by the officiating Muslim leader, though the couple did apply for and received a marriage license application form from the Secretary of State's office for the State of Tennessee.

Ultimately, following the filing of the divorce proceeding, Mr. Aghili submitted a motion for summary judgment arguing that no valid marriage had been established because the Muslim official who conducted the marriage ceremony was not qualified under state law to carry out such a task and, further, the state laws governing the filing of a marriage license had not been complied with by the couple. In effect, then, Mr. Aghili argued that the marriage was void precisely because state law requirements had not been met, a position that seems to comport precisely with the holding in *Vryonis*. This court reasoned, however, that such failures need not necessarily invalidate a marriage. Thus, it overturned a motion for summary judgment granted in Mr. Aghili's favor by the trial court.

Significantly, then, the court did not appear to place priority upon compliance with state law as against the attempt to establish a valid marital relationship pursuant to religious law. Indeed, this court broadly recognized the principle that marriages should be recognized as valid in the absence of compelling proof of their invalidity. As the court stated, "Tennessee protects the institution of marriage by presuming that regularly solemnized marriages are valid."[258] In other words then, the court seems to have reached the conclusion that, as a matter of law, greater value is to be placed upon the attempt to establish a marriage than upon enforcement of the technical rules imposed by the state identifying necessary requisites for the creation of such a legal relationship. The question then becomes what standard will be utilized to determine whether a serious attempt was made to establish a valid marital relationship.

Here, the only steps that were taken were those which were in keeping with Muslim religious demands. Accordingly, though the court does not state this explicitly, it appears that the attempt to comply with Muslim religious requirements outweighed the failure of the couple to adhere to state imposed technical requirements. In this sense, then, the

[258] *Aghili v. Elchahal*, at p. 788.

case of *Aghili v. Saadatnejadi* seems to stand in opposition to the holding of the court in *In re Vryonis*.

Finally, there is an interesting related case from the state of Virgina, *Farah v. Farah*.[259] This case bears some factual resemblance to both *Aghili* and *Vryonis* in that, here, a marriage was solemnized pursuant to Islamic law, but did not meet technical requirements imposed by Western legal codes. Unlike the cases of *Aghili* and *Vryonis*, however, the significant events related to the establishment of the marriage took place outside of the U.S.

In this case, two individuals, one a Pakistani citizen and the other an Algerian, both of whom were residents of the State of Virginia, were married in Muslim custom, through a proxy ceremony in England, at which neither was present. This proxy ceremony was followed by a requisite reception in Pakistan. After living as married for about eight months, the couple separated and Mr. Farah sought to have the marriage declared void. Ms. Farah, meanwhile, filed for divorce and sought economic support. The question for the Virginia Court of Appeals was whether this marriage should be deemed valid. The trial court had reasoned that the marriage should be deemed valid and had entered a divorce decree along with a significant economic award to Ms. Farah.

This case was complicated by the number of jurisdictions involved. Indeed, at trial, Mr. Farah offered evidence of the invalidity of the marriage pursuant to English law. At the same time, Ms. Farah argued that the marriage was concluded in Pakistan and offered evidence of the marriage's validity under Pakistani law, which is based, in some measure, upon Muslim religious law. Ultimately, the court reasoned that the jurisdiction with the greatest contact to this marriage ceremony was England and, accordingly, the failure of the couple to meet technical requirements imposed by English law rendered the marriage void.

Interestingly, however, the court went on to argue that the marriage should be deemed invalid even under the version of Islamic law imposed by Pakistan. The court based its opinion, in part, upon the fact that Ms. Farah was a member of a Muslim sect that was not recognized by the Pakistani government and, accordingly, would be deemed

---

[259] 429 S.E.2d 626 (Vir. Ct. App. 1993).

ineligible to enter into such a marital arrangement.[260] While the outcome in this case is similar in impact to the decision reached in *Vryonis,* it seems significant that the court felt compelled to address the implications of Pakistan's Islamic law regime upon this matter. In neither *Vryonis* nor *Aghili* were questions of the interpretation of Islamic law addressed specifically. This fact may prompt further questions regarding the preparedness of the U.S. judiciary to confront this body of law adequately in response to such situations.

The question of the preparedness of the U.S. judiciary to undertake a reasoned analysis of Islamic law was raised by Virginia Muslim jurist. In a 2000 speech, attorney and University of Richmond law professor Azizah Al-Hibri argued that the lack of exposure by American judges to concepts stemming from the body of Islamic law has led to problematic interpretations. Often, these flawed interpretations have been prompted or supported by personal biases or misinformed expert witnesses testifying on the subject of Islamic law, she argued. As she observed regarding those individuals typically employed in the U.S. as experts on the subject of Islamic law:

> Many Muslim men, whether imams of mosques or professors of religion, are not sufficiently familiar with Islamic law. Often, they confuse their cultural beliefs and practices with Islam itself. An American judge has no way of discerning the difference in the absence of more reliable sources of information. If I am a non-Muslim American judge and a Muslim expert witness, a Muslim professor of Islam (how more reliable can an expert witness be?) or the imam of a *masjid* walks into my court, then I am inclined to believe that I am going to get the real story. But that is not always the case. There are some important issues about who can, with authority, interpret Islamic laws, and the judges are not aware of this.[261]

As an exemplar of the consequences of failed interpretations of Islamic law, Al-Hibri pointed to an unnamed Virginia case in which a judge,

[260] Ibid., 629.

[261] "Muslim Marriage Contracts in American Courts," a speech to the Minaret of Freedom banquet, Bethesda, Maryland (May 20, 2000).

based upon apparently flawed expert testimony, reached the conclusion that the very nature of the Muslim marriage contract was in violation of state public policy and, accordingly, should be rendered null as a matter of law.[262] In effect, this decision placed at risk the marriages of every Muslim resident of the state of Virginia, she argued. Al-Hibri went on to observe that those who tend to be harmed the most by ill informed interpretations of Islamic law were the most vulnerable and these individuals are typically women.

Recent examples of cases in which marriages conducted pursuant to Islamic practice have been deemed valid offer some insight, as well, into the impressions or misimpressions of U.S. courts relative to the Muslim community. In *Hassan v. Hassan*,[263] a decision rendered by the Superior Court of Connecticut, the judicial body was faced with the peculiar task of determining the validity of a marriage both parties to the union deemed valid under Islamic law.

The issue of the validity of the marriage came before the court in conjunction with a paternity petition related to the Hassans' minor son. Mr. Hassan challenged the petition on the grounds that the couple was validly married, denying the court subject matter jurisdiction over the claim. The wife, meanwhile, countered with the argument that the marriage was void *ab initio*, under state law, because she was only a minor of 15 years of age at the time of the ceremony, and accordingly incapable of entering into such a union, and because the couple never lived together as husband and wife. Both parties acknowledged that an Islamic religious marriage ceremony had been performed, though there was conflicting evidence as to whether an Imam presided. Both parties acknowledged their belief that the ceremony was sufficient to establish a valid marital union pursuant to Islamic law.

In addition to the claim of minority of Ms. Hassan, the validity of the marriage ceremony was disputed under Connecticut law based, in part, upon the fact that the couple had never obtained a marriage license, as required by state law, and upon a claim that the credentials of the Imam, who was said to have conducted the service, were inadequate.

---

[262] Ibid.

[263] Slip Op. No. FA010632261; 2001 Conn. Super. LEXIS 2959 (Sept. 30, 2001).

Ultimately, the court determined that a valid marital relationship had been established between the couple, even though certain legal requirements imposed by the state for the formation of a marriage had not been met. As the court observed, "[t]he inescapable conclusion is that even though flawed in a number of respects, the *Hassan* ceremony established enough of a status of marriage between the parties as to require a court to disestablish it."[264] Perhaps, what is most interesting about this decision is the manner in which it was reached.

Great emphasis was placed, within the decision, upon the credentials of the Imam who apparently conducted the marriage ceremony. In particular, the court focused upon a state statute which authorizes "all ordained or licensed clergymen" to solemnize marriages.[265] In doing so, the court raised the question of whether the Imam would meet this statutory standard. The court reasoned that the Imam, in question, should be understood to meet this legal standard, though the court acknowledged that a further evidentiary hearing would be necessary to resolve the matter fully.

In reaching this point of decision, it is interesting to note that the court never addressed the scope of the term "ordained or licensed." The fact that Islam does not distinguish between a lay and clergy class, as does Christianity, was not addressed by the court. Indeed, while apparently recognizing the Imam as a type of ordained clergy, the court went on to argue that even if the Muslim leader did not meet this definitional standard, the marriage could still be deemed valid, if it met all requirements of the religious system recognizing it. In other words, irrespective of the nature of the credentials of the Imam or whether an Imam even participated in the ceremony, such a marriage would be recognized as valid so long as it met with the requirements of Islamic law.[266]

At the same time, the court failed to consider how or whether the form of "Islamic law" employed in the marriage ceremony might respond to some of the peculiarities affecting the marital union. These included such facts as the failure of the couple to cohabitate or to have

---

[264] Ibid., 30.

[265] Ibid., 4, citing Conn. Gen Statutes, section 46b-22.

[266] Ibid., 7. As the court states, "Thus even if the Imam's authority is not recognized or no Imam was actually present, the marriage is not void if it was solemnized in a manner recognized by Islamic law." Ibid.

consummated the relationship. In the end, it seems that the court placed primacy not upon the technical requirements for a valid marriage imposed under state law, but, instead, upon the consideration of whether the marriage was constituted appropriately under Islamic religious law. In that sense, then the case stands in contrast to a case like *In re Vyronis*, where emphasis is placed precisely upon the state requirements for the valid establishment of a marriage, as against any sort of religious criteria.

Further insight may be gleaned from an examination of the Texas case of *Shike v Shike.*[267] In this matter, the court accepted as valid the marriage of two individuals joined in a ceremony conducted in Pakistan pursuant to Islamic law. Interestingly, the validity of this marriage was accepted by the court with little or no detailed consideration of the nature of the marital proceedings undertaken in Pakistan, even though technical requirements imposed by the state, including the proper completion of the marriage license, appeared not to have been met.

The *Shike* case, in part, concerned a compensatory award made by the trial court to Mrs. Shike for damages totaling more than $1.5 million and resulting from alleged violent conduct within the marital relationship. Mr. Shike sought to invalidate the award based, in part, upon the claim that the couple had not been validly married and that, in treating the marriage as valid, the court had committed error. According to the testimony in the case, both of the Shikes participated in a Muslim ritual ceremony in Pakistan, which they each believed to be merely a ceremonial recognition of their engagement. Subsequently, the couple sought to be married formally by a Muslim official in the U.S., who was characterized by the court as "Mr. Shike's pastor."[268] The official determined that the couple had already been married in the ceremony in Pakistan and signed their marriage license without conducting any sort of further proceeding. Accordingly, Mr. Shike argued that a valid union between he and his wife had never been properly formed, due to the failure of the Muslim official to conduct the requisite ceremony prior to signing the marriage license.

The court reasoned that the signing of a marriage license merely served to confirm, under Texas law, an already valid and existing

---

[267] Slip op. No. 14-97-00888-CV; 2000 Tex. App. LEXIS 2733 (April 27, 2000).

[268] Ibid., 7.

marriage. Thus, if the license in the present matter was signed by an inappropriate individual or under improper circumstances, such events would not destroy the previously formed marital union. The court offered such reasoning without apparently reviewing or investigating the marital process employed in Pakistan or assessing whether it may have comported with other marriage requirements imposed by the state.

In part, it may be observed that the court appeared interested in reaching a necessary equitable result in this matter and, accordingly, found it important to recognize the validity of this marital union. At the same time, however, it is interesting to note the weight the court gave to procedures employed pursuant to Islamic law designed to establish a marital union. It gave decisive weight to these procedures, even while acknowledging the potential failure of efforts by the couple to comply with state requirements concerning the establishment of a valid marital union. Again, then, this case seems to stand in some contrast to decisions like those issued in the lines of cases including *In re Vyronis*.

From Beginning to End

In seeking to understand the manner in which U.S. courts have responded to claims of right established pursuant to Islamic law, useful insight may be gleaned from cases focused upon the termination of marriage, as well. Indeed, while issues related to the validity of a marriage are often intertwined with questions concerning the legitimacy of acts undertaken to terminate such relationships, it does appear that U.S. courts have found themselves responding to Muslim divorce cases more frequently. In large measure, these cases have focused upon the legality of divorce proceedings or upon the effectiveness of particular associated agreements. Yet, as with child custody decisions and matters concerning the validity of marriages, the results of these cases have been broadly mixed.

Perhaps, the most widely cited case recognizing the validity of a divorce decree granted by a state implementing a form of Islamic law is the matter of *Chaudry v. Chaudry*.[269] This matter involved a couple who were citizens of Pakistan. Mr. Chaudry resided in New Jersey, where he practiced medicine. Ms. Chaudry resided in Pakistan, where

---

[269] 159 N.J. Super. 566; 388 A.2d 1000 (N.J. Super. Ct. 1978).

she maintained the three children born to the couple. In 1972, the couple sought termination of their marriage and a divorce was granted by a court in Pakistan pursuant to principles of Islamic law. In accordance with this process, Ms. Chaudry was awarded the sum of approximately $1,500 as a part of the divorce,[270] an amount established in what appears to have been a dower arrangement, but which the court terms "an antenuptial agreement" made by the couple.[271] Subsequently, Ms. Chaudry brought suit in New Jersey, seeking to have the Pakistani divorce decree set aside and a new award for support entered.

At trial, the court determined that Mr. Chaudry had sufficient contacts with the State of New Jersey that it would be appropriate for it to assume jurisdiction over the matter. It further resolved that the limited award of support made by the Pakistani court, and rooted in the antenuptial agreement, was inconsistent with New Jersey public policy. It dismissed the Pakistani divorce decree, including the antenuptial agreement, and awarded Ms. Chaudry a new divorce and support in the amount of $430 per month.[272]

On appeal, the New Jersey Court of Appeals overturned the decision of the trial court, arguing that the Pakistani divorce decree should be recognized in accord with the doctrine of comity. In

---

[270] The actual amount set by this agreement was 15,000 Pakistani rupees, which was the equivalent of about $1,500, according to the court. Ibid., 1002.

[271] It may be argued that there is a significant difference between an agreement designated as a prenuptial arrangement versus one deemed to be a dower or *mahr* provision. The *mahr* provision is not made for the purpose of protecting the assets of a wealthier spouse, but for the purpose of ameliorating the harsh effects felt by women in the event of a unilateral divorce initiated by males in a marital relationship under Islamic law. See Lindsey Blenkhorn, "Islamic Marriage Contracts in American Courts: Interpreting Mahr Agreements as Prenuptials and Their Effect on Muslim Women," *Southern California Law Review* 76, no. 1 (Nov. 2002): 189-226. In particular, when mahr agreements are equated with prenuptials, they may have the negative effect of being understood as a substitute property division arrangement, preventing the woman from exercising rights under community property or equitable distribution rules. In the end, such an interpretation has the tendency to leave "Muslim women unfairly destitute." Ibid., 197.

[272] Chaudry v. Chaudry, 1002.

reinstating the initial divorce decree and its limited award of support, the court relied upon the testimony of a Pakistani lawyer who testified as an expert witness that, under the circumstances presented, neither alimony nor a separate award of maintenance to Ms. Chaudry would be permitted under Pakistani law, a system designed to reflect Islamic law.

The process followed by the Pakistani legal institutions in reaching a decision in this matter proved significant for the New Jersey appellate court in its ultimate judgment. According to the court, Mr. Chaudry effectuated the divorce by announcement (*talaq*) at the Pakistani consulate in New York in 1973 and served his wife with a copy of the document verifying this act. The divorce decree was reviewed and confirmed in a hearing by a Pakistani court in 1974, at which the wife was permitted to testify. The award was reviewed and reconfirmed by a Pakistani appellate court in 1975.[273] In the end, then, the New Jersey Court of Appeals determined that the legal process followed by the Pakistani consulate and courts was sufficient to ensure Ms. Chaudry was provided with a reasonable measure of due process and that the final verdict should be observed. It found no other fatal flaw in the decision, itself.

Meanwhile, not all foreign divorce decrees have fared as well in U.S. Courts. In the recent case of *In the Matter of Sonia Ramadan and Samer Ramadan*,[274] a foreign divorce decree was overturned by a U.S. court. The case is interesting due to the rather strained grounds upon which the decision appears to be based. In the matter, the Ramadans were married in their country of residence, Lebanon, in 1986, and subsequently moved to Massachusetts, shortly thereafter. At the time of the marriage, the couple entered into a marriage contract which provided for the payment by Mr. Ramadan of a delayed dower of 250,000 Lebanese lira to Ms. Ramadan, due at the time of the death of Mr. Ramadan or upon the termination of the marriage. The couple remained in the U.S. until 1992, when they returned to Lebanon. They lived in Lebanon from 1992 until 1997, before moving, again, to Egypt, where they lived until 1999. The couple returned to the U.S., taking up residence in New Hampshire in that year, and resided in the state until a divorce was sought in 2003.

---

[273] Ibid., 1004.

[274] 891 A.2d 1186 (N.H. Sup. Ct. 2006).

Mr. Ramadan sought to effectuate a divorce in October 2003 through the process known as *talaq*. This divorce by *talaq* was commenced through a formal public declaration by Mr. Ramadan of his intent to be divorced. In the present case, Mr. Ramadan declared to his wife three times, "I divorce you," in keeping with requirements of traditional Islamic law.[275] He subsequently flew to Lebanon to have the divorce legally recognized in the state. A short time later, at the request of Mr. Ramadan, a religious magistrate in Lebanon issued a decree declaring that the couple was divorced on the day when Mr. Ramadan uttered his declaration. Meanwhile, on the day following Mr. Ramadan's declaration, Ms. Ramadan filed a separate petition for divorce in a New Hampshire court.

The New Hampshire trial court reasoned that the attempt by Mr. Ramadan to effectuate a divorce pursuant to Islamic law principles and the subsequent action of the Lebanese religious magistrate were invalid and it failed to observe the resulting divorce decree. On appeal, the New Hampshire Court of Appeals was asked to overturn the trial court's decision and grant recognition to the decision of the Lebanese religious magistrate on the basis of comity. In response to the appeal, the court emphasized the discretionary nature of the principle of comity. As the court stated:

> We have recognized foreign divorce decrees as a matter of comity.... Comity, however, is a discretionary doctrine that will not be applied if it violates a strong public policy of the forum state, or if it leaves the court in a position where it is unable to render complete justice.[276]

The court went on to reason that it would create an undue economic burden, and, accordingly, violate public policy if Ms. Ramadan were forced to challenge the terms of the divorce in Lebanon. Moreover, the court determined that public policy of the state would be offended by the recognition of a divorce decree issued by a court in a foreign jurisdiction where the parties were not domiciled at the time of the commencement of the action.

---

[275] Ibid., 1188.

[276] Ibid.

Each of these conclusions, however, appears labored, when considered in depth. For example, with regard to the initial ground cited by the court, while it is true that some travel costs would have inured to Ms. Ramadan if she were forced to challenge the decision of the Lebanese court in Lebanon, it is, likewise, true that the Ramadans appeared to travel with some regularity to Lebanon. At the same time, while the parties may not have been domiciled in Lebanon at the time of the commencement of the action at issue in this case, the parties each appeared to maintain their Lebanese citizenship and what appeared to be relatively close ties to their native land. Thus, the issues of concern, cited by the court, may not appear nearly as compelling, upon second glance, as the court seems to assert. Still, the court appeared intent, primarily, upon ensuring that this divorce was not sanctioned by the state of New Hampshire. Thus, the concerns related to the violation of public policy may have served to mask a larger disdain for the practice of *talaq* divorce itself.

Perhaps, the seminal case in this line is the matter of *Shikoh v. Murff*,[277] a decision rendered by the Federal Court of Appeals. In the case, Mr. Shikoh, a Muslim practitioner and a resident of Pakistan, came to the U.S. to pursue certain educational goals. Prior to arriving in the U.S., Mr. Shikoh had been married and had three children born to the marriage. After residing in the U.S. for eight years, Mr. Shikoh sought a divorce from his wife. He approached Sheikh Daoud Ahmed Faisal, Spiritual Head and National Director of the Islamic Mission of America, Inc., for the propagation of Islam, at his office in Brooklyn, New York, requesting approval of the divorce. The Sheikh granted the divorce to Mr. Shikoh and prepared a document memorializing the action, which was submitted to and filed by the office of the Consulate General of Pakistan in New York.[278]

Approximately 17 months after the divorce was granted to Mr. Shikoh, he married an American citizen in New York. Approximately six months after the wedding to his American wife, he sought permanent resident status from the U.S. Immigration and Naturalization

---

[277] 257 F.2d 306 (2nd Cir. Ct. App. 1958).

[278] Ibid., 307. The document included the declaration by the Reverend Sheikh that said divorce was being pronounced, "in exercise of the authority vested in him in accordance with the laws of Islam and in conformity of the laws of the Government of the United States of America." Ibid.

Service ("INS"), based upon his marital status. The INS determined that the divorce was improper and, therefore, Mr. Shikoh's subsequent re-marriage was deemed void. His application for permanent resident status was, accordingly, denied.[279]

In its review of the action of the INS, the Federal Court of Appeals observed that religious divorces have been broadly accepted by U.S. courts in instances where several conditions prevailed. In particular, divorces have been recognized by U.S. courts in instances where they were granted by the foreign country of domicile of the parties; where both the husband and wife were validly subject to the jurisdiction of the officiating agent issuing the divorce; and where the action was recognized as valid by the government of the state implicated.[280] In other words, comity, according to the court, typically should be granted in instances where such qualifications have been met, even where the divorce is made pursuant to religious practice.

The court, meanwhile, distinguished the present matter based upon the observation that the officiating representative who granted the divorce, Sheikh Faisal, acted not in Pakistan, but in New York. The court reached this resolution even while acknowledging that both the parties continued to be residents of Pakistan, Sheikh Faisal was acting in accord with the laws of Pakistan and the divorce was submitted to and, apparently, recognized by the Consulate of Pakistan. As the court stated:

> Though a divorce secured in the manner indicated in the case at bar would appear to be valid when obtained in Pakistan, and if so obtained might well receive recognition here,

---

[279] Ibid.

[280] In part, the court relied upon the language of English jurist Lord Penzance, who said, "Different communities have different views and laws respecting matrimonial obligations, and a different estimate of the causes which should justify divorce. It is both just and reasonable, therefore, that the differences of married people should be adjusted in accordance with the laws of the community to which they belong, and dealt with by the tribunals which alone can administer those laws." Ibid., 309, citing Wilson v. Wilson, L.R. 2 P. & D. 442.

> nevertheless it was not valid when obtained in the territorial jurisdiction of New York.[281]

In what may be viewed as one of the most interesting cases in this line, *Seth v. Seth*,[282] a divorce procured in Kuwait pursuant to Islamic law principles was deemed invalid as a matter of public policy. In the matter, Mr. Seth had a first wife whom he married in India in 1957. After about nine years, Mr. Seth took up residence with a second woman. Approximately nine years later, Mr. Seth and the second woman converted to Islam and were married in a Muslim ceremony in India. A year later, Mr. Seth sought a divorce from his first wife in Kuwait by following the Muslim *talaq* process. Mr. Seth, subsequently, re-married the second woman in a Muslim ceremony in Kuwait. The following year, in 1977, Mr. Seth and his new wife were granted permanent resident status in the U.S. and established a domicile in the country.[283]

Ultimately, when Mr. Seth's second wife filed for divorce in Texas, the question of the validity of the marriage came before the court. Focusing upon what it defined as the "harshness" of the *talaq* divorce process, the Texas Court of Appeals determined, as a matter of law, that such a procedure should not be recognized in the State of Texas. As the court stated:

> The harshness of such a result to the non-Muslim divorced wife runs so counter to our notions of good morals and natural justice that we hold that Islamic law in this situation need not be applied. [284]

And while the court may have been concerned about the potential impact of the divorce upon the first wife, it is interesting to note the extent to which the court strained in order to assert jurisdiction in the matter. While the court observed, curiously, that both the jurisdictions of India and Kuwait had closer connections to the matter than did the State of Texas, Texas still had sufficient contacts with the Seths to act

---

[281] *Shikoh v. Murff*, 309.

[282] 694 S.W.2d 459 (Tex. Ct. App. 1985).

[283] Ibid., 461.

[284] Ibid., 463.

upon this matter, due to the economic and personal investments made by the couple during their residency in the state.

Dower Agreements

In regard to dower arrangements and other Muslim marriage contract provisions, courts have again responded in a mixed fashion to the validity and enforceability of such agreements. In addition to the *Chaudry v. Chaudry* case, considered above,[285] a number of court decisions have emerged which treat such contract provisions favorably. Among these is the decision in the recent New Jersey case of *Odatella v. Odatella*.[286] In the matter, Mr. and Ms, Odatella were married by an Imam at a ceremony in New Jersey in 1996. Prior to the ceremony, the families of the bride and groom met to negotiate terms of the marriage contract and this discussion was videotaped. The resulting agreement called upon the groom to provide his wife with one gold coin as an immediately payable dower, with an additional $10,000 to be provided as a postponed dower, payable to the wife at an undesignated time in the future.[287]

Eventually, Ms. Odatella sought specific performance of the contractual dower provision by Mr. Odatella in conjunction with a mutually desired divorce. At trial, Mr. Odatella sought to obviate the dower agreement, arguing that it was unconstitutionally impermissible for a U.S. court to enforce what amounted to a religious arrangement. Mr. Odatella further argued that the postponed dower arrangement was too vague to be enforceable due to the fact that there was insufficient specificity concerning the circumstances that would prompt the payment of the sum. In effect, he argued that the only way to determine the true terms of the arrangement would be to introduce

---

285 See page 21, et seq.

286 355 N.J. Super. 305; 810 A.2d 93 (N.J. Super. Ct. 2002).

287 Ms. Odatalla argued in the case that the postponed dower was payable upon her demand, at any time, in accord with Islamic law principles. However, she noted that such a demand would traditionally only be made upon the death of the husband or termination of the marriage. Ibid., 99-100.

prohibited parol evidence,[288] which would serve to explain the terms of the arrangement intended by the parties.

The court disagreed with each of Mr. Odatella's arguments. With regard to the issue of constitutionality, the court reasoned that such a contractual arrangement, while made as part of a religious ceremony, could be enforced by a U.S. tribunal so long as such enforcement could be based upon "neutral principles of law and not on religious policy or theories."[289] With regard to the argument that the dower agreement was too vague to be enforceable, the court, likewise, disagreed with Mr. Odatella, reasoning that parol evidence should not be excluded when its sole purpose is to interpret written terms of a contractual agreement, rather than to add to them.[290] In other words, while parol evidence might be excluded in instances where it serves to change contractual terms or add to them, such oral evidence could be validly admitted when it serves simply to explain otherwise valid contractual terms. Ultimately, the court found the terms of the postponed dower arrangement to be reasonably ascertainable and enforceable.

A similar result may be witnessed in the case decision in *Akileh v. Elchahal*.[291] Interestingly, however, in this matter, the court recognized a specific public value in the recognition of such Muslim marital contracts. The matter sprang from the relationship of Syrian-born Asma Akileh, who moved to the U.S. in 1990, where she met Lebanese-born Safwan Elchahal, who was also residing in the U.S.

---

[288] The parol evidence rule is a legal principle, derived from the common law, that forbids the introduction of extrinsic information or evidence, including communication between the contracting parties, that would change or add to written terms of an original written contract or agreement. In general, the principle rests upon the proposition that the written contract is the definitive statement of the intended contractual terms.

[289] *Odatella v. Odatella*, 101.

[290] Ibid. As the court explained, "The 'parol evidence rule' purports to exclude testimony 'only when it is offered for the purpose of 'varying or contradicting' the terms of an 'integrated' contract; it does not purport to exclude evidence offered for the purpose of interpreting and giving a meaning to those terms. The terms of any contract must be given a meaning by interpretation before it can be determined whether an attempt is being made to 'vary or contradict' them." Ibid.

[291] 666 So. 2d 246 (Fl. Ct. App. 1996).

The two decided to marry and terms of a marital contract were set, according to which Mr. Elchahal would pay his bride $1 at the time of the marriage with a $50,000 postponed dower agreement. The couple was married in a Muslim ceremony by an Imam in Tampa, Florida, in 1991. Within a year following the marriage ceremony, Ms. Akileh contracted a form of venereal disease from her husband and, upon realizing her condition, left her husband. She subsequently sought a divorce and payment of the postponed dower.[292]

The trial court determined that the postponed dower agreement was unenforceable due to a lack of consideration offered on the part of Ms. Akileh and due to the fact that there was no clear meeting of the minds as to the terms of this arrangement. In other words, as in the *Odatella* case, the argument was made that the terms of the agreement were too vague to be enforced. As concerned this latter argument related to the vagueness of the marital contract, the trial court focused on the fact that Ms. Akileh and Mr. Elchahal disagreed as to whether a woman initiating a divorce would be entitled under Islamic law to claim payment of a postponed dower. In regard to the question of the sufficiency of consideration, the trial court apparently reasoned that the wife offered no contribution worthy of solidifying such a contractual arrangement. The appellate court disagreed with the reasoning of the trial court on both grounds and upheld the postponed dower arrangement.

As concerned the issue of the claimed vagueness of the marital contract, the appellate court reasoned that subjective interpretations of the parties to a contract should not serve to destroy the agreement, itself, where an objective interpretation was attainable. In the present instance, then, the private arguments of Ms. Akileh and Mr. Elchahal concerning the nature of the contract were not sufficient to render the arrangement void. As concerned the sufficiency of consideration, the court ruled that entry into the marriage could be sufficient consideration, alone, to establish a valid and binding contractual arrangement. Ultimately, the court overturned the decision of the lower court, determining that the marital contract should be recognized and fully enforced.

Importantly, the court further recognized the purpose of such an arrangement to be to protect the wife economically in the event of a

---

292 Ibid., 247.

future divorce.[293] In other words, the basic system of Islamic law applicable to the present case served a useful and desirable public good – that of ensuring the availability of some means of support for a divorced wife. Accordingly, it was not, according to the court, relevant to the enforceability of the agreement whether the husband or wife initiated the divorce. Interestingly, then, the court's commentary appears to imply that such an outcome, as was produced here, was not only consistent with the public policy of the state, but produced a desirable result.

The Supreme Court of the State of New York has similarly upheld such a postponed dower agreement, as a part of a marital contract struck pursuant to Islamic legal principles. In *Aziz v. Aziz*,[294] the court, with little difficulty or discussion, found that such arrangements were consistent with basic public policy considerations affecting contractual arrangements codified under state law.

While these cases offer examples of matters in which such Islamic legal principles associated with dower agreements have found some receptivity by U.S. courts, they stand in contrast to another group of decisions that seem to offer significantly different conclusions. Perhaps, the most interesting case in this group may be the recent California case of *Shaban v. Shaban*.[295] The case seems to stand in direct contradiction to the decision in the *Odatella* matter. In the case, a couple that was married in a Muslim ceremony in Egypt sought a divorce, after living in the U.S. for 17 years. In the divorce proceeding, Mr. Shaban sought enforcement of a marriage contract, which, in part, provided that in the event of a future divorce marital property would be divided in accord with the requirements of "Islamic law,"[296] and, further, that upon the event of divorce or death of the husband, the wife's support would come in the payment of a postponed dower of 500 Egyptian pounds.

Despite the apparent definiteness of the terms associated with the payment of the dower, the court reasoned that the contract was too indefinite to be enforced without the use of parol evidence,[297] to aid in

---

[293] Ibid., 248.

[294] 7 N.Y.3d 739; 853 N.E.2d 229 (N.Y. Ct. App. 2006).

[295] 88 Cal. App. 4th 398; 105 Cal. Rptr. 2d 863 (Cal. Ct. App. 2001).

[296] Ibid., 401.

[297] Ibid., 406-407.

construction of the terms of the agreement. The court went on to point out the very breadth of the term "Islamic law," itself, noting that any agreement that claimed to be subject to such a system is highly indefinite, given the multiplicity of forms of this regime in effect around the globe. The indefiniteness, according to the court, was compounded by complications related to translation of original sources.[298] While the factual details of the cases differ to some degree, it is interesting to note the fundamentally different conclusions drawn by the *Sheban* court and the *Odatella* court concerning the enforceability of Muslim marriage contracts.

This general rejection of Muslim postponed dower arrangements has been reinforced by other judicial opinions. In the case of *In re Dajani*,[299] the court was faced with the task of determining the enforceability of a postponed dower agreement that called for the payment to the wife of approximately $15,000, following the death of her husband or the dissolution of the marriage. In the matter, the wife had brought the claim for divorce and the court was asked, specifically, to determine whether a spouse seeking divorce could simultaneously attempt to enforce such a postponed dower arrangement. Ultimately, the court reasoned that the enforcement of such a provision would be contrary to public policy due to the fact that it would facilitate or prompt the termination of marriages by offering a financial incentive to undertake such action.[300]

The holding in *Dajani* rests on the heels of an earlier California case rendering void a Jewish marital contract arrangement recorded in a *ketubah*.[301] In the case, the court acknowledged that the arrangement recorded in the *ketubah* was designed to provide some economic protection to a wife within a system that generally provided much greater rights to the male partner in terms of the ability to initiate a divorce. In other words, such a provision had a balancing effect, likely

---

[298] As the court observed, "even the term "Islamic law" is relatively uncertain. There are at least four schools of interpretation of Islamic law: the Shafi'i, Hanafi, Maliki, and Hanbali." Ibid., 408.

[299] 204 Cal. App. 3d 1387; 251 Cal. Rptr. 871 (Cal. Ct. App. 1988).

[300] Ibid., 1389.

[301] *In re Noghrey*, 169 Cal. App. 3d 326; 215 Cal. Rptr. 153 (Cal. Ct. App. 1985). A *ketubah* is a Jewish religious device used to memorialize the marriage of a couple.

tempering the husband's willingness to exercise his broad rights. Thus, the enforcement of a contractual provision establishing a financial payment scheme due in the event of a divorce might serve the positive effect of dampening the willingness of male partners to initiate the termination of a marriage. Still, the court voiced concern that the financial incentive might serve the opposite purpose with regard to the wife, since she would be the recipient of proceeds. Ultimately, the court reasoned:

> An antenuptial agreement, the terms of which encourage or promote divorce, is against public policy and is unenforceable. This state's highest court has stated the matter thusly: "Contracts which facilitate divorce or separation by providing for a settlement only in the event of such an occurrence are void as against public policy."[302]

The holdings, then, in this case and in *Dajani*, seem to stand in contradiction to the decision in *Akileh v. Elchahal.*

Questions and Interpretations

In the end, these cases serve to raise a number of important issues related to the enforcement by U.S. courts of arrangements initiated under regimes recognizing some form of Islamic law. Among these issues is the question of the impact of the varied conclusions reached by the courts. What does it mean for U.S. courts to have arrived at such starkly different opinions on the enforceability of Muslim marriage arrangements, divorce decrees and associated agreements? What are the implications for continued relations between governmental institutions, including the judiciary, and Muslims based upon this experience? Have these varied positions created inequities? To what degree might they impact the perceptions of Muslims related to the trustworthiness of such institutions?

As has been already observed one of the hallmarks of a functioning system of justice is consistency of judgment. In order for litigants to place trust in such a system, believing that any judgment will comport with objective standards, the system must be transparent. Where

---

[302] Ibid., 329-330.

decisions in regard to particular issues are widely divergent, there can be no reasonable expectation of outcome. Transparency gives way to confusion and the fear that decisions are turning not upon objective criteria, but upon personal preference and even bias. The apparent unevenness of decisions related to the implementation of Islamic law in matters of marriage and divorce may serve to promote considerable uncertainty and anxiety on the part of potential Muslim litigants residing in the U.S. Indeed, such mixed results may even serve as a strong incentive for such potential litigants to avoid U.S. courts altogether, perhaps, leaving them to resort to inferior processes, and, perhaps, even to modify their own practice of the Muslim faith.

In some regards, it may be argued, a transformation of Islam in the United States is already taking place. As is discussed later, significant attention has begun to be paid to the nature of the ethical obligations imposed upon Muslims living in non-Muslim regions of the world. Thus, it has been argued by some among the Muslim leadership that adherents living in regions where the Islamic religion constitutes a minority faith may not be obliged to abide by precisely the same legal and ethical demands that govern the lives of their brethren living in other parts of the globe. This, of course, is a topic of some controversy, with many arguing that such efforts to modify religious practice would effectively emasculate the Islamic system. It is also true, as is considered later in this work, that Muslim communities throughout the West have sought novel processes for the enforcement of Islamic ethical norms, designed to provide some avenue for resolving disputes that allows individuals to avoid U.S. courts.

Finally, one may question whether the attempt of American courts to interpret Islamic law in accord with Western judicial norms and expectations transforms the very nature of this religious system, upending its own internal structures. Indeed, it may be asked whether the dismissal or voiding of fundamental rights rooted in Islamic law and claimed by Muslim practitioners, based upon American public policy concerns, serves to diminish the authority of the religious system, as a whole, for practitioners residing in the U.S. And, if so, what impact may such a result have upon the adherence by Muslims to the broader slate of ethical demands carved into the system?

CHAPTER 6

Abandoning Tradition?

So when people see that the Muslims are trying to say that Islam is flower power, Islam is a new vitamin packed cereal or Islam is a new species of Christianity or whatever they are saying to try to win the hearts of the Christians and Jews, you are not gonna win their hearts until you quit making sajdah with your head upon the ground my friends in that sense, but stand your ground and say this is the way I am, like it or don't like it.

A modernist is someone with an inferiority complex, so he's not of the Ahl ul dhikri, not someone who knows well about the things of his deen.[303]

While the larger emphasis of this analysis has focused upon the reaction of outside forces, in particular governmental and social institutions, toward the presence of Muslims within traditionally non-Muslim regions of the world, it is also worthwhile to consider the internal response of Islamic societies to this modern reality. Generally,

---

303 "Modernism and Minority Fiqh," from the website The Muslimah (September 4, 2007), http://themuslimah.com/?p=47 (accessed September 10, 2007).

there have been many different reactions within the Muslim community toward the social and institutional challenges confronted by practitioners of the faith living in the West. Indeed, the diversity of responses to the challenges confronted by Muslim minority groups is, in many respects, as broad as the religious community, itself. Still, there are common concerns and responses that bind certain groups of Muslim thinkers as they consider the experience and plight of Islamic practitioners living as minorities around the globe. This chapter considers some of the responses of Muslims to their brethren living principally in the West.

Within the larger global Muslim community, there are thinkers and leaders who have embraced the idea of a reformation within Islam of certain of its institutions, arguing that, in general, the religious system was designed to be responsive to the reality of evolving and changing social norms. In other words, these so-called "modernists" have adopted a sort of pragmatic approach toward the implementation of ethical, moral and ritual obligations associated with the practice of the faith. According to those adopting this position, the Muslim system is designed to conform in certain respects to the social realities of a transformed global social landscape.

With regard to the system of Islamic law, in particular, this modernist position is often associated with a continual reformation in terms of the interpretation and implementation of Qur'anic standards, which is deemed essential for the sustenance of a dynamic faith community. Of course, this is not meant to imply that the Qur'anic substance of the legal system is, itself, subject to revision. Yet, the way in which Qur'anic dictates are understood may vary according to the practical circumstances confronted by the practitioner, according to those holding this position.

As may be gleaned from the quote with which this chapter opens, not all would embrace this position. Indeed, many within the Muslim community have taken the position that such modernist tactics amount to an abandonment of core traditional obligations essential under the Islamic system of faith. For such individuals, virtually any reformation of the Muslim system would serve to irreparably damage the religious institution. Accordingly, the response to the modernists' campaign has been to encourage a sort of retrenchment among Muslim faithful aimed at the protection of traditional understandings associated with the practice of the faith.

While this introduction poses a sort of duality between what may be labeled a modernist camp and a traditionalist camp, it should be observed that the positions staked out by Muslim thinkers exist on a sort of continuum, with individual members of the larger religious community embracing ideas that may veer toward either one of these poles, though they may not agree with either position on all issues. Why have Muslims embraced such differing positions relative to the implementation of ethical, moral and ritual obligations associated with the tradition? Perhaps, a number of reasons may be cited. Chief among them, however, may be differences of opinion concerning the origins of key aspects of the Islamic tradition.

The Relationship Between Islam and Islamic Law

What, one may ask, is the relationship between Islamic law and the larger Muslim tradition? And, in response, it must be admitted that there have been many different perspectives voiced by students of the Islamic tradition related to the nature of this relationship. This very question, then, is one filled with great complexity. Indeed, whole volumes have been written on this and associated subjects and any detailed and comprehensive response to this question is, accordingly, beyond the scope of this project. Still, it is worthwhile to pay heed to at least a couple of the key controversies that affect any attempt to define the relationship between the ethical and ritual components of the Muslim tradition and the larger theological and social systems that serves to define Islamic belief and practice.

Part of the controversy associated with this line of inquiry stems from differing assumptions related to the origins of Islamic law. When did an observable system of enforceable ethical and social norms, treated as law, actually emerge from within the larger Muslim community? As alluded to earlier in this work, this seemingly simple question is itself not very easily answered. Again, there are a host of responses that have been proffered, some from the academic arena and others from the sphere of Muslim religious practice. Here, however, the focus is on two potential responses, which effectively represent positions situated on either end of the spectrum of discussion related to this debate.

As may be gleaned from a cursory review of literature in the field, some seek to trace the origins of Islamic law directly to the events associated with the life of Muhammad. An example of the staking out of such a position may be witnessed in the recent popular work, *The Evolution of Fiqh*.[304] This work pinpoints the initial stage in the establishment of the system of Islamic law as taking place during the lifetime of Muhammad, and identifies the religious leader himself as an active participant in the process of crafting such an ethical system and the first true Islamic judge. Thus, the Qur'an is described as being a sort of repository of law, directing the daily activities of the earliest Muslims, as well as those who have followed in the tradition. The entirety of Islamic law produced during this period, according to the author of this text, is understood to be revealed, though it is derived from separate foundational sources – the Qur'an and the *Sunnah*.[305] As the volume further argues:

> This period (the lifetime of Muhammad) marked the beginning of the evolution of *fiqh* and it was during this period that the foundations for the science of deducing laws from the Qur'an and the *Sunna* were laid by the Prophet.[306]

The author identifies the cumulative final personality of the Muslim system of religious law as a product of the early caliphate and the Islamic leadership during the reins of both the Umayyad and Abbasid dynasties. Collectively, then, the early leadership of the Muslim community, beginning with Muhammad and continuing for several centuries, is recognized as contributing toward the cultivation of a mature *shari'a* or *fiqh* system, featuring a defined set of ethical obligations binding all followers and an intricate process of interpretation.

New systems of legal reasoning or interpretive methodologies employed that depart from the foundations laid during this formative period of the development of Islamic law, then, may represent a significant departure from or even an undermining of the original guidance rooted in the revelations received by Muhammad. And while this understanding of the development of the *shari'a* system is embraced by many inside and outside the larger Muslim community, it

---

[304] Abu Ameenah Bilal Philips (Riyadh, Saudi Arabia: International Islamic Publishing House, 2000).

[305] Ibid., 29.

[306] Ibid., 37.

is, likewise, criticized by some, on the grounds that it is more of an idealized re-creation of the history of the development of Islamic law by sympathizers within the religious system, than a historically accurate synopsis.

This position, then, stands in contrast to the arguments of the controversial Western scholar and commentator on Islamic law, Joseph Schacht. Though it was published more than 40 years ago, Schacht's volume, *An Introduction to Islamic Law*,[307] has become a primary resource for students of Islamic law in the West, and particularly those students who enter this field with a limited exposure to the Muslim faith. Schacht saw Islamic law as an important part of the social apparatus of the Muslim community. He attributed significance to Islamic law in terms of the effect it has had upon the personality of the Muslim community. However, he believed this ethical system had little connection with the events leading to the original establishment of the Muslim faith as a religious order. Indeed, he argued that the very origins of the system of Islamic law should be traced back to a period no earlier than several decades following the death of Muhammad.

As Schacht argued, "[d]uring the greater part of the first century (of development of the Muslim community) Islamic law, in the technical meaning of the term, did not as yet exist."[308] In other words, according to Schacht, the establishment of this system of law was a latter development within the Muslim community and one that did not always seem to reflect the basic teachings contained in the Qur'an, nor was it directly connected with the prophetic work of Muhammad. As Schacht further argued, law was a subject typically segregated from the sphere of religion during the lifetime of Muhammad and in the era immediately following his death. Further, as he observed, "as far as there were no religious or moral objections to specific transactions or modes of behavior, the technical aspects of the law were a matter of indifference to the [early] Muslims."[309]

Schacht evidences his case for the segregation of Islamic law from the prophetic work of Muhammad through various means. On the one hand, he observes that the legal principles that stem from Islamic law are not always consistent with Qur'anic dictate. Thus, for example, he

---

[307] (Oxford: Clarendon Press, 1964).

[308] Ibid., 19.

[309] Ibid.

points to the general preference under Islamic law for the utilization of live testimony of witnesses to evidence claims being brought, while denying the "validity of written documents." This, he says, directly contradicts the Qur'anic text of Sura II, verse 282, which seems to sanction and encourage the practice of committing contractual arrangements to writing.[310] Such contradictions between the requirements of Islamic law and the substantive content of the Qur'an should not be present if the former was truly a product of the latter, Schacht reasoned.

At the same time, Schacht pointed to a host of commonalities between requirements imposed and methodologies employed under Islamic law and those of other legal systems known in the region surrounding the Arabian Peninsula. Accordingly, for example, he argued that the idea of providing security for a debt was derived from Roman law and written into the *shari'a* tradition. As well, methods of legal reasoning, he proposes, were borrowed from Jewish law.[311]

As Schacht reasoned, the existence of the commonalities between these varying systems, which were in existence prior to the establishment of the Muslim diaspora, suggests a host of sources, extending well beyond the Qur'an and the *Sunnah*, that were at work in influencing the construction of Islamic law from its earliest origins. It is such evidence, then, that led Schacht to the conclusion that the system of Islamic law is to be differentiated from the broader religious tradition known as Islam.

In effect, he sees the system of Islamic law as a social institution crafted by the political order that controlled the Arabian Peninsula during the time period extending from the middle to the latter portion of the first century of the development of the Muslim faith. For the

---

[310] Ibid. Sura 2, verse 282 is translated by Abdullah Yusef Ali as stating, "When you deal with each other in transactions involving fixed obligations for a fixed period of time, reduce them to writing. Let a scribe write down faithfully as between the parties...."

[311] Schacht, *Introduction to Islamic Law*, 21. Schacht argues that elements of Roman and Byzantine law, the canon law of the Eastern Church, Jewish law and Sassanian law may each be glimpsed within the content of the broader system of Islamic law. As well, of course, borrowings from these systems stand in addition to the incorporation of elements from traditional Arab custom, as well.

purpose of acquiring legitimacy and support, the system was eventually associated with the Muslim religious movement. Islamic law, however, is distinguishable from the Muslim faith both in terms of its later origin and its unorthodox content.

Separating Law from Practice

This brief consideration of the historical controversies associated with the origin of Islamic law exposes a secondary, but vital additional practical inquiry. What is the relationship, in application, of Islamic law to the Muslim system of religious practice? In other words, are the two so deeply intertwined that they stand effectively as a seamless whole or may one be separated and examined without invoking appreciable harm upon the substance of the other?

On one hand, it is observed by some that the very substance of Islam lies in its ethical content. According to those embracing this stance, which may be termed a sort of traditionalist position, the practice of Islamic law may be equated with the very practice of the Muslim faith, itself. Thus, the ritual and communal components of this tradition cannot be severed meaningfully from its legalistic components.

A voice for this traditionalist position may be seen in the person of Sayyid Qutb. The beliefs, rituals and legal code that define the Muslim system of faith are part of a seamless whole, according to Qutb. Collectively, they serve as the "uniform" expression of submission to the divine.[312] Islamic law, he argued, is a creation of Allah in the same way that laws governing the functioning of the natural world are expressions of the work of the divine. Such laws must be observed by the faithful, accordingly. As he wrote:

> Thus the *shari'a* which Allah has given to man to organize his life is also a universal law, as it is related to the general law of the universe and is harmonious with it. Thus, obedience to the *shari'a* becomes a necessity for human beings so that their

---

[312] *Milestones* (Kuwait: International Islamic Federation of Student Organizations, 1978), 161.

> lives may become harmonious and in tune with the remainder of the universe....[313]

As he further emphasized, the keeping of Islamic law is vital to participation in the Muslims faith. Indeed, it is "more important than the establishment of Islamic belief," he argued. This is true because no individual can truly claim Muslim identity without submitting to this divine system of order.[314] This theme is reiterated in Qutb's earlier volume *Social Justice in Islam*, when he states that Islam is "at once worship and work, religious law and exhortation."[315]

In his own work examining the Islamic law tradition, J.N.D. Anderson sought to identify the essential traits that mark the relationship between Muslim faith and ethical practice. In so doing, he described Muslims as recognizing the system of Islamic law to be divinely ordained, independent of secular influence, compose of a set of norms to which Muslims are "under a perpetual duty to conform," possessive of an eternal quality, and beyond human conceptions of good and evil.[316]

This characterization of the Muslim understanding of the nature of Islamic law seems consistent with the assertions of many active and current leaders in the larger community who continue to embrace a sort of traditionalist position. An example may be Imam Yusef Kavakchi, the spiritual leader of the Islamic Association of North Texas, which describes itself as one of the largest Muslim communities in North America. A trained scholar in the field of Islamic law, having studied the subject at Attaturk University in Turkey, Kavakchi insists on the integrated nature of the entirety of the Muslim system of faith, including its system of religious law. As Kavakchi states:

> In Islam, creedo, belief and the ethical system are one. Actions cannot be separated from creed. They are one. And wherever they live, in a ditch, under the ocean, on Mars, on

---

313 Ibid., 165.

314 Ibid., 166.

315 John Hardie, trans. (Oneonta, N.Y.: Islamic Publications International, 2000).

316 *Islamic Law in the Modern World* (New York: New York University Press, 1958), 8-11.

> Sputnik, these things cannot be compromised.... It is not divisible.... You cannot lessen the value of or belittle any aspect of [the Muslim law system].[317]

In his desire to ensure that Islamic law is being fully and adequately employed within the confines of Western Muslim communities and particularly those in the U.S., Kavakchi argues further for the necessity of the establishment of a specially designated court, with trained personnel, designed to handle cases involving claims of Muslim litigants. In the absence of such a court, he suggests the creation of an arbitration system that could provide an alternative forum that would be less-expensive and swifter in its actions. Still, his broader emphasis upon preserving and applying Islamic law is worthy of note.

On the other side of this controversy lie those who may seek to differentiate Islamic law from the substance of Islamic practice. In part, this opposing view is represented by some of the same thinkers who, like Schacht, see the system of Islamic law as a latter addition to the larger religious system. Thus, for Schacht and others, such as Ignaz Goldziher or John Wansbrough, the appendage of religious law can be extracted from the larger religious system without damaging the larger faith system.

At the same time, some may argue that the severability of Islamic law from the larger corpus of the Muslim tradition is evidenced by the willingness of the religious community to exempt certain of its members from particular ethical demands. The most obvious example of such a recognized exemption relates to Muslims living in regions of the globe that are primarily non-Muslim in terms of religious orientation. As the *Shorter Encyclopedia of Islam* observes regarding the application of Islamic law, "even Muslims are not bound by some of its prescriptions outside [those areas that are not part of the majority-Muslim geographic sphere]."[318] Thus, as some understand the operational structure of the religious system, Islamic law, in whole or in part, may be set aside in particular circumstances, especially for those living in regions of the world where its application is unduly burdensome. Yet, such an exemption for some from specified ethical obligations under the religious system is not be equated with a failure

---

[317] Interview, Dallas, Texas, July 6, 2006.

[318] (Leiden, Netherlands: E.J. Brill, 1953), 525.

on the part of affected individuals to adhere to the broader Islamic faith tradition, it is argued. For such individuals, then, Islamic law has effectively been severed from the substance of the larger faith system.

A Modernist Call

In general, this effort aimed at redefining Islamic law, and the manner in which it is imposed within regions where Islam is a minority faith, may be referred to as the construction of a "*fiqh* of minorities," or in its more popular Arabic title, *fiqh al-aqalliyyat*. What is *fiqh* of minorities? The online Muslim journal *Milli Gazette* has defined the concept in this way:

> [Fiqh of minorities] is based on the idea that the Muslim jurist must relate the general Islamic jurisprudence to the specific circumstances of a specific community, living in specific circumstances where what is suitable for them may not be suitable for others. Such a jurist must not only have a strong background in Islamic sciences, but must also be well-versed in the sociology, economics, politics, and international relations relating to that community. The purpose of Fiqh Al-Aqalliyyat is not to recreate Islam, rather it is a set of methodologies that govern how a jurist would work within the flexibility of the religion to best apply it to particular circumstances.[319]

This "modernist" willingness to reconsider the applicability of Islamic law and its scope, especially as it relates to Muslims living in regions of the globe where they constitute a minority, has been embraced by various faith-based groups in the U.S., the most notable ones being the Islamic Council of North America, the Islamic Circle of North America and other similar organizations. While the events of September 11, 2001 may have served to curb or temper the efforts of some to pursue such a reform-minded path, certain Muslim thinkers have sought a reconsideration of the application of Islamic law

---

[319] Taha Jabir Al-Alwani, "Fiqh of Minorities I," *Milli Gazette* 5, no. 9 (May 1, 2004), http://www.milligazette.com/Archives/2004/01-15May04-Print-Edition/0105200444.htm (accessed August 4, 2008).

specifically for faith practitioners residing in regions of the world that are predominantly non-Muslim, especially in the West.

In regard to these efforts, Yusuf Talal DeLorenzo, former Secretary of the Fiqh Council of North America and Chief Shariah Officer for Shariah Capital, Inc.,[320] has observed that a major objective for the larger Islamic community should be to "develop a *fiqh* for Muslims living in non-Muslim societies."[321] His call underscores a desire for the development of a special system of law for Muslims living in areas where they constitute a minority. While it is unclear precisely how the obligations confronted by Muslims under such a system would differ from those imposed by more traditional forms of Islamic law, the new ethical structure would apparently serve the purpose of alleviating the burdens practitioners living in the West feel with regard to the task of balancing perceived moral and ethical expectations derived from Islam with secular demands. DeLorenzo is not alone in this effort.

In a statement deemed controversial or, perhaps, even heretical by many Islamic traditionalists, at least one leading American Muslim has argued that Islamic law should be shaped broadly by its context. Speaking for a growing modernist Muslim community in the West, Khaled Abou El Fadl has asserted that the strength of the Islamic moral system lies in its adaptability to present circumstances.[322] Abou El Fadl perceives an undue rigidness in the decisions of Muslim jurists in some parts of the world. Thus, the application of Islamic legal decisions arising from contexts quite distinct from that prevailing in the U.S. should not be determinative for Muslims residing in the country. Indeed, American Muslims, this progressive commentator suggests, are obliged by their religious tradition to respect U.S. law and social practice even when the adherence to these social norms runs contrary to traditional Muslim expectations.

---

[320] See "Questioning Shari'ah Conversion Technology: Yusuf Talal DeLorenzo," *Dinar Standard*, Issue 29 (Feb/March 2009), http://www.dinarstandard.com/finance/DeLorenzo012308.htm (accessed July 7, 2009).

[321] "The Fiqh Councilor in North America," in *Muslims on the Americanization Path?* Yvonne Y. Haddad and John L. Esposito, eds. (Oxford: Oxford University Press, 2000), 70.

[322] "Conference of Books Revived," *The Minaret* (October 1996): 43-44.

Similarly, the applicability and even the validity of Islamic law requirements have been questioned where they directly conflict with broadly accepted Western ethical norms. Abdullahi Ahmed An-Na'im has observed that numerous Islamic law provisions contravene broadly accepted modern notions of universal human rights and, accordingly, such demands should be abandoned.[323] As well, there have been calls for the broad reinterpretation of Islamic law in an effort to incorporate basic values of gender equality.[324] While these individual thinkers may be singled out for special attention here, others in the reformist camp may be viewed as desiring even broader changes.[325] Such reformers seek to constrain the role of Islamic law in the lives of Muslims living in the U.S. and the West, in general.

Among the groups seeking to lead the effort to develop and establish a system for the implementation of a formal *fiqh* of minorities applicable to the specific situations encountered by North American Muslims, is the Fiqh Council of North America, of which DeLorenzo formerly served as Secretary. In a recent advisory publication, the organization outlined its intended mission, which includes the offering of "Shari'a-based advice" to Muslim practitioners residing in North America concerning religious practice and conflicts with secular obligations; to consult with Islamic law experts around the globe on issues of significance to practitioners living in the West; to research particular issues of law, as they arise and to "develop a *fiqh* for Muslims living in non-Muslim societies."[326] The statement goes on to

---

[323] "Shari'a and Basic Human Rights," in *Liberal Islam*, Charles Kurzman, ed. (Oxford: Oxford University Press, 1998).

[324] See Mohommed A. Muqtedar Khan, *American Muslims: Bridging Faith and Freedom* (Beltsville, Md.: Amana Pub., 2002): 90-94.

[325] See generally Azzam Tamimi, "The Origins of Arab Secularism," in *Islam and Secularism in the Middle East*, John Esposito and Azzam Tamimi, eds. (New York: New York University Press, 2000). Tamimi points particularly to the writings of Ali Abdel Raziq and the community of his followers. Ibid., 25.

[326] Yusuf Talal DeLorenzo, "Fiqh and the Fiqh Council of North America," http://www.islamicity.com/politics/SHARIAH.HTM#S2 (accessed July 24, 2008). Specifically, the group identifies its objects as the following: "1) To consider, from a Shari'ah perspective, and offer advice on specific undertakings, transactions, contracts, projects, or proposals, guaranteeing thereby that the dealings of American Muslims fall within the parameters of

observe that the traditional system of Islamic law "pays little or no heed to the Fiqh of Muslim minorities." Accordingly, as the group observes in its statement of purpose:

> It is therefore essential that the councilor strive to interpret the teachings of Islam in a way that is consistent both with the higher principles of the Shari'ah and with the circumstances of Muslims living in predominantly non-Muslim societies. Such Fiqh might be known as the Fiqh of Muslims in non-Muslim environments, and its applications in today's world are probably without limit.[327]

Founders of a Movement

Such efforts to craft a specialized Islamic law or *fiqh* system in the U.S. have been acknowledged more recently in a report from the Hudson Institute's Center on Islam, Democracy and the Future of the Muslim

---

what is permitted by the Shari'ah; 2) To consider issues of relevance to the community and give, from a Shari'ah perspective, advice and guidelines for policy, procedure, and practice. Such advice may take the form of position papers, fatawa, research papers, sample forms for legal agreements, or whatever else is deemed effective; 3) To consult, on issues requiring specialized knowledge and experience, with professionals or subject specialists; 4) To establish and maintain working relationships with Shari'ah experts worldwide, including muftis, university professors, researchers, Shari'ah court justices, and members of national and international Fiqh councils and academies; 5) To assist local and national organizations in the resolution of conflicts; 6) To advise in the appointment of arbiters, and review arbitration proceedings and decisions for their consistency with Islamic legal principles; 7) To commission research on relevant Islamic legal issues; 8) To maintain and develop a comprehensive Shari'ah library; 9) To anticipate and serve the particular needs of minority groups within the community; youth, women, prisoners, recent converts, etc.; 10) To develop a Fiqh for Muslims living in non-Muslim societies." Ibid.

[327] Ibid.

World.[328] The report refers to the ongoing effort of many Muslims living in the West to cultivate new understandings regarding the nature of *shari'a* and its applications to practitioners living in non-Muslim countries as a vital event in the ongoing effort of this religious sub-community to define itself. It further attributes the initiation of this effort to devise a defined *fiqh* of minorities primarily to the efforts of al-Alwani and Yusef al-Qaradawi, a Muslim leader and thinker from Qatar, who has been viewed as a figure of some controversy in the West.

This movement to cultivate a *fiqh* of minorities is in its formative stages and may be dated back to about 2001. At the heart of this effort, according to the Hudson Institute report, lies the belief that the self-identity of U.S. Muslims is being compromised as a byproduct of living in the West, and the further concern that Islam, in its present state, is not capable of surviving in regions of the globe beyond the bounds of Muslim-majority states.[329]

The creation of a *fiqh* of minorities would address these concerns by cultivating an environment within which Muslims living in regions where they constitute a minority would be better able to adhere to essential ethical and ritual expectations. In so doing, it is believed, the very self-identity of Muslims living in the West would be re-invigorated. The cultivation of a *fiqh* of minorities would presumably involve the re-consideration of basic obligations recognized as part of the system of Islamic law. The system would also involve the establishment of some form of *ulema,* which is knowledgeable about circumstances in the West and is able to render reasoned opinions concerning controversies as they arise within these minority pockets of Muslims scattered across the globe. As well, some mechanism would be established that is designed to facilitate communication and interaction between the Muslim leadership in the West and those guiding relevant majority communities.[330]

In his role as one of the leading proponents of this movement, Al-Qaradawi has emphasized some of these goals in his volume entitled,

---

[328] Shammai Fishman, "Fiqh al-Aqalliyyat: A Legal Theory for Muslim Minorities," Research Monographs on the Muslim World Series, No. 1, Paper 2 (Washington D.C.: Hudson Institute, October 2006).

[329] Ibid., 3.

[330] Ibid.

Priorities of the Islamic Movement in the Coming Phase.[331] In particular, he cites the importance of efforts of the larger Muslim community to support those living as minorities in Western countries by recognizing the peculiar circumstances they confront. Such support, he suggests, will serve to preserve the Islamic identities of these individuals and to ensure that a vital Muslim presence remains in these regions. Among the particular goals he suggests related to Muslim minority communities is precisely the establishment of an educated Western *ulema*, which can answer their questions when they ask them, guide them when they lose their way and reconcile them when they differ.[332]

In terms of the process that might be followed to produce a "*fiqh* of minorities," al-Alwani offers some speculation in his own work, when he issues a call to the Muslim community:

> Review the topics covered by this science (fiqh), and eliminate those without relevance to the modern scholar or jurist. These might include, *Hukm al Ashya' Qabl al Shar"* "Rulings before the Shari'ah", *Shukr al Mun'im* "How one is required to thank the Almighty Bestower", *Mabahith Hakimiyyat al Shar'* "Studies about the Sovereignty of the Shari'ah", and excessive concern with definitions. We should also dispense with disputes concerning the uncommon *Qira'at Shadhdhah* "Alternate Recitations" of the Qur'an, and the Arabic nature of the entire Qur'an. Likewise, we should now end the long disagreement about single-narrator Hadith by saying that if such a narration is proven to have met the conditions of being authentic *Sahih* it will be acceptable, and laws may be derived from it.
>
> Moreover, we should re-examine all the conditions, laid down by certain early jurists, that seem to have been dictated by circumstances. For example, the condition that a Hadith should not contradict the general principles they established, that it should not be narrated by other than a *Faqih*, that it

---

331 (1990), http://www.witness-pioneer.org/vil/books/Q_Priorities (accessed September 12, 2008).

332 Ibid.

> should not contradict *al Qiyas*, or the traditions of the people of Madinah, or the explicit meaning *Zahir* of the Qur'an. Or the condition that a Hadith, if it deals with a common issue or hardship or affliction, must be widely known. All of these conditions should be rejected, and the same must be done with other conditions which were and are still controversial and a source of disagreement among Muslims, and which still occupy the time of scholars.[333]

In effect, then, al-Alwani appears to suggest a process through which the precise expectations of behavior for Muslims associated with the Islamic system of religious law be reconsidered in light of modern circumstance. Of course, even as al-Alwani acknowledges, this should not be taken as an invitation to place at risk identifiable prescriptions derived from the Qur'an or *hadith* deemed to be reliable, but to prompt a re-examination of interpretations that are the products of particular circumstances and times.

In an enlightening blog, al-Alwani also speaks to the particular problems faced by Muslims living in the West and the necessity for establishing a *fiqh* of minorities. As concerns the self-identity of Muslims living in the West, al-Alwani argues that popular presumptions associated with the faith and misconceptions that Islamic law is in some manner antithetical to personal freedom have led to a generalized observation that Islamic identity and Western values are incompatible. These factors, he suggests, have worked together to create a "psychological barrier" that diminishes respect for the Muslim faith among both adherents and non-practitioners residing in the West.[334] This diminishment of respect for Islam has led to the development of an "inferiority complex" affecting Muslims living in the West. Thus, Muslim practitioners have often been led to believe that they may only "fit into" the local societies of North America and

---

333 *Usul al Fiqh al Islami*, http://www.witness-pioneer.org/vil/Books/TA_uaf (accessed September 18, 2007).

334 Taha Jabir Al-Alwani, "Problems facing Muslim communities in the West" article cited from the website Islamonline.net (April 10, 2005), http://www.islamonline.net/livedialogue/english/browse.asp?hGuestID=9Vgi9 (accessed February 12, 2009).

Europe by effectively abandoning ethical, moral and ritual demands of their own faith.

The work of al-Alwani and al-Qaradawi has inspired others to consider approaches to the interpretation of Islamic religious law that effectively reduce burdens on practitioners living as minorities in the West. An example may be Louay Safi, who argues that Muslims should "liberate themselves from traditionalism" and re-engage those "universal truths," which he suggest lie at the heart of the Muslim system of faith.[335] In so doing, he argues, Muslims will be placed in a better position to embrace significant civic roles in their Western communities, even while maintaining a strong connection to their faith system.

At the same time, the very failure of Muslims in the West to reconsider the requirements of their faith may have served to limit their own influence in this region to which they have migrated. For example, Parvez Ahmed, in a 2007 speech, suggested that, despite the presence of Muslims in the United States for more than a century, the minority religious community has failed to play a role of significance in terms of affecting public policy or social dynamics. Further, the failure of the American-Muslim community to engage in the task of religious reformation may leave community members residing in the West isolated and disenfranchised permanently. As he observed, "Muslim societies in the past have often mired in the malaise of dogma and a failure to contextualize teachings of the Qur'an and the Prophetic traditions." Yet, he suggested that recent changes in the attitudes of Muslims, especially those living in the West, may lead to an alteration of this state. As he further observed:

> Today more and more Muslims are reviving critical inquiry (*ijtihad*) into both the Quran and the *Sunnah* (the traditions of Prophet Muhammad). New Muslim thinkers are provoking debate and counter arguments, often leading to renewed understanding of Islam's congruence with modernity. More and more Muslims in America are thus being better able

[335] "The Creative Mission of Muslim Minorities in the West," 12.

> balance between the demands of their faith and the challenges of modernity.[336]

For Ahmed, like al-Awani, a key first step in the process of establishing such a *fiqh* for minorities lies in resurrecting the legal concept of *ijtihad*, or reasoning. Though historically an important aspect of the Islamic legal process, many argue *ijtihad* was effectively abandoned as a formal source of legal reasoning some six centuries ago. Al-Alwani and others, meanwhile, suggest that *ijtihad* must be reinvigorated and through its use, Islamic law may be reconceived in a manner that allows it to be more fully embraced even by Muslims living in diverse locations across the globe.

The question of how Islamic law is to be understood by minority Muslims may affect the very vitality of the faith system in the future, according to some. Thus, it is argued that absent such a reconsideration of Islamic law, the system as a whole may simply fall into disuse and a state of irrelevancy for those living outside regions where political structures intentionally enforce its strictures. In considering the specific example of Nigeria and the efforts of the government of this African nation to impose Islamic law in portions of the country that are majority Muslim, Allan Christelow documented a litany of challenges that plagued the effort. The experience there, he suggested, has led even Muslim leaders in Nigeria to question whether Islamic law "can only truly be restored in a setting where there is an Islamic state and an Islamic society."[337]

At the same time, the numbers of individuals who see a future for Islam in the West is significant. Indeed, the fundamental institutions of Islam may be readily adaptable to a diversity of differing cultures and environments without threatening the essential characteristic of the faith, according to some. As is argued by one Muslim scholar, the very adaptability of the system represents a strength, while the failure of leaders to recognize this feature may work to the detriment of the faith

---

[336] Parvez Ahmed, "American Muslims: Integration and Disenfranchisement," in *Changing Identities--Evolving Values Is There Still a Transatlantic Community?* Esther Brimmer, ed. (Washington D.C.: Brookings Press, 2006).

[337] Allan Christelow, "Islamic Law and Judicial Practice in Nigeria: An Historical Perspective," *Journal of Muslim Minority Affairs*, Vol. 22, No. 1 (2002): 185-204, 198.

community. Inflexibility, which he equates with a "one size fits all" approach can actually serve to prompt extreme and exclusive interpretations of the faith. As he observes:

> While the underlying intention of this "one view fits all" approach is noble, which is to promote unity among Muslims, such a perspective could also lead to problems. One could fall into the grave mistake of applying the rulings made by the classical *ulama* without understanding the context in which the opinions were decided upon hundreds of years ago.
>
> This mistake could lead to extremism, as the subscriber of such a view may accuse those who differ with him on the grounds of differing contexts or considerations as lesser Muslims. This "one view fits all" perspective will inevitably cause the imposition of one view on others, which does not fit the pluralistic nature of creation.
>
> I would argue that the notion of a 'European Muslim' or 'Singaporean Muslim' is not fundamentally wrong in Islam. Instead, it is part of being contextual in practising the religion, which is one of the fundamental characteristics of Islam.[338]

The Outcry of the Traditionalists

Yet, not all Muslims are pleased with this attempt at re-defining the manner in which Islam is practiced, regardless of where the affected adherents happen to reside. As the Hudson Institute report observes, efforts to establish a *fiqh* of minorities or a specialized ethical and ritual system designed to accommodate the unique needs of Muslims living in such far-flung regions as Europe and North America have been criticized by many adherents of the religious system. These criticisms have been largely based upon two primary grounds.

---

[338] Muhammad Haniff Hassan, "Can Islam be Contextualized?" RSIS Commentary No. 66, An Institute of Defense and Strategic Studies Commentary, produced by the S. Rajaratnam School of International Studies, Nanyand, Singapore (September 30, 2005), http://www.rsis.edu.sg /publications/commentaries.asp?sel Year=2005 (accessed February 6, 2009).

First, it is argued that there is only a single recognizable mode of Muslim practice and, accordingly, to invent a new system is to diverge from true Islam. This broader systematic argument stands alongside a second and more specific set of criticisms that claim proposed changes to the *fiqh* system to accommodate interests of Muslims living in non-Muslim countries afford unwarranted leniencies that alter the very fabric of individual Islamic religious practice.[339] Indeed, the concern of traditionalists may well be summed up in the statement of one Muslim religious scholar who has observed, "Western-educated intellectual" Muslims have produced religious communities in the U.S. that are "devoid" of respect for or understanding of Islamic law or tradition.[340] This position is expressed by others, as well. Often, through the adoption of highly charged language, some have voiced strong opposition to efforts to reform the system of Islamic law by Western adherents. Such steps are equated with the effective abandonment of true Islam as may be witnessed in an excerpt from an online blog by a Muslim leader, who cautions his advisees:

> Some, in an effort to be modern, have said that it is acceptable to accept man-made systems, as long as they do not contradict Islam, to keep up with the times. Some Westernised people have gone as far as declaring a Bid'a (instinctual observation), stating that the practical Ahkam Shar'eea that are extracted from their detailed evidences are merely human knowledge and a man-made Fiqh. But the truth is that the Shar'eea is a Divine revelation whose primary source is the Book of Allah, and is clarified by the Sunnah of the Messenger of Allah (sallAllahu 'alayhi wasallam).
>
> Now, a large variety of what is falsely labeled as different types of "Fiqh" have been hatched, that essentially aim to twist the Ahkam Shar'eea, and escape having to abide by the

339 *Fiqh al-Aqalliyyat: A Legal Theory for Muslim Minorities*, at p. 12.

340 Muhammad Khalid Masud, "The Obligation to Migrate: The Doctrine of Hijra in Islamic Law," in *Muslim Travelers*, Dale Eickleman and James Piscatori, eds. (Berkeley: University of California Press, 1990): 29-48. See also Ali Asani, "On Pluralism, Intolerance and the Qur'an," *American Scholar* 71, No. 1 (Winter 2002): 52-60.

> commands and prohibitions of Allah. They give these new false types of "Fiqh" titles that have no truth to them, such as the "Fiqh of Reality" (Fiqh al-Waqi'), "Fiqh of Minorities" (Fiqh Al-Aqaliyyat), "Fiqh of Defeat" (Fiqh Al-Hazima), "Fiqh of Balancing" (Fiqh Al-Muwazanaat), "Fiqh of Priorities" (Fiqh Al-Awlawiyyat), and the "Fiqh of Results" (Fiqh Al-Ma-alaat).
>
> ....
>
> The careful observer of these calamities can only attribute them to two reasons: One, either these people are afflicted with ignorance of the nature of Islam, and a loss of trust in its laws, which has led these people – assuming their sincerity – to drown in the muddy swamp of reality. Rather than changing the reality in a fundamental and revolutionary way, we see them taking the reality as their source of thinking instead of their object of thinking, in order to change it.
>
> Or, the second possible reason is that some of them are agents working for the colonialists, and are hateful of Islam, injecting poison into the healthy parts, so that the Ummah is lost in the ruins of helplessness. All this in order that they lose their cultural identity, their civilization is killed, and that the Ummah can melt into the Western culture, allowing the West to rid themselves from the greatest challenge they face in the coming decades.[341]

Other Muslim leaders have offered more pointed criticisms of any effort to craft a "Fiqh of Minorities." In part, it is argued that the effort to reform Islamic *fiqh* serves as an attempt to cloak actions and activities that are clearly in conflict with ethical norms firmly established in the Muslim system beneath a false veneer of legitimacy. The legitimization of such activities eases the strains associated with Islamic practice and allows adherents to more fully conform to the behavioral norms adopted by cultural groups in non-Muslim regions of

---

341 Walhamdulillahi Rabb Al-'Alameen online blog, http://aligarians.com /mehfil/index.php?topic=3869.0; wap2 (accessed September 12, 2007). Al-Alameen is a contributor to the online site www.khilafah.com, often described as a web presence designed to articulate a radical version of Islam.

the globe. Reformist positions have also been described as being in direct conflict with the true spirit of Muslim practice and "a symptom of a corrupt thought process."[342]

In addition to general concerns related to the preservation of a "traditional" form of Muslim practice, some likewise perceive reform efforts as being part of a larger political agenda directed at Islamic society. Thus, the establishment of a minority *fiqh* system would serve to divide the Muslim Diaspora, itself, they predict. As has been observed by a noted Syrian Muslim leader:

> It is not a coincidence that the call to "Fiqh of Minorities" has come together with the plan aimed at dividing Islam. In an age in which the leaders of the ideological attack are planning, throughout the world, to divide the single global Islam into various local Islams, that differ and are in conflict with one another, this ideological attack follows in succession the voices calling to "Fiqh of Minorities" and these grant legitimacy to one another. In clarification of the matter, [Fiqh of Minorities] is nothing other than an Islamic garb that is appropriate for the Islam that is thriving today in the West, in Europe and America, not the other Islam that is prevalent in the traditional Muslim lands.[343]

The image painted here is one of a Western Muslim community divided between conflicting loyalties. Such divided loyalties may serve to alienate Muslims from their own religious tradition and community, it is argued. As a popular Islamic website warns its readers:

> At the forefront of the challenges facing the Muslims in the West are the continuous calls for complete integration, thereby abandoning any overt form of an Islamic identity or character. Debates in Governments and media on how to integrate the Muslims are frequent and indicative of the prevailing

---

[342] Asif Khan, *The Fiqh of Minorities: The New Fiqh to Subvert Islam*, Dawud Masieh, ed. (London: Khilafah Publications, 2004), 42.

[343] Shaykh Muhammad Sa'id Ramadan al-Buti, "Fiqh of Minorities," Mahdi Locke, trans. (2008), http://marifah.net/articles/Bouti-MinorityFiqh.pdf (accessed March 13, 2008).

> environment in the West. Even the reaction of Muslims to diverse controversial events, such as, the publication of "The Satanic Verses", the war in Iraq and the discrimination of Muslims in society have been addressed in a way to provide further justification for integration.[344]

For religious practitioners sympathetic to arguments against the crafting of a minority *fiqh*, a more acceptable course of actions may lie in the establishment of a Muslim judicial system within the U.S., designed to preserve and promote long-held Islamic moral ideals.[345] And in the absence of a formal Islamic judicial system in the West, systems of private justice have emerged, with imams serving Western communities of Muslims by establishing "Islamic arbitration committees."[346]

It may be noted that it is not traditionalist Muslims alone who have criticized those seeking to reform the Islamic *fiqh* to accommodate the practicalities of life in West. Some outside the Muslim community, have reacted with suspicion to efforts aimed at reforming understandings associated Islamic law. As Shammai Fishman has argued, the purpose of the establishment of a minority *fiqh* may have less to do with the desire to bridge relations between Muslims and Western societies hosting them, than with a long-term effort to increase Muslim political and economic influence in the West. As he argues:

> In dealing with these political questions, Muslim Minority Jurisprudence is geared towards the Muslim community to

---

[344] "Fiqh al Aqaliyaat – A Jurisprudence to Assimilation," website Ummah Forum (July 28, 2003), www.ummah.com/forum/showthread.php?t=20319 (accessed March 10, 2008).

[345] There are at least three organized groups that appear to desire the establishment of formal *fiqh* councils in the United States. These are the Shari'a Scholars Association of North America, MSA and ISNA. The creation of one or more such councils would provide American Muslims with a venue to seek advice on the resolution of practical issues in a manner consistent with Islamic law principles. It has been speculated by some that these councils might be structured to provide mediation or other more formal dispute resolution processes, as well.

[346] Leonard, *Muslims in the United States*, 99.

> gain a certain type of political power at the expense of the sovereign governments of the Western states. On the other hand, it is geared away from accepting life within the framework of western society as it is, or even the very existence of the states in which they live.[347]

For Fishman, the move toward the establishment of a *fiqh* designed for minorities is attracting an alarming broad base of support from global Muslim leaders. In general, these individuals are associated with what is perceived to be an accommodating brand of Islam, he argues. Yet, the ulterior motives of this rising majority, he cautions, are heavily anti-Western.

Ultimate Questions

The viability of the effort to construct a *fiqh* of minorities is unclear. The ultimate success of such an effort will depend finally upon the willingness of the broader Muslim community to embrace a common vision for this system and to establish a functioning internal hierarchy that will be able to defend and sustain the system. Still, apart from these operational practicalities, Muslims, as a community, are faced with a much greater philosophical dilemma. Can the majority of Muslims reach agreement on whether such reforms are compatible with the larger system of faith they embrace? Is a *fiqh* of minorities, in the end, a necessary accommodation, providing Muslims with the ability to balance desires to follow Islam with the demands of living within Western society, or is it merely an abomination of an otherwise pristine religious system?

While many Muslims have reached their own personal conclusions regarding these issues, a community consensus seems distant, even despite the arguments of individuals such as Al-Awani. These questions, it seems, will bear directly upon the experience of Muslims residing in the U.S. and other countries of North America and Europe well into the future. Still, however such issues are resolved, Muslims

---

[347] Shammai Fishman, "Some Notes on Arabic Terminology as a Link Between Tariq Ramadan and Sheikh Dr. Taha Jabir al-Alwani, Founder of the Doctrine of 'Muslim Minority Jurisprudence'(*Fiqh al-Aqaliyyat al-Muslimah*)," (online) www.e-prism.org (accessed February 22, 2009).

and Westerners, alike, will be affected. The final resolution of these broader issues, then, necessarily demands the participation of not just members of the Muslim community living in the West, but Muslims across the globe and their non-Muslim neighbors. Yet, even when confronted by this conflict, some Muslim leaders have expressed optimism that Muslim ideals and Western priorities can be reconciled. As the Muslim scholar Imad-ad-Dean Ahmad has observed:

> The reconciliation of Islamic law with secular government is easy for us Muslims living in America. The American government is secular, and we only have to resolve to live our lives in accord with Islamic law, establishing our own institutions (schools, Islamic centers, social service and arbitration agencies) in compliance with our understanding of that law.[348]

Of course, even despite this optimistic pronouncement, it appears that there is no shortage of devils lurking in the details associated with Ahmed's vision of social cohesion and inter-cultural compatibility.

---

[348] Imad-ad-Dean Ahmed, "Reconciling Secular Government with Islamic Law," A Paper for the 6th Annual Conference of the Center for the Study of Islam and Democracy: Democracy and Development—Challenges for the Islamic World, April 22-23, 2005, Washington D.C. (online) www.minaret.org (accessed February 12, 2008).

CHAPTER 7

A Parallel System of Justice?

> *Young women killed for dating. Limbs amputated for petty theft. Makeshift courts deciding the fates of members of local Muslim communities. The Western world has grown accustomed to hearing about the brutalities of Islamic law. However, these primitive practices are no longer limited to the remote tribal areas of Pakistan, the backward kingdom of Saudi Arabia, or oppressive, mullah-dominated Iran. Today, thanks in large part to a massive flow of immigration from Muslim countries, sharia law and medieval customs are becoming increasingly common in the heart of Christian Europe.*[349]

The questions of how and whether to accommodate Islamic law in some form have occupied the attentions of government officials and ministries throughout North America and Europe in recent decades. Following the terrorist attacks in New York of September 11, 2001, these questions have garnered heightened attention and, with general concerns related to terrorism growing, they seem to have become more difficult to resolve. As the brief excerpt from an article appearing in *The National Review*, quoted above, indicates, the very issue of

---

[349] Lorenzo Vidino and Erick Stakelbeck, "European Dishonor: *Sharia* on the Old Continent," *National Review* (December 3, 2003), http://www.nationalreview.com/comment/vidino-stakelbeck200312030840O .asp (accessed November 12, 2007).

whether to accommodate Islamic legal norms is one that often generates significant popular anxiety and ire, which is felt acutely by elected political leaders.

Still, it is important and worthwhile to consider the manner in which certain governments have tackled these questions. Indeed, it is possible that, in the experience of other nations, there may be found essential lessons that could inform the U.S. and Western states still grappling with these basic issues.

What are the options available for Western governments as they consider the relationship between their own legal systems and the set of ethical norms bound up in the *shari'a*? On a foundational level, it may be argued that there are available three essential approaches that have been employed in certain Western states to date, which offer some reasonable accommodation of Islamic legal norms.

In this chapter, attention is given to one of these approaches – the establishment of a parallel system of justice through the use of arbitration. The establishment of religious arbitration systems has been considered by some as a viable and potentially advantageous alternative to the utilization of secular courts to entertain certain types of disputes involving Muslims and members of other religious groups. In both the U.S. and Canada, the subject of religious arbitration is quite controversial, but also increasingly discussed. This chapter examines the experience of religious communities in both Canada and the U.S. as they have flirted with the use of religious arbitration systems.

Canada's Experiment with Arbitration

Islamic law has been the subject of significant dispute in Canada, with the epicenter of the debate being located in the province of Ontario. The province of Ontario was drawn into the limelight on this subject with the passage of provincial legislation, in 1991, that the renowned and sometimes reviled commentator Daniel Pipes cynically described as "what seemed at the time to be an enlightened, multicultural piece of legislation."[350] The *Arbitration Act,*[351] as it came to be known, required

---

[350] See "Enforce Islamic Law in Canada?" *New York Sun* (September 27, 2005) http://www.danielpipes.org/article/2989 (accessed November 20, 2007).

[351] Arbitration Act, 1991, S.O. 1991, c. 17, for excerpts of the act, see Appendix A, below.

that the courts of Ontario enforce as law the decisions of voluntary arbitration panels, authorized to render judgments on matters falling within a defined scope. The act was deemed to apply not only to commercial endeavors, but also to private conflicts rooted in religious law.

The results of such arbitration would be enforceable by the government of Ontario under the act, so long as decisions were not in direct conflict with the laws of Canada. Thus, the act came to be seen as a potential vehicle through which various religious minorities might be able to fulfill their desire to impose and enforce religious law in Canada.

Ultimately, Jewish, Muslim, Christian and other religious groups embraced and used the act to impose religious law within their respective communities. While the *Arbitration Act* was always controversial, public concern about the law grew in 2003, when an organization known as the Islamic Institute of Civil Justice ("IICJ") was organized for the stated purpose of establishing a formal arbitration body that would apply principles of Islamic law and be available to all Muslims in the province of Ontario. According to the proposal, the IIJC planned to provide forums for arbitration on matters of family or personal law and inheritance.

Ultimately, the response to the IIJC proposal was broad and much of it highly critical. Voicing particularly strong resistance to the IIJC proposal were various women's groups, including the Canadian non-profit group Metropolitan Action Committee on Violence Against Women and Children. The popular objections to the *Arbitration Act* led to its amendment in 2005. Under the amendment, arbitration decisions imposing religious law would no longer be enforceable by Ontario courts. However, for the purposes of this analysis, it is worthwhile to consider the short-lived Ontario *Arbitration Act* as a potential model for the treatment of religious law by Western governments. Further, it is informative to examine the various arguments that led to the emasculation of the act's original design.

a. The Ontario *Arbitration Act*

In general, it may be observed that rights asserted pursuant to Islamic law have not fared well in the Canadian court system. An example of the responses of Canadian courts to such claims may be the recent Ontario case of *Khan v. Khan*.[352] In the matter, Ms. Khan sought support from her husband following the termination of their marriage. Mr. Khan countered that the Islamic marriage contract that bound the couple, an agreement signed and effectuated in Lahore, Pakistan, precluded such an award of support. He further argued that if the provision of the marriage contract that precluded such an award was declared void, then the entirety of the marriage proceeding must be deemed void, leaving Ms. Khan without a claim in either event. Ultimately, the court found the marriage contract to be valid, but the provision denying support to be void as an "unconscionable" agreement. In effect, then, the provision of the contract related to support, which was instituted pursuant to a legal regime imposing Islamic law, was held to be unenforceable in Canada.

This matter may be compared with the Ontario case of *Kaddoura v. Hammoud*,[353] in which a divorced spouse sought to enforce terms of an Islamic marriage contract that called for the payment of a delayed dower sum of $30,000 (also known as a *mahr*). Curiously, in the *Kaddoura* case, the court did not find that the contract was void as an unconscionable agreement, but, instead, ruled more broadly that the dower, as a religious arrangement, was not subject to review in the Canadian civil courts. As the court observed:

> The *mahr* and the extent to which it obligates a husband to make payment to his wife is essentially and fundamentally an Islamic religious matter. Because *mahr* is a religious matter, the resolution of any dispute relating to it or the consequences of failing to honour the obligation are also religious in their content and context. While not, perhaps, an ideal comparison, I cannot help but think that the obligation of the *mahr* is as unsuitable for adjudication in the civil courts as is an obligation in a Christian religious marriage, such as to love, honour and cherish, or to remain faithful, or to maintain the marriage in sickness or other adversity so long as both parties live, or to raise children according to specified religious doctrine. Many such promises go well beyond the basic legal

---

352 O.J. No. 1923 (Ontario Ct. of Justice, 2005).

353 168 D.L.R. (4th) 503 (Ontario Ct. Gen. Div., 1998).

> commitment to marriage required by our civil law and are essentially matters of chosen religion and morality. They are derived from and are dependent upon doctrine and faith. They bind the conscience as a matter of religious principle but not necessarily as a matter of enforceable civil law.[354]

The very breadth of the ruling seems to implicate a strong resistance by the court to any sort of claim rooted in principles stemming from religious ethical systems.

In a significant and interesting Calgary case, *Hassan v. Hassan*,[355] the court was faced with the task of determining the validity of a marriage established in Canada pursuant to an Islamic ceremony. In a holding that appears to stand in stark contrast to the Tennessee appellate court decision of *Aghili v. Saadatnejadi*,[356] the court determined that, while the marriage ceremony complied with requirements of Islamic law and though the couple lived together as husband and wife following the ceremony, the union, itself, was void due to the failure of the parties to comply with technical requirements, including licensing regulations. In other words, priority was given to technical legal requirements over religious standards for the determination of the validity of a marriage.

These cases and others paint a picture of a Canadian judiciary that is not particularly friendly to systems of religious law. The Ontario *Arbitration Act* appeared to provide a mechanism through which religious communities could enforce private systems of law, while avoiding the challenging task of seeking to defend those same systems in the Canadian courts. Under the *Arbitration Act*, courts were specifically precluded from intervening in or interfering with any agreement by parties to submit controversies or claims to an arbitration panel applying a defined set of law, except to prevent unfair treatment of a party or to enforce the final award of the arbitrator.[357] As well, courts were directed to enforce the final determinations of such arbitration panels.

---

[354] Ibid., 511.

[355] A.J. No. 955; 2006 ABQB 544 (Alberta Ct. Queen's Bench, 2006).

[356] See chapter five, note 256, above.

[357] Arbitration Act of 1991, Section 6.

While the *Arbitration Act* imposed few limits on the use of the alternative system of dispute resolution, certain strictures were established to guide the proceedings of panels. Among the limitations imposed were the requirements that the participants voluntarily submit to the jurisdiction of the arbitration panel; that the arbitration not result in the ordering of individuals to undertake acts that would be illegal under Canadian law; that the private systems of law employed not deal with criminal matters; and that the arbitrations be conducted fairly and the parties be treated equally.

For more than a decade, the *Arbitration Act* was used by religious groups in Ontario to establish parallel justice systems. The legislation was controversial throughout its existence. However, it was the public announcement of the IIJC of the organization's intent to establish a broad and centralized system of *shari'a*-based tribunals focused upon issues of family law that prompted heightened public angst. The vocal public reaction led to the June, 2003, appointment of former Ontario Attorney General Marion Boyd to conduct a formal review of the social implications of the *Arbitration Act*. After meeting with more than 50 affected groups associated with the controversy, an extensive report, popularly referred to as "the Boyd Report"[358] was issued in December, 2004.

In some respects, the Boyd Report only served to exacerbate the ongoing controversy related to the utilization of religious law in Ontario. While suggesting the placement of certain limitations upon the arbitration system designed to ensure the fairness of processes employed, the Boyd Report went on to recommend that private arbitration continue to be available for the resolution of issues relating to inheritance and family law matters in Ontario. The report, further, specifically recommended that such arbitration tribunals be allowed to employ systems of religious law. As the report observed in its opening executive summary:

---

[358] *Dispute Resolution in Family Law: Protecting Choice, Promoting Inclusion*, website of the Ministry of the Attorney General for the Province of Ontario (December 20, 2004), http://www.attorneygeneral.jus. gov.on.ca/english/ about/pubs/boyd/ (accessed July 10, 2007); *see also* Appendix B, below, for the Executive Summary of this report.

> In fact, religious arbitration is already being conducted by several different faiths. Although some participants in the Review fear that the use of arbitration is the beginning of a process whose end goal is a separate political identity for Muslims in Canada, that has not been the experience of other groups who use arbitration. As well, Canada's First Nations people are the only minority group that has a defined right to negotiate with the Canadian state about political autonomy. Canada is a multicultural society and the fundamental tension that must be addressed is between respect for the minority group and protection of a person's individual rights within that minority. The Review found that secular state laws do not treat everyone equally because people's individual backgrounds lead to differences in the impact of these laws. If the state allows cultural groups complete freedom to define family and inheritance matters those groups may trample on the rights of individuals within the group and may discriminate in ways that are unacceptable to Canadian society. The Review concluded that cultural groups should not be permitted to stop people from having access to laws and processes that are available to all.[359]

In effect, then, the Boyd Report sought the preservation of an arbitration system designed to accommodate claims rooted in religious law, with the addition of certain safeguards designed to overcome fears voiced by the general public. In so doing, the report emphasized the importance of reinforcing "multiculturalism" as a social guiding principle and underscored the observation that "freedom of contract" should apply not merely to commercial matters, but to religious and family matters, as well.

The recommendations were accompanied by the admission that the preservation of a purely secular system of laws might lead to discriminatory results. In the end, the report argued that a system which accommodates both secular law and religious law offers the greatest potential for the avoidance of discriminatory results.

---

[359] Ibid., 4.

b. From Enthusiasm to Anxiety

The Boyd Report provided a foundation for a divisive and broad public debate concerning the *Arbitration Act.* Strong arguments were made both for and against the utilization of arbitration panels to enforce religious law in Canada. Much of the debate centered specifically upon Islamic law.

At the heart of the debate concerning the *Arbitration Act* were questions related to the compatibility of Islamic law with social expectations deeply rooted in Canadian life and fundamental rights guaranteed under the country's laws. Perhaps, the most vocal complaints related to the emerging private systems of religious law in Canada came from groups seeking to represent the interests of the most vulnerable in society, particularly women and children. In part, concerns expressed by commentators focused upon the ability of women and children to protect their own rights and interests within the scope of the arbitration system, given the economic and social challenges afflicting these groups. Statistical evidence was offered, as part of the debate, to show the economic vulnerability of Muslim women, in particular, within Canadian society. As was observed in the publication *Canada Issues*, while the Islamic community grew rapidly in Canada between 1991 and 2001, Muslim women were among the most economically disenfranchised groups in the nation.[360] As the article observed:

> The 2001 Census reports that the Muslim population has grown 128% over the past decade to approximately 580,000, [2% of the Canadian population] of which 276,075 were women. Based on 2001 Census, recent research of Dr. Daood Hamdani released by [the Canadian Council of Muslim Women] shows that Muslim women are among the poorest women in Canada, are underemployed despite high levels of education and tend to work part-time in low-paying jobs. Muslim women have a higher rate of unemployment and a

---

[360] Rezia Jaffer, "Religion, Pluralism and Faith-based Arbitration: Consequences for Canadian Muslim Women," *Canadian Issues* (Spring, 2005): 82-86. Jaffer wrote the article as president of the Canadian Council of Muslim Women.

> lower rate of labour force participation compared to other women. Compared to other women, twice as many Muslim women remain separated; fewer of them are divorced and marital breakdown among Muslim women aged 18-24 is higher than their peers.[361]

The article went on to question whether, given the economic conditions confronted by many Canadian Muslim women, such individuals would have the ability to freely choose to submit to arbitration to resolve private disputes. The ability of women to make informed and independent choices about whether to submit to the jurisdiction of such arbitration panels was limited, according to some, because they tended to reside within "religious or cultural enclaves," to possess limited English language skills, to be unaware of their rights under Canadian law, and to lack the economic means to overcome these limitations.[362]

The group Women Living Under Muslim Laws produced an analysis critical of the Boyd Report, which similarly observed that Muslim women in Canada were routinely marginalized, both economically and socially. Such marginalization limited the freedom of women to choose whether to participate in a religious system of adjudication.[363]

As the report suggested, women who chose not to submit to arbitration were frequently ostracized within their own communities. Further, women involved in abusive situations frequently reported feeling that they had "little choice" but to participate in religious arbitration that would often protect the abusers.

Another major set of concerns associated with the *Arbitration Act* related to the long-term impact of the use of alternate dispute resolution in Canada to impose religious law upon individual minority communities. The maintenance of a separate judicial system would

---

[361] Ibid., 83.

[362] Ibid., 84.

[363] Pamela Cross, "An Analysis of Marion Boyd's Review 'Dispute Resolution in Family Law: Protecting Choice, Promoting Inclusion,'" *Women Living Under Muslim Laws*, Dossier 27 (December, 2005), http://www.wluml.org/english/pubsfulltxt.shtml?cmd[87]=i-87-531766 (accessed September 10, 2007).

result in the segregation and further marginalization of minority groups, it was feared by opponents of the act. As one commentator observed, the formal establishment of an Islamic arbitration panel would "ghettoize Muslims and will lead to a two-tiered legal system – one for Muslims and one for everyone else."[364]

One of the most divisive issues in the debate regarding the *Arbitration Act* concerned the extent to which application of the act would either enhance or retard the ability of the Canadian social system to accommodate differing cultural groups. In large measure, the *Arbitration Act* was viewed by its supporters as an effort consistent with the larger national priority of encouraging "multiculturalism" in Canada. In other words, the Ontario government was seen as providing significant support to religious minority groups, precisely by allowing them to establish state-sanctioned judicial institutions. Such support would ultimately encourage broader participation by affected minority groups in the social sphere. Yet, some questioned this conclusion, arguing that multiculturalism would actually be deterred, rather than promoted, by this scheme. Scholar Ayelet Shachar argued that the *Arbitration Act* would lead to greater social disenfranchisement and economic adversity for participants, rather than increased broad social cohesion.[365]

The debate, he suggested, was wrongly characterized as an "either-or choice" between "loyalty to the faith and governance by the state."[366] Yet, as he argued, such a forced choice can only lead to ostracism by the larger Canadian populace.

It was concern regarding the impact of arbitration upon specific sub-groups, such as women and children, and the potentially divisive effect of the establishment of parallel judicial systems that appeared to be determinative in the Canadian debate. At least in part, it was such commentary that prompted revision of the *Arbitration Act*, leading to the exclusion of religiously-oriented arbitration panels from the protections afforded by the Act.

---

[364] Jaffer, "Religion, Pluralism and Faith-Based Arbitration," 85.

[365] "Religion, State and the Problem of Gender: New Modes of Citizenship and Governance in Diverse Societies," *McGill Law Journal* 50 (February, 2005): 49-88.

[366] Ibid., 63.

Of course, even though the *Arbitration Act* was ultimately modified to exclude religious panels from its protections, many compelling arguments were made in favor of the original version of the act. In addition to pointing to enhanced multiculturalism as a potential benefit of the act, proponents argued that use of arbitration in Ontario would afford litigants a less expensive and swifter process to resolve personal disputes and the proceedings would eliminate the need for underground tribunals, which are out of the reach of government oversight. One vocal proponent of the *Arbitration Act* was attorney and Muslim activist Faisal Kutty, who observed that arbitration panels in Canada had proved to offer a sound and transparent vehicle for the resolution of a wide range of disputes.[367] Precisely because of the oversight employed by Canadian courts, the decisions of arbitration panels had been viewed positively and with respect, he argued. Further, such arbitration panels provided a "less disruptive alternative to the adversarial litigation process."[368]

Meanwhile, in response to the claim that society's most vulnerable would suffer through the application of the *Arbitration Act*, proponents argued that the availability of an alternative dispute resolution system had actually served to protect the interests of this group. The act, it was claimed, had kept such matters from being resolved through "back-door" processes that are beyond the reach of state review. Thus, the elimination of the arbitration system, according to Kutty, would "push the practice of religious arbitration outside the legal system."[369] The consequences of such underground panels would be broad, he argued. In part, such underground systems of dispute resolution would be less likely to protect specific individual rights, than would regulated arbitration panels.

As well, the interpretation of religious law employed by such underground tribunals would likely be more stringent and lead to more onerous results. Additionally, he argued that such underground

---

[367] "Canada's Islamic Dispute Resolution Initiative: Hysteria and Racism," published on the website www.islamonline.net (Jan. 13, 2005), http://www.islamonline.net/servlet/Satellite?c=Article_C&cid=156077845426 &pagename=Zone-English-Muslim_Affairs%2FMAELayout (accessed December 2, 2007).

[368] Ibid.

[369] Kutty, "Canada's Islamic Dispute Resolution Initiative."

tribunals might utilize oppressive mechanisms to compel participation in ways that would be abhorred by state-sanctioned arbitration panels. Ultimately, in the view of Kutty, the interests of minority sub-groups, including women and children, would likely be better protected within an arbitration system that is overseen by secular courts than would be the case in the absence of such supervision.

The availability of institutional oversight of arbitration panels proved to be one of the strongest selling points of act proponents. Such oversight could serve to ensure that individual rights would not be ignored through the institution of specific safeguards. Among the safeguards suggested were specific processes designed to ensure the adequacy of the training of religious arbitrators and the provision of mandatory counseling for participants intended to communicate the full extent of their personal array of rights related to the resolution of personal claims.[370] Other specific safeguards were also suggested, including the incorporation of a mandatory system of counseling on individual rights.[371]

---

[370] See also Riad Saloojee, "How Sharia Law Could Work in Ontario," *Calgary Herald* (June 9, 2004): A16. Saloojee argues that the voluntariness of such an arbitration process could be protected by ensuring that all participants receive independent legal advice relative to the effect of decisions and rights related to appeals. He also suggests that mandatory counseling concerning legal rights be provided for immigrants. He agreed that a regulatory scheme designed to ensure the adequacy of training of arbitrators would be important, and he further emphasized the need for transparency, arguing that some version of all decisions of arbitrators should be made a part of the public record. Ibid.

[371] Shachar, "Religion, State and the Problem of Gender," 75-76. In particular, the author suggests the inclusion of the following safeguards in any proposal to establish a religiously-based arbitration system:

> 1. Introduce a requirement of mandatory and independent legal advice for each party *before* entering the binding arbitration process. The purpose of this consultation session would be to inform the parties about the legal consequences of the following choices:
>
> (i)Choice of forum, that is, turning to binding religious arbitration as opposed to a civil court; and (ii) Choice of law under the tribunal. For instance, the arbitration could follow the norms of secular family law

Echoing similar sentiments was a *Toronto Star* column, which argued that, while the proposal to establish a formal Muslim arbitration system in Ontario had been characterized as an act tantamount to the introduction of Taliban-style justice in the Western nation, the essence of the plan amounted in actuality to an attempt by a single Muslim group to exert rights already exercised by many other religious groups in Canada, including Mennonite and Catholic Christians, Jews and Ismaili Muslims.[372]

The "hysteria" surrounding the discussion, the columnist observed, ignored the fact that, even under the *Arbitration Act*, arbitration judgments inconsistent with fundamental rights protected under Canadian law would be subject to review and correction by national courts. Moreover, much of the opposition to the *Arbitration Act* was fueled by two "very small" Muslim groups, The Canadian Council of Muslim Women and the Muslim Canadian Congress, each with less than 1,000 members, who, it was argued, did not represent the interests and opinions of a majority of Canadian Muslims. A similar theme was apparent in a 2004 editorial in the *Globe and Mail*, which argued:

> or those of religious law. In the latter case, the parties must specify which school of Muslim jurisprudence is to be followed. The parties could further agree to apply a combination of secular and religious sources of law according to subject matter. For example, the requirements set as default rules in Canadian secular laws could be selected as binding on property-related questions, while the relevant school of Muslim law would formulate the status dimension of the divorce settlement.
>
> 2. Permit a non-governmental organization to act as amicus curiae to assist women, should they desire it, in making these choices.
>
> 3. File a written affidavit confirming the consultation session and the choices made by each party with a civil registration authority or local court.

Ibid., 76.

[372] Haroon Siddiqui, "Sensationalism Shrouds the Debate on Sharia: Haroon Siddiqui says Hysteria Shows a Lack of Faith in Canada," *The Toronto Star* (June 12, 2005): A17.

> "Canada is founded upon principles that recognize the supremacy of God and the rule of law," says the very first line of the Charter of Rights and Freedoms. This is a country that respects freedom of religion.
>
> Those who fear fundamentalism should accept that deep religious expression is not necessarily a sign of militancy or extremism. Besides, fundamentalism, in its peaceful manifestations, cannot be squashed by state edict. The Islamic civil tribunal may yet send a message that Muslims can be who they are and still be as Canadian as anyone else.[373]

In general, Kutty and others supportive of the *Arbitration Act* reasoned that the criticisms leveled against this alternative judicial process, particularly as it relates to situations in which religious law would be imposed, were "paternalistic" in that the state was viewed as the only viable protector of individual interests and rights and the religious communities and individuals, themselves, were deemed incapable of carrying out such a function.

c. The Future of Western *Shari'a*-based Arbitration

The polemic debate outlined, in brief above, seems to reflect significant popular anxiety and, perhaps, a bit of misinformation. The question that may be asked, based upon the experience in Canada, is whether such a system offers any sort of workable model that could be embraced in the West. Part of the difficulty in implementing any such system, according to scholar James Thornback, is the manner in which Islam is portrayed in Western media.[374] As he has argued, the debate in Ontario amounted to a polemic attempt to describe Islam and the *shari'a* system as either the ultimate "bad" or the ultimate "good," with little reasoned and balanced consideration of the serious issues that lie between these positions. As he observed:

---

[373] "An Islamic Court? Here? Why Not?" *The Globe and Mail* (August 28, 2004): A14.

[374] James Thornback, "The Portrayal of Sharia in Ontario," *Appeal* 10 (2005): 1-12.

> The question that Canadians should be asking is not whether Sharia is Good or Bad. Rather, we need to examine family law in Ontario and the rest of the country to decide whose interests we want to protect and whose interests are being protected. Does family arbitration exist simply to save the government money, or are there genuine benefits to those who use it? Should the government respect the choice of individuals and allow them to resolve their disputes in the manner they choose, or should the government step in and impose solutions? How do we ensure that domestic contracts, whether they are arbitration agreements or not, are based on the true and informed consent of both parties?[375]

Ultimately, Thornback seems convinced that a form of *shari'a*-based arbitration, incorporating significant safeguards, could provide the blueprint for a workable system that responds to the concerns and goals of practicing Muslims, as well as non-Muslims, interested in the adherence to religious law even while residing in a Western environment.

Based upon the experience of other religious groups, perhaps Thornback is correct. In Canada, several religious groups seemed to meet with success in their application of the *Arbitration Act* and it was only the public unveiling of a plan to construct a Muslim arbitration center that pushed the entire system into turmoil. A similar pattern may be identified in the United States, as the Jewish community, acting in certain jurisdictions, has created an arbitration system to resolve claims under religious law. Thus, a foundation for successful implementation of an arbitration system is present in North America. Whether the Muslim community, in practice, would be allowed to take advantage of this foundation fully is unclear.

Arbitration, U.S. Secular Courts and the Muslim Community

The experience of religious groups in the U.S., including the Muslim community, with alternative dispute resolution mechanisms is quite varied. In many respects, Muslims are just beginning to explore the

---

[375] Ibid., 12.

extent to which such legal tools may be used for the purpose of employing religious law. At this juncture, then, Muslims in the U.S. stand in the shadow of certain other religious communities that have experimented with the use of alternative dispute resolution systems for a couple of decades in an effort to craft venues capable of securing religious law norms. Perhaps, the best example comes from the Jewish community, where arbitration has come to play a significant role in the communal life of members of certain sects.

Portions of the American Jewish community have begun to carve a workable system for the employment of religious law, at least within certain contexts. For the purposes of the present analysis, the question may be asked whether the experiences of American Jews in seeking to establish a viable private religious forum may provide a road map for Muslims living in the United States. As well, it is important to consider some of the limitations and hurdles confronted by the Jewish community in their efforts and the extent to which such constraints might affect similar efforts on the part of the Muslim community.

a. Arbitration in the U.S. Jewish Community

Through reliance particularly upon statutory enactments creating mechanisms for the application of binding arbitration procedures, Jews, especially of the Orthodox and Conservative branches of the larger Diaspora, have established forums for the resolution of varying disputes through the application of religious law. In effect, these forums, while technically employing binding arbitration, are acting as rabbinical courts. Panels of one to three rabbis typically oversee the arbitration.[376] The system is described as "well-organized" and broad in its geographical reach.[377] Perhaps, the most noted example of such a forum is the Beth Din of America, an extension of the Rabbinical Council of America, which was established in New York in 1960. According to Rabbi Jonathan Reiss, Beth Din of America ("Beth Din")

---

376 Caryn Litt Wolfe, "Faith-based Arbitration: Friend or Foe? An Evaluation of Religious Arbitration Systems and their Interaction with Secular Courts," *Fordham Law Review* 75 (October 2006): 427-469, 438.

377 Ibid.

provides dispute resolution services undertaken in accord with Jewish law in three primary areas.[378]

The most prevalent type of matter heard by the Beth Din rabbinic panels relates to the granting of divorces. In part, the necessity for this service stems from the demand by Orthodox and Conservative branches of Judaism that adherents seeking a divorce receive religious sanction for the termination of the marriage. In the absence of such sanction, any attempt to effectuate a divorce is deemed ineffective.[379]

Through forums established by the Beth Din, couples can obtain a *get*, which, in accord with Jewish law, is a document that serves to effectuate a divorce, releasing parties from continuing obligations to their spouses. In addition, the forums may provide a venue to resolve varying types of intra-community disputes ranging from commercial to familial and to overcome internal disputes that prevent parties from obtaining final resolution of pending controversies. The website of the Beth Din organization expands this list by observing that its rabbinic courts also entertain issues regarding the validity of a marriage and personal religious status, as well as matters of internal dispute of varying types within a gathered Jewish community.[380]

There are key advantages cited that may serve to encourage Jews to submit claims to the Beth Din. These include the utilization of notable rabbis and lay "experts" to oversee and guide the dispute resolution process, the adherence to secular state law regarding arbitration in order to ensure the effectiveness of judgments, and the low cost of litigating matters through the system.[381] At the same time, Rabbi Reiss has identified certain obstacles that may serve to deter some in the U.S. from accessing the services of private rabbinical courts, such as those organized by Beth Din. Some members of the

---

[378] For general background information on Beth Din of America, see the website of the organization at www.bethdin.org.

[379] Lawrence Warmflash, "The New York Approach to Enforcing Religious Marriage Contracts: From *Avitzur* to the *Get* Statute," *Brooklyn Law Review* 50 (Winter 1984): 229-243.

[380] "Our Services," website of Beth Din of America, www.bethdin.org/services.htm (accessed December 14, 2007).

[381] Rabbi Jonathan Reiss, "Jewish Divorce and the Role of Beit Din," Jewish Law Articles, www.jlaw.com/Articles/divorcebeit.html (accessed December 14, 2007).

Jewish community, he suggests, fear that rabbinic courts may lack the sophistication to effectively respond to complicated or technical issues. Some females cite fears that the rabbinic court system and the Jewish religious law, in general, is biased in favor of male litigants.

Such fears that women may be treated differently than men may stem specifically from the priority given to the husband in terms of obtaining a *get*. In particular, under Jewish law a *get* may not be granted without the express approval of the husband. It is the husband who must initiate the *get*. The authority to initiate a *get* is not traditionally extended to the wife under Jewish law. As one commentator has explained:

> The Jewish law of divorce has evolved over time. According to Biblical law, the husband had the power to divorce his wife at will. In the tenth century, Gershomides, the leading Rabbinic sage, issued a decree that is still binding, requiring that the woman willingly accept the *get* for it to be valid, thus preventing men from divorcing their wives without their consent. Since the tenth century, Jewish law has required the *get* (similarly to the *ketubah*) to be given willingly by the husband and to be accepted willingly by the wife. This approach of Jewish law is analogous to the common law requirement that contracts are invalid if entered into under duress.[382]

A related concern is the fear that certain parties may abuse the system in order to obtain personal advantage. The most obvious example of a matter in which the rabbinical court system might be used to personal advantage relates to situations wherein a husband seeks to withhold his agreement to the issuance of a *get* if he disagrees with the terms of a divorce arrangement.

---

[382] Michelle Greenberg-Kobrin, "Civil Enforceability of Religious Prenuptial Agreements," *Columbia Journal of Law and Social Problems* 32 (Summer, 1999): 359-398, 364.

b. Advantages and Hazards of Religious Arbitration in the U.S.

While arbitration has provided a useful vehicle for the employment of religious law by portions of the American Jewish community, its utilization is not without some risk. U.S. Courts, in general, were reluctant to enforce arbitration schemes until the latter part of the 20th century. As one commentator has suggested, early courts feared that recognition of the judgments of private systems of dispute resolution served to usurp their own authority, giving citizens license to make and implement their own personal law to the detriment of public law.[383] Since this time, their use has become dramatically more widespread.[384] Arbitration is utilized in the resolution of a variety of types of disputes ranging from commercial to labor-oriented conflicts. Still, the application of arbitration practice to the resolution of disputes under religious law represents a very small part of the larger realm of alternative dispute resolution.

Authorization for the use of arbitration as a vehicle for the resolution of private disputes generally stems from state statutory law. Accordingly, the system of laws governing arbitration may vary from state to state in the United States. While acknowledging these potential jurisdictional variations, there are a common set of pitfalls that may provide obstacles to those seeking to resolve disputes through arbitration panels employing religious law.

First, in order to bring a matter before an arbitrator to be resolved, there must be a valid agreement or contract executed by the involved parties expressing willingness to have the matter resolved through such a process. As may be seen in the case of *Sieger v. Sieger*,[385] any attempt to compel the application of religious law or the submission of matters to the jurisdiction of religious tribunals, in the absence of such a voluntary agreement, will be rejected by the courts generally. For a body to be empowered to compel such action is considered a violation

---

383 Michael Grossman, "Is this Arbitration? Religious Tribunals, Judicial Review and Due Process," *Columbia Law Review* 107 (January, 2007): 169-209, 172.

384 Wolfe, "Faith-based Arbitration," 435.

385 297 A.2d 33; 747 N.Y.S.2d 102 (N.Y. Supreme Court, 2002).

of the First Amendment's protections of religious activity contained in the Free Exercise and Establishment Clauses.[386]

As well, arbitration statutes tend to view agreements by parties to arbitrate as being akin to other contracts and, thus, apply general relevant restrictions. Thus, courts will review contracts requiring parties to submit disputes to arbitration to determine the validity of such agreements. In instances where such agreements are challenged, courts will seek to determine whether the parties have expressed valid assent to the contractual terms that bind them to the use of arbitration.

The New York case of *Meisles v. Uhr* offers an example of an agreement to arbitrate that was voided by a court.[387] In the matter, two individuals formed a partnership that owned and managed parcels of real property and, in forming the relation, the individuals signed an "irrevocable consent to arbitrate" future conflicts before a rabbinic court. Ultimately, the pair decided to terminate the relationship and issues related to the termination were aired before a rabbinic panel. The decision of the rabbinic court was challenged by one of the parties in the Supreme Court of New York for Kings County. The court vacated the decision of the rabbinic court and the agreement to arbitrate on the grounds that the agreement was lacking in sufficient specificity.[388] As well, such agreements may be subject to challenge based upon claims that their enforcement would produce an unconscionable result.[389]

In addition to such challenges aimed at the original agreement to arbitrate, the final award of any arbitration panel is likewise subject to challenge based upon a number of potential grounds. These may include the claim that the award was procured through "corruption,

---

[386] The First Amendment to the U.S. Constitution provides, "Congress shall make no law respecting an establishment of religion, or prohibiting the free exercise thereof." In general, these clauses have been interpreted as prohibiting the establishment of a state religion or interfering with the practice of religion by a group or individual in the absence of a "compelling state interest." These clauses have been interpreted as extending beyond Congressional legislative action to include action of the executive and judiciary branches of the Federal government, and to actions of the states.

[387] 547 N.Y.S.2d 502 (1989).

[388] Ibid., 509.

[389] Wolfe, "Faith-based Arbitration," 443.

fraud, or undue means." As well, such awards may be challenged based upon the claim that the arbitrator was guilty of misconduct or exceeded his or her authority in rendering a decision.[390] At the same time, a court may vacate the decision of an arbitrator based upon its determination that the individual acted in disregard of legal rules or that the award rendered would violate public policy.[391] The potential for the vacation of a rabbinic panel's award may be witnessed in the case of *Stein v. Stein*,[392] where such an award was voided in part, based upon the failure of the arbitrator to adhere to certain procedural safeguards demanded by secular court practice, including the imposition of a waiting period between serving a party and the initiation of dispute resolution proceedings.[393]

Public policy grounds have been asserted in order to limit the scope of arbitration awards employing religious law in certain contexts, due to concerns related to prejudice. Thus, child custody decisions, for example, made by arbitration panels may often be disregarded and in their place secular legal standards would typically be employed. As well, concerns of violation of public policy may be raised in response to the perceived paternalistic emphasis that is said to mark both Jewish and Islamic systems of religious law.

In the case of Beth Din, specific guidelines have been created and are employed in matters of arbitration that are designed to protect the decisions of its panels from such challenges. These procedures are crafted to reflect and ensure compliance with the requirements of New York state law related to binding arbitration. The procedures offer guidance on a range of issues including service of process upon relevant parties, matters of evidence, and the identification of applicable law.[394] In addition to such guidelines, the Beth Din offers various standardized documents, including a form agreement to submit a dispute to a Beth Din arbitration panel, a form prenuptial agreement and guidelines for a *get* proceeding.

---

[390] Ibid.

[391] Ibid ., 444.

[392] 707 N.Y.S.2d 754 (N.Y. Supreme Court, Queens Co., 1999).

[393] Ibid., 759.

[394] "The Beth Din of American Guide to Rules and Procedures 1997," website of Beth Din of America, www.bethdin.org/services.htm (accessed December 14, 2007).

While any attempt to utilize religious arbitration in the U.S. may be beset by pitfalls and challenges, the alternative dispute system may likewise aid in avoiding constitutional concerns. It has been argued that many issues rooted in religious law claims cannot be fully addressed by secular legal courts, without prompting an infringement upon First Amendment protections. Indeed, the resolution of such claims often requires a determination of matters rooted in religious doctrine. Yet, any determination of religious doctrine violates the constitutional requirement of separation of church and state. On the other hand, to fail to offer some vehicle through which such disputes may be resolved may result in a violation of the constitution's Free Exercise clause. Accordingly, at least one commentator has argued that the only viable pathway between these twin constitutional requirements may be to establish arbitration panels capable of resolving disputes rooted in religious doctrine.[395] Indeed, the difficulties associated with resolving issues rooted in Islamic Law may be greater than those stemming from other religious systems.[396]

c. The U.S. Muslim Response to the Arbitration Model

As one commentator has suggested, arbitration has generated "mixed views within the Muslim community."[397] In part, the reluctance of some Muslims to embrace arbitration stems from suspicion of the

---

[395] Charles Trumbull, "Islamic Arbitration: A New Path for Interpreting Islamic Contracts," *Vanderbilt Law Review* 59 (2006): 610-647.

[396] Ibid., 622. As Trumbull argues,

> The interpretation of Islamic legal terms raises unique constitutional concerns. First, …there is no separation between the secular and the religious in Islamic law, making it difficult for a court to only examine the "purely secular terms" of the contract. Second, when interpreting Islamic legal terms, courts must necessarily make determinations of religious doctrine because there is no single authoritative opinion in Islam.

[397] R. Seth Shippee, "Blessed are the Peacemakers: Faith-based Approaches to Dispute Resolution," *ISLA Journal of International and Comparative Law* 9 (Fall 2002): 237-255, 248.

process. That suspicion is based partly upon the wide array of successful challenges that have been brought against decisions of arbitrators in secular courts. Such challenges range from procedural complaints to charges that the individual decisions of arbitrators are incompatible with notions of justice.[398] Further, as has been observed, if decisions from arbitrators lead Muslims back into the secular court system through such a challenge, it may be perceived that no true advantage has been gained through the utilization of the alternative dispute mechanism.

Still, others in the Muslim community point to the apparent success of certain Jewish groups in arguing for greater utilization of arbitration. Among the advantages cited include the ability of arbitration panels to employ Islamic law on a more informed and consistent basis than could be accomplished through the use of other available legal mechanisms in the U.S.[399]

As well, there is some enthusiasm for the prospect that decisions of arbitrators are technically binding, even despite the technical hurdles that often plague attempts to enforce such decisions. For those seeking to encourage the use of arbitration within the Muslim community, the model cited is typically one that is similar to that used by Jewish groups. In particular, some have called for the development of recognizable "Muslim arbitration boards" designed to offer *shari'a*-based dispute resolution that is broadly accessible to adherents of the Islamic faith living in the U.S.[400]

At the same time, it is observed that many Muslims in the U.S. have come to view mediation, rather than arbitration, as offering greater promise in terms of bringing individuals toward a more reliable outcome. Further, mediation is viewed by some as better representing the true spirit of Islam, due to its emphasis upon attaining a mutual agreement among parties to a controversy.[401] Mediation may provide a more comfortable environment for parties. Often, each party to a dispute will offer input on the selection of a mediator. Alternatively,

---

398 "Mediation: Solving Marital Disputes Mutually," from the website of SoundVision.com, http://www.soundvision.com/Info/marriage/conflict/mediation.asp (accessed December 28, 2007).

399 Ibid.

400 Shippee, "Blessed are the Peacemakers," 248.

401 Ibid., 247.

each party may name a mediator that he or she trusts. These multiple mediators would then work together to seek resolution of the conflict. In some instances, mediators will be Imams or family members.[402] By involving members of the parties' community of reference, it is argued that decisions derived from mediation have a greater likelihood of being observed due to social pressure. As well, it is argued that mediation has a greater likelihood of bringing parties to reconciliation. As Shahina Siddiqui, executive director of the Islamic Social Services Association of the United States and Canada (ISSA), has observed:

> The job of the [Muslim] mediator is to listen to both sides, to help [the parties] identify what the problem is, where the conflict is, and then allow each client to listen to each other.[403]

The challenges associated with this dispute resolution system, meanwhile, include the fact that decisions stemming from mediation are not legally binding or enforceable in U.S. courts. The fact that mediation is not technically binding may be countered, according to one Muslim attorney, by the preservation of any ultimate agreement stemming from the process in a formal contract that is accepted and acknowledged by each party. Indeed, such written agreements, he suggests, may offer a greater likelihood of being enforced than arbitration agreements.[404]

From Canada to the U.S.: Assessing the Future of Muslim Arbitration

Arbitration offers some promise to the Muslim community in the U.S. While the availability of religious arbitration may vary from state to state, due to the patchwork of laws that govern the employment of alternative dispute mechanisms, a precedent has been set within certain jurisdictions for the accommodation of tribunals employing religious law. Statutory laws permitting the use of arbitration have been

---

[402] Ibid.

[403] "Mediation: Solving Marital Disputes Mutually," from the website of SoundVision.com.

[404] Ibid.

embraced by certain Jewish and even Christian communities, with often positive result.

Indeed, it has been argued that U.S. courts may have flirted with the very boundaries of their own jurisdiction by undertaking matters that demand the interpretation of religious terms or questions.[405] For courts to make such determinations would violate the First Amendment of the Constitution. Thus, the only appropriate venue for the resolution of such questions may be precisely arbitration panels, it is argued.

Still, as Muslims have acknowledged, the attempt to employ arbitration to resolve religious disputes in binding fashion offers certain difficulties. There are numerous grounds upon which arbitration proceedings and final judgment of arbitrators may be challenged. It is often true, then, that the arbitration designed to keep litigants out of secular courts may propel these same parties into proceedings before a state judge in which the process employed, itself, comes under scrutiny. This practical reality has prompted some within the Muslim community to resist the use of arbitration.

More important than the legal challenges to arbitration may be the more practical questions raised in opposition to the process. The experience associated with the Canadian *Arbitration Act* provides a useful test case. Ultimately, it was public criticism and anxiety that prompted the act to be amended in Canada to exclude religious arbitration. It must be recognized that the public outcry that prompted the emasculation of the *Arbitration Act* came only in response to the proposed formation of Muslim religious tribunals under the law.

At least within Canada, a similar outcry did not apparently beset the arbitration panels earlier established by Jewish or Christian groups. Accordingly, it is important to question the extent to which a similar response may follow any attempt to establish a formal Muslim arbitration system within the U.S.

As has been observed, the support shown to the arbitration process by courts and legislators in the U.S. is a relatively recent phenomenon. Arbitration has come into vogue only since the 1960s or 70s in the U.S. Utilization of arbitration for the purpose of enforcing religious law represents only a small fraction of controversies resolved by this form of dispute resolution. Yet, the extent to which the support of this

---

[405] Charles Trumbull, "Islamic Arbitration: A New Path for Interpreting Legal Contracts," *Vanderbilt Law Review* 59 (2): 609-646.

system would persist among legislators and courts in the face of efforts to establish a broad *shari'a*-based tribunal is unclear. Indeed, based upon the experience of Canadian Muslims in what many would consider to be a much more accommodating political environment, it is unclear how willing members of the Islamic community of the U.S. may be even to risk proposing the creation of such a tribunal.[406]

Issues related to potential gender bias are also relevant to the consideration of any proposal to establish a Muslim arbitration system. As was the case in Canada, it may be expected that any attempt by Muslims in the U.S. to create recognizable panels designed to employ religious law may come under attack based upon perceptions that the system of Islamic law is imbued with a paternalistic bias. Such cries would add to the larger public concern related to the employment of Islamic law. As well, claims of gender bias may lead to efforts to attack such systems on public policy grounds. Indeed, it may be expected that an argument would be made asserting that the employment of any system of laws that treats individuals differently based upon gender is an act that is inconsistent with inherent notions of equality that lie at the heart of U.S. law at every level.

Finally, it may be asked what the result would be of a system that permitted the widespread establishment of arbitration panels employing religious law. If the technical issues could be effectively straddled and the public relations battles won, what precisely would the Muslim community have gained? What would the impact be upon the larger U.S. society of the insertion of such tribunals into the social fabric?

For Muslims, the gain would lie in the establishment of a parallel system of justice over which they would exercise control. Yet, who within the diverse community would provide leadership and direction for this tribunal? What part of the highly diverse American-Muslim community would they represent? Undoubtedly, many would feel disenfranchised. One may question whether a significant portion of the Muslim community would feel sufficiently disenfranchised to prompt them to disregard such religious courts altogether, even while they perceived secular courts to be enforcers of a legal regime that is at times in conflict with their chosen system of faith. As well, it is

---

[406] For a general consideration of the impact of social bias in the West affecting Islam, see Sherene Razack, Casting Out: The Eviction of Muslims from Western Law and Politics (Toronto: Toronto Univ. Press, 2008).

possible that such a system may be plagued by continuing concerns regarding issues of equal treatment of litigants and the extent to which agreements to submit matters to arbitration may have been motivated by duress.

Of course, the issue of whether to allow religious tribunals in the U.S. is not one that affects only those who are adherents of the faiths implicated. The larger society would see many matters being resolved by tribunals that would be far less transparent than secular courts. As well, the social costs associated with problematic decisions issued by such tribunals, especially those that inflict economic harm upon vulnerable individuals, would frequently be borne by the social infrastructure in the form of economic and social support. In an environment where the stakes are high for religious groups and the larger social infrastructure, decisions concerning the utilization of arbitration by Muslims and others are of genuine significance.

What is the solution to these apparent conflicts and challenges? As is considered later in this work, the best solution may lie in the re-thinking of the relationship between the U.S. judiciary and the various religious groups in the country that seek accommodation for their private systems of law and ethics.

CHAPTER 8

Other Paths

Since the death in January [2006] of Dr Zaki Badawi, his colleague at the Muslim College in west London, [Maulana Shahid] Raza has taken on his mantle as a leading representative of mainstream opinion among Britain's 1.6 million Muslims. Born in India, he came to Leicester in 1978 as principal iman at the city's Central Mosque. He is executive secretary of the Muslim Law (Sharia) Council for the UK as well as one of the leaders of the British Muslim Forum, an organisation representing 300 mosques around the country. "I want respectful integration of the Muslim community into the mainstream," he says of the main thrust of his work. "We still have a lot to do to deepen our dialogue. We constantly explain to our community and our youngsters Islam's messages of peace, dialogue and tolerance. However, every night on the TV they watch scenes from Iraq, Palestine and Afghanistan, humiliating Muslims."[407]

---

[407] Peter Stanford, "The Chosen Ones," *The Independent* (Dec. 17, 2006), http://findarticles.com/p/articles/mi_qn4159/is_20061217/ai_n16898513 (accessed December 1, 2007).

What are the options available for Western governments as they consider the relationship between their own legal systems and the set of ethical norms bound up in the *shari'a*? On a foundational level, it may be argued that there are available three dominant approaches that have been employed in certain Western states to date, which offer some reasonable accommodation of Islamic legal norms.

One approach implicated by the analysis of the previous chapter involves the legal sanction of the use of arbitration or another alternative dispute resolution process to establish alternate forums through which religious legal norms may be applied. This may be accomplished through the utilization of existing laws regulating and authorizing the use of alternate dispute resolution systems within a specific jurisdiction, where such laws exist. Alternatively, legislative action of the type undertaken in Canada may be required to provide a foundation for such accommodation. The alternate dispute resolution process that is most likely to be employed in this regard is binding arbitration, due to the enforceable nature of rulings procured through such a process. In the case of the Ontario *Arbitration Act*, bodies were authorized to utilize binding arbitration for the purpose of enforcing religious norms. It is binding arbitration that has been called upon by the Jewish community in the United States, as well, to establish a forum capable of administering religious law. In general, such a system makes use of a voluntary commitment by religious adherents to submit to the authority of private tribunals in order to establish alternative tribunals. Such forums, however, are not without their detractors, nor are they without significant risks.

In this chapter, other potential approaches to the accommodation of systems of religious law are considered. The first approach is one in which religious law receives formal sanction to be implemented and interpreted by secular courts, under specified conditions. In practice, such accommodations have tended to be restricted to issues of personal status, including such matters as divorce and marriage. As well, under certain circumstances, issues of a transactional nature have been brought under the scope of such systems.

Such processes, however, can be complicated. As secular courts seek to grapple with systems of religious law, they are often beset by challenging potential conflicts among competing interest groups. On the one hand, there is the interest of the individual in retaining a connection with foreign legal norms that are familiar and which, in the case of religious law, may be understood to be of keen spiritual importance. On the other hand, in Western democracies, there are significant state interests in transparency and in the consistency of decision-making within the jurisdiction. Such goals may be compromised through the introduction of competing systems of law. In general, then, the introduction of foreign systems of law into the judicial system of specific jurisdictions is an effort that is complex and often controversial. For the purposes of this analysis, Germany will serve as the representative example of a Western state providing an environment within which such accommodation is being made in limited instances.

An additional approach that may be followed is one that may be termed *collaborative engagement*. In such an approach, the minority community seeks some compromise that affords them some limited opportunity to impose and enforce religious norms. In part, this may stem from an effort designed to bring the spirit of the foreign law into some conformity with key social and legal norms embraced by the majority state. As well, the religious minority community may seek to prompt policy and legal system reforms within the relevant state through activism, designed to generate greater openness to its religious priorities. Through the establishment of formal or informal groups, the minority community gains a voice of significance within the spheres of judicial leadership and public policy formation, through which accommodations may be pursued. Such collaborative engagement may originate through focus upon common concerns and goals shared by the minority community and the dominant social institutions. As an example of such social engagement, this analysis will examine the experience of specific organized Muslim groups in England and their interactions with institutions of the British government.

In the end, the central question posed here is the extent to which any of these approaches may serve to inform, in a useful manner, ongoing relations between Muslims and the U.S. judiciary and policy-makers.

Germany: Limited Enforcement of Muslim Legal Norms

Issues and concerns regarding the relationship between Germany's Muslim populace and the judicial apparatus of the state have assumed greater prominence in recent years, as the size of the minority community in this European territory has grown. With approximately three million Muslims, Germany hosts the largest Islamic community in Europe, outside of France.[408] The growth of this community from relative obscurity has occurred over a remarkably short time frame, with the first significant migration of Muslims into Germany coming only during the decade of the 1960s.[409] Islam is now thought to be the fastest growing religious community in Germany. Serving this expanding population of Muslims is a series of more than 2,000 mosques scattered throughout the country.[410]

Broadly, the right of religious adherents to practice their chosen faith is enshrined in the German Constitution. According to Article 4, Section 1 of the Constitution, "Freedom of faith and conscience, and freedom to profess a religious or philosophical creed, shall be inviolable." As Article 4, Section 2 adds further, "The undisturbed practice of religion shall be guaranteed." Yet, even such broad ranging guarantees of religious freedom are not absolute. Accordingly, the manner in which German courts have defined religious practice and categorized particular religious activities is key to understanding the broader legal experience of the Muslim minority community.

a. *Shari'a* in German Courts

The relationship between the courts of Germany and the *shari'a* system is complex and rooted in issues related to citizenship. As has been observed, the ideal of "German nationhood" colors laws affecting the rights and status of citizens and minorities. The ideal was born out of historical conflict between the Germanic region and Napoleonic forces and identifies the historical societal desire to preserve an ethnically and philosophically homogeneous community, even in the face of outside

---

[408] Central Intelligence Agency, *The World Fact Book*, https://www.cia.gov/library/publications/the-world-factbook/geos/gm.html (accessed December 2, 2007); and U.S. Department of State, "Background Notes: Germany," http://www.state.gov/r/pa/ei/bgn/3997.htm (accessed December 2, 2007).

[409] Mathias Rohe, "The Legal Treatment of Muslims in Germany," Speech before the International and European Forum on Migration Research, Turin, Italy (June 19-21, 2003), http://www.zr2. jura.uni-erlangen.de/Islamedia/ Puplikationen/The%20Formation%20of%20a%20European%20Sharia% 2001-08-2003.pdf (accessed November 27, 2007).

[410] Ibid.

threat.[411] Accordingly, German law has traditionally made it difficult for immigrants of non-Germanic heritage to claim citizenship. Indeed, until 1999, one had to provide evidence of at least a single German ancestor to stake a valid claim for citizenship.

Issues of citizenship are important within the German legal structure, for it is the law of the region in which one's citizenship resides, rather than where one is domiciled, that is applied in resolving conflicts rooted in matters related to private law, including family law. In other words, even though an immigrant may establish a new home in Germany, issues related to his or her personal status will typically be determined through the application of the law of the individual's state of origin. Thus, German private law seeks to sustain the connection between individuals and the laws of their native lands. As noted German legal scholar Mathias Rohe has observed regarding the treatment under German law of foreign legal systems:

> In the area of civil law, which essentially regulates legal relations between private persons, the welfare of those persons is of prime importance. If someone has organized his/her life in accordance with a certain legal system, this should be protected even when the person in question changes his/her place of abode. Accordingly the law of the state of origin which is familiar to the person in question should continue to be applied when the person crosses the borders.[412]

Among other legal systems, Rohe pays particular attention to the application of Islamic law in Germany. The phrase used by Rohe and others to underscore German openness to the application of Islamic law in its courts is "*Shari'a* in Germany." This phrase is a subtle but important reminder of the deference afforded to this system of religious law in Germany, but even such deference may not be extended to the

---

411 Pascale Fournier, "The Reception of Muslim Family Law in Western Liberal States," website of the Canadian Council of Muslim Women (September 30, 2004), http://nji.ca/nji/CCIAWJ/papers/new/56_Pascale%20paper.pdf (accessed November 12, 2007), 15.

412 Mathias Rohe, "Islamic Law in German Courts," *Hawwa: The Journal of Women in the Middle East and the Islamic World* 1, no. 1 (March, 2003): 46-59, 47.

point that national interests are negatively impacted. Thus, when the German courts apply religious law for the purpose of resolving private concerns, such ethical systems are interpreted to ensure that specific requirements or demands do not conflict with designated social standards or individual rights.

In particular, the result derived from the imposition of *shari'a*, or any other foreign system of law, must not conflict with basic "rules of German public order."[413] Accordingly, while a preference is given to the enforcement of foreign laws in private conflicts in which the parties are citizens of another state, the resolution must not contradict basic German civil rights. Still, the German courts will be reluctant to strike down such efforts to enforce the foreign system of law, unless the conflict with basic German rights is clear. As Rohe observes further:

> First we have to keep in mind that the public order within the framework of Private International Law does *not* have the function of controlling foreign legal provisions on the basis of their compatibility with corresponding domestic provisions. As mentioned above, the public order prevents the application of foreign rules only if this application would lead to a *result* which is *obviously incompatible* with the main principles of German law including the constitutional civil rights. To give a practical example of the divergence between the two positions: The husband's unilateral right to divorce *(talak)* obviously contradicts the constitutional equality of the sexes (Art. 3, German *Grundgesetz* or Constitution) as well as the special protection of marriage and family (Art. 6 German *Grundgesetz* or Constitution). Nevertheless, German courts have accepted this kind of *talak* in cases where the prerequisites for a judicial divorce according to German family law were equally fulfilled. Furthermore, the German public order is only concerned if the case in question has a sufficient connection to the German legal order, which usually would be so if one of the parties is a German citizen or has a German domicile.[414]

---

[413] Ibid., 48-49.

[414] Ibid., 50-51.

Thus, the application of a religious law system, such as the shari'a, in Germany depends not precisely upon the compatibility of its requirements with those imposed at the federal level, but upon its avoidance of "obvious incompatibility." Even when such obvious incompatibility exists, this may provide grounds for the rejection of the foreign law system only if one or more of the litigants possess sufficiently strong ties to Germany such that the imposition of the result would create an apparent injustice. Again, the strong preference under German law, then, in matters of dispute involving immigrant and ethnic minority parties, is to recognize and honor outcomes that would be rendered pursuant to systems of foreign or religious law.

The employment of *shari'a* law in Germany by German courts has produced some curious results. Thus, if a couple marries in a state implementing some form of *shari'a* law and, subsequently migrates to Germany without obtaining German citizenship, a future divorce application and claims for spousal support would be determined pursuant to the *shari'a* system employed in the pair's native land. The interpretation of the *shari'a* system requirements, meanwhile, would be undertaken by the German courts.[415]

At times, the results stemming from the employment of a *shari'a*-based legal regime may appear to be at odds with German social priorities. For example, polygamous marriages are expressly forbidden in Germany. Indeed, it is impossible for a valid polygamous marriage to be effectuated in Germany. However, for Muslims, polygamous marriages have been treated as legally valid and binding so long as the marriage is concluded in a country permitting such arrangements.[416] Importantly, then, women living within such a marital arrangement while residing in Germany will have access to the panoply of rights available to other spouses, including social security benefits and inheritance. At the same time, wives within such a marital union have not routinely been granted the specific right to join husbands already in Germany. As well, German courts have generally enforced Muslim dower arrangements, though they have refused to classify such

[415] Fournier, "The Reception of Muslim Family Law in Western Liberal States," 20.
[416] Ibid.

arrangements as either part of a marriage contract or as spousal maintenance.[417]

As concerns marriage termination, German courts have generally refused to recognize the *talaq* divorce, opining that the process is contrary to constitutional guarantees of gender equality. Yet, in one case, where both the husband and the wife were present in the courtroom and the husband sought to dissolve the marriage by pronouncing the *talaq* as a part of the proceeding, the judge recognized the attempt and gave it judicial weight.[418]

b. The Effect of Legal Recognition

One may question the impact of the recognition of foreign *shari'a*-based systems by German courts. What is the result of the meshing together of *shari'a*-based legal precepts with German constitutional demands and state social policies? Is the resulting curious hybrid system truly in keeping with the spirit of Islamic law? In great measure, the response to this question may be in the eye of the Muslim beholder.

Indeed, as German scholar Rohe has observed, Muslims living in Europe are not of a single mind in terms of how they, themselves, should interpret and respond to obligations imposed pursuant to Islamic law. Muslims, living as members of minority communities in Europe, North America, and other areas of the globe, are faced with a choice regarding the manner in which they respond to their environment. They can seek to maintain an affiliation with a traditional form of religious and ethical practice, resisting any broad embrace of the surrounding culture. Those embracing such a position would likely resist any "Western" influence upon the *shari'a*, and argue for the imposition of a pristine traditional form of Islamic law. They, in turn, may voice concern regarding the mingling of Islamic ethical standards and German law.

Alternatively, some Muslims have adopted a broader interpretation of Islamic law, seeking to widen the scope of the system to allow for independent reasoning, especially with reference to minority and immigrant members of the Islamic community living in the West. Individual Muslims adopting such a stance may be more willing to

---

417 Ibid., 22.

418 Ibid., 23.

embrace certain modifications of Islamic law, but may, still, point to unassailable core ethical principles.

At the same time, other Muslims have sought new ways of interpreting the essential sources of Islamic law, leading to the production of a reformed *shari'a*.[419] Those embracing the latter path may well find the production of a *shari'a* that leans upon both Islamic sources and Western European social norms to be an acceptable vehicle. While such a stance may not be one that is likely to be embraced by all Muslims living in the West or Europe, specifically, it does appear to be seen as a viable position for some. As has been observed with regard to one specific community of Muslims living in Germany:

> To avoid possible conflicts and to refute fears of legal and cultural upheavals, the Central Council of Muslims in Germany, one of the leading Muslim organizations in Germany on a federal level, promulgated a charter on Muslim life in German society. It stressed that Muslims are content with the harmonic system of secularity and religious freedom provided by the Constitution and that they don't intend to create a "state of God" there.... [I]t is pointed out that Muslims willingly accept the German legal order including the rights of women to take part in elections actively and passively, the right to change the religion and the provisions of German Family Law, the Law of Inheritance and Procedural Law.
>
> It is equally stressed that the Qur'an forbids all kinds of compulsion and force in matters of faith. Obviously these Muslims have gained the impression that they are able to manage their life within the wide scope of religious freedom granted by German law itself.[420]

---

419 Mathias Rohe, "The Formation of a European Shari'a," in *Muslims in Europe: From the Margins to the Centre*, Jamal Malik, ed. (Munster: Lit Verlag, 2004): 161-184.

420 Rohe, "The Legal Treatment of Muslims in Germany," 19.

Thus, for some Muslims living in Germany, Europe and North America, the marriage of Western social priorities and traditional Islamic law may lead to the production of a practical and useful ethical system, understood to adhere to essential religious demands, even while other members of the faith community would see such intermingling of social systems as being directly contradictory to core expectations of Islam, expressed in traditional religious law and its sources.

Yet, for many in the Muslim leadership in Germany and other Western states, what is at stake is not merely a set of technical rules imbedded in a system of religious law. Instead, it may be feared that the infringement upon the system of law represents the first step in a broader assault upon Muslim religious ideals and sensibilities. As one scholar has suggested, in states like Germany, and in others throughout Europe and North America, "there is strong pressure to conform to the West's prevailing cultural norms."[421] And since the individual's identity as a Muslim may not be embraced by those within the larger cultural system in which she resides, she may feel compelled to distinguish between her inner religious commitment and her outward social practice. This process of segregating religious and social practice is termed, by some, the "Protestantization" of Muslim experience in the West.[422] Such Western social pressures may serve to draw an individual toward the support of more liberal interpretations of the nature and applicability of Islamic law.

Conversely, the Muslim leadership in the West may serve as a countervailing influence, often promoting a more conservative or strict interpretation of the requirements associated with the Islamic faith. It is argued by some that this tendency toward conservatism stems from the nature of preparatory training received by Muslim religious leaders. Most Muslim community leaders in the West hail from and have been trained in other regions of the world, from the Middle East to North Africa. Accordingly, they may often possess only a limited

---

[421] Hans-Christian Jasch, "Dialogue with Islam and Integration of Muslims in Italy and Germany: A Comparison of the Political Conditions and Legal Frameworks for Mechanisms of Dialogue with Islamic Faith Communities in Both Countries," *German Law Journal* 8, no. 4 (April 2007) http://www.germanlawjournal.com/ article.php?id=811 (accessed November 10, 2007).

[422] Ibid.

understanding of Western culture and social norms. As has been observed:

> These Imams have frequently been educated and trained abroad and are sometimes also paid by foreign institutions like the *Diyanet*, the Turkish religious authority. They are often unfamiliar with the morals and customs of their European host countries and only stay for a limited time before going back to their countries of origin. In many cases these *imams* remain "outsiders" with little interest to integrate into and understand the societies of their host-countries. Some are even beholden to foreign interests since the sending authorities and states consider these *imams* as a means of maintaining influence over Muslim immigrant communities in the West thus guaranteeing the flow of remittances that are still an important contribution to the economies of many countries of origin. Efforts at integration by European states are therefore also sometimes regarded in a critical manner.[423]

Thus, instead of embracing processes aimed at "integrating" Muslim culture and practice into the Western social environment, many Islamic religious leaders may favor efforts designed to further segregate the minority communities they represent from the broader social culture. In this way, a sense of "cultural autonomy" may be maintained even in the face of social pressures to conform.

c. The Future for Muslims in Germany

While German courts have undertaken the task of applying Islamic law in accord with constitutional requirements, the application of this religious system of law is undertaken only in the presence of specific circumstances. For Muslims, then, there may be a desire for greater judicial recognition of principles of Islamic law. At the same time, certain German groups have voiced concern about the recognition and enforcement of Islamic law by institutions of the European state. With this struggle in the foreground, it is worthwhile to consider events that

---

[423] Ibid.

may shape the future of the relationship between Germany and its Muslim minority community.

Since the terrorist attacks in New York on September 11, 2001, Germany has sought to nullify any attempts by individuals or groups to radicalize Muslim communities in the nation. Through this effort significant attention has been placed upon the "integration and participation" of Muslims groups in the larger German society.[424] As a part of this effort, in September 2006, German Minister of the Interior, Dr. Wolfgang Schauble, initiated the *Deutsche Islam Konferenz* ("DIK"), a program designed to establish a continuing dialogue between officials of the German government and appointed representatives of the Muslim community. The stated purpose of the DIK is to expand the integration of the Muslim community into German society and to offer specific recommendations for improving the experience of Muslims on a range of specific priorities, including Islamic education, the training of Imams and the adherence of Muslims to cultural and religious activities.[425]

---

[424] Ibid., 23.

[425] See "The German Conference on Islam (DIK)," website of the German Federal Ministry of the Interior, http://www.bmi.bund.de/cln_028/nn_1026710/Internet/Content/Themen/Deutsche__Islam__Konferenz/DatenUndFakten/Islamkonferenz__Kurzinfo__en.html (accessed December 12, 2007). As the Ministry states regarding the purpose of the DIK:

> The Conference is intended to be a long-term process of negotiation and communication between the German state and representatives of Muslims living in Germany, to continue for two to three years. Through the discussion process, the conference strives to achieve a broad consensus on respecting the same principles of social and religious policy, with a special emphasis on absolutely upholding and respecting the principles of liberal democracy as enshrined in the Constitution. The Conference is intended to address the question of how to reconcile religiously based Muslim behaviour and practices with the German constitutional order, whether and how Islam can comply with the requirements of German state law on religion, and how modern Islam can grow and develop in Germany.

Ibid.

The motto for the DIK is "Muslims in Germany – German Muslims." This motto seems intended to reflect the desire of organizers that Muslim groups in the European state be fully integrated into German society. Organizationally, the DIK is composed of 15 representatives of the German government and 15 representatives of the greater German Muslim community. All members have been appointed to the committee by Minister Schauble and the representatives of the Muslim community were chosen from a broad cross-section of Muslims groups, an act designed to engage the largest possible segment of Islamic practitioners.[426] Among the groups represented on the DIK are the Turkish-Islamic Union ("DITIB"), the Central Council of Muslims in Germany ("ZMD"), the Islamic Council, the Association of Islamic Cultural Centres ("VIKZ") and the Alevite Community in Germany.[427]

The DIK does not have decision-making authority. Instead, it is organized to make recommendations to the government, which should be acted upon within a defined period of two-to-three years. The DIK, then, is organized in a manner similar to that of advisory panels established by other European governments, including Italy. The aim of such committees has been to ensure the greatest possible access by Muslims to traditional religious practice, while avoiding infringement upon the personal rights of members of the broader public and social priorities of the community. Included among the goals of such advisory groups have been efforts to expand the access of Muslims living in Europe to Islamic law systems for the purposes of resolving matters of personal status, finance and contract administration.

While the process of dialogue has essentially only just begun in Germany, the effort raises questions related to the future of Islamic law

---

[426] "Federal Minister of the Interior Dr. Wolfgang Schauble Opens the First German Conference on Islam in Berlin "Muslims in Germany – German Muslims," website of the German Federal Ministry of the Interior (May 20, 2008), http://www.bmi.bund.de/cln_028/nn_1026710/Internet/Content/Themen/Deutsche__Islam__Konferenz/DatenUndFakten/Islamkonferenz__Kurzinfo__en.html (accessed December 12, 2007).

[427] For a useful discussion of the relationship between these groups, see Wolf Aires, "Germany's Islamic Minority," in *Regulating Religion: Case Studies from around the Globe*, James T. Richardson, ed. (New York: Kluwer Academic Pub., 2004): 103-112.

within the European state. In particular, the dialogue process may serve as a foundation for the German Muslim community to seek broader implementation of *shari'a*. In light of the work of the DIK and growing political prominence of the Muslim community in Germany, the German government will be pressed to consider additional accommodations for the Muslim community. At the same time, the dialogue process may lead to the articulation by the Islamic community of specific political goals. And it is clear, based upon remarks by German minister Schauble, that the outcome of the process of dialogue between Muslims and the national government of this European state is far from resolved. As he observed:

> We have to give the Muslims time. What is not negotiable and cannot be postponed, however, is the legal system and values anchored in our Basic Law. The Islam Conference has argued over the question whether there is a system of values extending beyond the Basic Law. This system encompasses more than the articles of the Basic Law but can also be shaped by the religions and the people. If Muslims accept the fundamental parameters of the Basic Law, then they can take part in shaping this system. And to do so, they need time. The state monopoly on the use of force, which seems to be dissolving in today's globalized world, was the answer when Christians of different confessions were unable to live in peace. Religious freedom doesn't release anyone from the obligation to respect the universality of human rights.[428]

For the American judiciary, meanwhile, the German experience provides an example of an apparently successful limited introduction of *shari'a* into the court system. While the constitutional and legal underpinnings that undegird questions related to choice of law decisions may not be identical in the U.S., the German example offers evidence, perhaps, that a limited recognition of Islamic law can be undertaken by Western courts without a serious infringement upon

---

428 "We Must Give the Muslims Time," From the Website of the German Federal Ministry of the Interior, http://www.en.bmi.bund.de/cln_028/nn_148130/Internet/Content/Nachrichten/Medienspiegel/2008/05/Minister__FAZ__Feuilleton__engl.html (accessed September 23, 2009).

cultural and social priorities. As well, through the introduction of the DIK, the German experience may provide further guidance to U.S. courts and legislators in the future regarding the potential for social dialogue and collaboration between Muslim groups and Western governments.

England: Seeking Influence

Perhaps, the 2007 commentary in the London *Daily Express* is sufficient, alone, to underscore the sensitivities that accompany questions regarding the status of Muslims in the West. From the screaming headline, "Now Muslims Get their Own Laws in Britain,"[429] to the text of the commentary itself, the anxieties of some in England regarding the presence and activities of Muslims within the European state are made starkly clear. As the commentary warns its readers:

> Muslim radicals have established their own draconian court systems in Britain.
>
> Controversial Sharia courts have been set up in major towns and cities to impose Islamic law and enable Muslims to shun the legitimate British legal system.
>
> Last night religious leaders and politicians expressed outrage that Sharia law is gaining an increasing foothold in our society.
>
> Critics insisted that the Government is allowing a two-tier legal system to flourish in the name of political correctness and that the authority of UK justice is being undermined.
>
> The *Daily Express* can reveal that one of the controversial

---

[429] Paul Jeeves, "Now Muslims Get their Own Laws in Britain," *Daily Express* (May 1, 2007), http://www.express.co.uk:80/posts/view/5795 (accessed June 17, 2007), see also Martyn Brown, "Now Muslims Demand Full Sharia Law," The Daily Express (October 15, 2009), http://www.express.co.uk/ posts/ view/134080/Now-Muslims-demand-full Sharia-law (accessed October 15, 2009).

courts has been set up in the home town of the 7/7 London bombings ringleader.

The concern voiced by the *Daily Express*, and echoed by others in England, relates to the emergence of a Muslim community group known as the Islamic Shari'a Council. Though its work is not technically sanctioned by the British government, nor are its decisions enforceable by the secular courts, the Islamic Shari'a Council ("the Council") was created for the purpose of bringing together representatives from a cross-section of individual Muslim groups from throughout England, including the Central Mosque of London and the Islamic Cultural Centre of London, to provide guidance to adherents of the faith on issues related to Islamic law and relations with British governmental institutions.

In particular, the Council, which traces its origins to meetings of Muslim community leaders beginning in 1982, is working to assemble a diverse collection of Islamic scholars from across Britain to entertain and advise both Muslim adherents and the larger social community regarding issues that affect the Islamic faith and its followers residing in Europe. On the group's website, the Council is described as functioning as a "quasi-Islamic Court."[430] The Council declares itself to be "widely accepted among Muslims in the U.K." and to represent all the "major schools of thought" of Sunni perspective.

The Council is described as having been fashioned in response to "an acute sense of alienation" felt by Muslims in England as they sought to resolve matters particularly of personal status. One of the specific concerns affecting Muslims living in England that motivated religious leaders to establish the Council was the recognition that resolutions of personal matters issued by English courts, applying regimes of secular law, would not be recognized by foreign *shari'a* courts. This fact, it is feared, could create particular legal hazards and hardships for immigrant Muslims as they return to their home countries. Thus, in many instances, the Council serves the function of seeking to inform the deliberations of English courts and sanctioning

---

430 "Feelings of Alienation are felt by Many Muslims, Male and Female," website of the Islamic Shari'a Council, http://www.islamic-sharia.org/about-us/about-us-6.html (accessed September 10, 2009).

the decisions of such bodies so that the court orders may receive recognition well beyond the shores of the U.K.

As well, the Council responds to the unfortunate reality that the very use of secular courts by members of the Muslim community may lead them to experience alienation and ostracism. For example, if one is not divorced pursuant to Islamic law, even though she may have received a secular divorce, any latter re-marriage will often be viewed as an adulterous act and children produced form that latter union may be deemed illegitimate. The Council, then, seeks to provide a venue within which Muslims may have matters resolved pursuant to principles of Islamic law even within the confines of a secular environment.

In many ways, the tribunals organized by the Council resist popular negative stereotype by embracing social norms of the surrounding secular environment. Often in the West, Islamic law has been linked through the popular media to images of seemingly harsh punishments ranging from stonings to the severing of body parts as recompense for crimes. However, the images painted of the work of the Council in England are far more sedate and familiar, both in terms of process and decision. A reporter from London's *The Guardian* described what he termed a "typical" Council experience:

> In the back room of a converted corner shop in east London, Sheikh Maulana Abu Sayeed is trying to save another marriage. He stretches across his desk and gently holds the hand of a young man with five o'clock shadow, whose eyes are red and swollen from crying. For more than an hour the man has been pleading with Sayeed to ask his ex-wife to give him a second chance. And for more than an hour, Sayeed has been quietly telling him that if his ex-wife does not want him back, there is nothing he can do. As the fraught meeting continues next door, one of Sayeed's colleagues at the Islamic Sharia Council in Leyton explains with a shrug, "He has come to us to ask for help, but if the woman is adamant and she doesn't want to reunite, what can we do?"[431]

---

[431] Dan Bell, "In the Name of the Law," *The Guardian* (June 14, 2007), available at http://www.guardian.co.uk/g2/story/0,,2102434,00.html (visited January 18, 2008).

The caricature of Islamic law that prevails among portions of the larger population of the West seems to bear little resemblance to the image painted here. Yet, according to the article, such a scene is common among tribunals organized by the Council across England. Absent are the brutal punishments and the oppressive interpretations of the Qur'an that some might expect. Instead, the Council is described as providing a significant and vital community service that benefits not merely Muslims, but the larger social sphere. In particular, the Council is described as providing to British Muslims "guidance" on how to live within a secular environment in a manner that is consistent with the religious ideals that lie at the foundation of the Islamic faith and does not infringe negatively upon the lives of others.

Though it is not universally true, the matters that the Council typically entertains tend to fall into the broad categories of personal and family relations. The Council reports that it had rendered decisions in more than 7,000 cases by 2007. Of those cases, more than 90 percent are said to relate to issues concerning the award and validity of marriages and divorces. The Council also issues *fatwas* on matters relating to Muslim practice and conduct, and hears individual disputes stemming from a range of potential controversies.[432]

Through its work, the Council often plays the role of providing significant support to the English judicial system. For example, by issuing parallel decisions, the Council may prompt individuals, who would likely ignore secular court orders regarding such matters as the payment of spousal or child support, to adhere to mandated requirements. As well, the Council may provide a more comfortable setting for the initiation of a divorce, where one of the parties is reluctant to undertake action within the English courts. Likewise, the Council employs more than 25 attorneys and, through its operation, provides guidance on matters of Islamic law to various individual attorneys, law firms and English courts.[433]

Even though the Council has not generally been recognized as having the authority to issue binding judgments in England, its decisions have become a part of the legal landscape of the country.

---

[432] "Feelings of Alienation are felt by Many Muslims, Male and Female," website of the Islamic Shari'a Council.

[433] Rohe, "The Formation of a European Shari'a," 12.

Indeed, the "mediation" processes orchestrated by the Council, while not enforceable in secular courts, have been sanctioned by judicial and governmental bodies in England, a fact that seems to dismay some. Thus, as has been suggested by at least one scholar, the Council has served to establish the foundations of an "Angrezi Shariat."[434] In other words, it may be argued that, in England, the secular system of justice is being shaped, to some degree, by the work of Muslim communities, even while the *shari'a* being employed by organizations like the Council is responding to its Western environment, as well.

The suggestion that such extra-judicial Muslim tribunals have laid the foundation for an Angrezi Shariat, or an indigenous *shari'a*, stems from the practical observation that the law being applied by such bodies is neither Islamic law nor British common law entirely, but a mixture of both. This hybrid law is one that seeks the preservation of core ideals lying at the heart of the Islamic ethical system. Yet, in practical terms, it also seeks to avoid direct conflict with or challenge of English law. The resulting system often produces certain curious results, such as the need for marriages and divorces to be solemnized twice, once by a secular court and a second time by a religious tribunal. Still, the process results in decision-making that appears to respond to the practical needs of Muslims living in Britain.

Meanwhile, the system may be subject to criticism on varying grounds. Among the concerns directed toward this emerging indigenous *shari'a* system is the fear that Muslims are being forced into "underground courts," that are not transparent, may not be responsive to the fundamental individual rights guaranteed by English law, and may be ill-equipped to deal adequately with matters of complexity. As well, there are concerns regarding the equality of treatment of litigants, especially women, within the system. Additionally, there are concerns related to the lack of a venue for reconsideration or appeal of decisions by bodies such as those organized by the Council.

It is such concerns that may prompt some calls for greater recognition of principles of Islamic law through some sanctioned legal process within Britain. Acknowledging growing pressures in this regard, the leader of the Church of England suggested publicly, in a highly controversial statement, that Islamic law must be recognized at

---

[434] Ibid.

some level by the British government. As he observed during a 2008 interview in response to the question of whether some form of Islamic law can and should be recognized by the British government and the state judiciary:

> It seems unavoidable and indeed as a matter of fact certain provision of Sharia are already recognised in our society and under our law; so it's not as if we're bringing in an alien and rival system; we already have in this country a number of situations in which the law the internal law of religious communities is recognised by the law of the land as justified conscientious objections in certain circumstances in providing certain kinds of social relations, so I think we need to look at this with a clearer eye and not imagine either we know exactly what we mean by Sharia and not just associate it with what we read about Saudi Arabia or wherever.[435]

If Islamic law can be formulated to accommodate certain key demands of a secular legal system, then perhaps the secular system may evolve to accommodate Muslim religious priorities, as well. It is this assumption that appears to motivate the work of certain groups within England seeking to provide Muslims with a voice on issues of public policy. One such organization is the Muslim Council of Britain ("MCB"). Founded in 1997, the group has worked to provide the larger community of Muslims living in England a collective voice and representation on issues of public policy. The stated aims and objectives of the organization offer a succinct summary of the issues of concern pursued by organizational leadership. These aims and objectives are:

- **i** To promote cooperation, consensus and unity on Muslim affairs in the UK.
- **ii** To encourage and strengthen all existing efforts being made for the benefit of the Muslim community.

---

[435] Interview of Rowan Williams, Archbishop of Canterbury by BBC Radio 4 (February 7, 2008), http://www.archbishopofcanterbury.org/1573 (accessed February 9, 2008).

iii To work for a more enlightened appreciation of Islam and Muslims in the wider society.
iv To establish a position for the Muslim community within British society that is fair and based on due rights.
v To work for the eradication of disadvantages and forms of discrimination faced by Muslims.
vi To foster better community relations and work for the good of society as a whole.[436]

At least to a limited extent, this effort to build "cooperation" within the Muslim community of Britain and between representatives of Islam and the larger social system of the United Kingdom, has been embraced by some, including certain figures within the English government. An example of such positive interaction between Muslim groups and the English government may be witnessed in the efforts of the MCB to play a leadership role in the formation of a panel designed to oversee British mosques and to set training standards for imams serving in the country. The proposal to create a government sponsored "Mosques and Imams National Advisory Body" ("MINAB") came as a recommendation from a terrorism task force established following the 2005 London train bombings. The MCB was one of four Muslim groups to be publicly identified with the formation of the advisory body.[437] In addition, groups sponsoring the MINAB include the British Muslim Forum, a group founded in 2006 and which claims to represent some 300 U.K. mosque communities, and the Muslim Association of Britain. To date, those involved in MINAB have done little more than undertake organizational activities, including the drafting of a constitution for the body.[438] Thus, it is not clear how the MINAB will function in practice.

Yet, even at this preliminary stage, not all have voiced confidence regarding the MINAB or its proponent MCB. In debate before the

---

436 "The Aims and Objectives of the Muslim Council of Britain," website of the Muslim Council of Britain, http://www.mcb.org.uk/aim.php (accessed February 18, 2008).

437 Dominic Casciani, "Watchdog for UK Mosques Launched," BBC News (July 27, 2006), http://news.bbc.co.uk/1/hi/uk/5120338.stm (accessed December 30, 2007).

438 Ibid.

British House of Commons, Michael Gove, a member of parliament, voiced strong reservations about the Muslim leadership appointed to this fledgling mosque oversight body, arguing that "foxes" had been placed in charge of the proverbial "chicken coop."[439] MCB and the organizational structure of the MINAB have both, likewise, been criticized as yielding to extremist elements. The draft constitution of the MINAB has come under specific scrutiny for its plan to include one representative from "every mosque or Islamic centre that provides basic service"[440] on its governing General Council.[441] This plan is seen as problematic due to the claim that as many as half or more of such mosques in Britain are believed to have ties to extremist organizations.[442]

At the same time, in what may be described as a pragmatic effort by the government of England to lend support to aspects of the Muslim community that it deem to be most compatible with the secular landscape of the United Kingdom, it is argued that certain groups have been given preferential treatment, leading to diminished influence for groups like the MCB. In an October, 2006, speech, Ruth Kelly, the British Secretary of State for Communities and Local Government and Minister for Women, voiced criticism of unnamed Muslim groups that

---

[439] The House of Commons, Debate concerning Treasury and Work and Pensions, Testimony of Michael Gove, Column 873 (November 27, 2006), http://www.publications.parliament.uk/pa/cm200607/cmhansrd/ cm061127/ debtext/61127-0012.htm, (accessed January 5, 2008).

[440] See Constitution of Mosques and Imams National Advisory Board (MINAB), Article 5(b), http://www.bmf.eu.com/english/news/ news19%20MINAB%20Constitution.html (accessed December 30, 2007).

[441] "Campaign to Reform Mosques Hijacked by Extremists," The website of The Centre for Social Cohesion, http://www.socialcohesion.co.uk/ blog/2007/10/campaign_to_reform_mosques_hij.html (accessed December 30, 2007).

[442] Andrew Norfolk, "Hardline Takeover of British Mosques," The Times of London (September 7, 2007), http://www.timesonline.co.uk/tol/comment/faith/ article2402973.ece (accessed December 27, 2007). According to the article "almost half" of the approximately 1,350 mosques scattered across England are "controlled" by the Deobandi Muslim sect, described as "a hardline Islamic sect whose leading preacher loathes Western values and has called on Muslims to shed blood for Allah." Ibid.

were failing to tackle the issue of terrorism in a satisfactory manner. The speech served as a call for Muslim organizations to do more and, according to some, represented a significant shift in government policy. As Kelly stated in her speech:

> So I promise we will increase our commitment to work in partnership with you and communities throughout Britain who show through their words and actions that are determined to take on the extremists and defend values that the vast majority of us share.
>
> It is not good enough to merely sit on the sidelines or pay lip service to fighting extremism. That is why I want a fundamental rebalancing of our relationship with Muslim organisations from now on. Since taking up my post, I have actively sought to develop relationships with a wider network of Muslim organisations, including those representing young people and women.
>
> In future, I am clear that our strategy of funding and engagement must shift significantly towards those organisations that are taking a proactive leadership role in tackling extremism and defending our shared values. It is only by defending our values that we will prevent extremists radicalising future generations of terrorists.[443]

Among the targets of the message of the speech was said to be the MCB and it is argued that relations between the British government and this Muslim group have "deteriorated significantly" since the Kelly statement. In particular, it is argued that the British government, backed by the U.S. administration of George Bush, entered into a strategy to gradually shift support away from organizations like the MCB and toward others that were more willing to offer broad support to its anti-terror agenda. The most prominent winner in this shifting of resources

---

[443] "Britain: Our Values, Our Responsibilities," A speech delivered by British Secretary of State Ruth Kelly, The House of Local Government, London (October 11, 2006), http://www.communities.gov.uk/ archived/speeches/ corporate/values-responsibilities (accessed December 28, 2007).

may have been the Sufi Muslim Council, a group described as open to the British government's anti-terror plans, but representing a relatively small slice of the larger British Muslim population concentrated predominantly in Northwest England.[444]

By late 2007, a new pathway had begun to be explored in England. Founded in 2007, the Muslim Arbitration Tribunal ("MAT") began offering formal arbitration services to Muslim litigants that were akin to those contemplated in Ontario, Canada. The panels conducted by the MAT focus predominantly upon matters of family law, but also consider issues in the field of inheritance law and contract law.[445] The panels operate under the jurisdiction of the 1996 U.K. Arbitration Act. In general, the arbitration panels have met with some hesitation and controversy. With the Conservative Shadow Home Secretary Dominic Grieve observing, upon being questioned about the MAT:

> If it is true that these tribunals are passing binding decisions in the areas of family and criminal law, I would like to know which courts are enforcing them because I would consider such action unlawful. British law is absolute and must remain so.[446]

Though it is not certain how many matters have been entertained by arbitration panels in the U.K., a 2009 report suggested that there were some 85 forums conducting sharia-based arbitration hearings across Britain.[447] Still, when questioned about the arbitration panels

---

444 Wendy Kristianasen, "Britain's Multiculturalism Falters," *Le Monde* (February 1, 2007), http://magazines.documenta.de/frontend/ article.php?Idlanguage=1&NrArticle=472 (accessed December 12, 2007).

445 See "Types of Cases that we Deal With," from the website of the Muslim Arbitration Tribunal, http:// www.matribunal.com/cases.htm (accessed August 12, 2009).

446 Abul Taher, "Revealed: U.K.'s First Official Sharia Courts," *The Times of London* (September 14, 2008), http://www.timesonline.co.uk/tol/comment/faith/article4749183.ece (accessed September 19, 2009).

447 Steve Doughty, "Britain has 85 Sharia Courts: The Astonishing Spread of Islamic Justice Behind Closed Doors," *The Daily Mail* (June 29, 2009), http://www.dailymail.co.uk/news/article-1196165 (accessed September 19, 2009).

during debate before the British House of Lords, the Parliamentary Under-Secretary of State for the Ministry of Justice, Lord William Bach, responded emphatically, "Sharia law has no jurisdiction in England and Wales."[448] Even so, he acknowledged the introduction of the "voluntary" arbitration panels in England, while agreeing that concerns related to the arbitration panels of specific affected groups, including women, should be heard by the government.

What will the end result of this interaction between England's governing institutions and the Muslim community be? In particular, to what extent will these relationships lead to clarification in the manner in which Islamic law is applied in England? English barrister Ahmad Thompson, a partner with Wynne Chambers, which claims to be one of the largest law firms in the U.K. focusing upon matters related to the intersection of Islamic and secular law, has argued for the legal recognition of the right of Muslims in England to resolve personal disputes pursuant to the *shari'a*, as one route toward alleviating the anxiety felt by members of the British Muslim community. He is not alone, with some pointing to the experience of British rule in India, wherein various systems of religious law were accommodated by the judiciary based upon the desires of the Indian populace, as a model that could be employed in the United Kingdom. As Thompson observed in an article published in the English online legal resource *Family Law Week* in 2007:

> If the decisions and judgments of these religious courts were recognised as valid by English law – but only enforceable through the civil courts, then a great case load burden would be lifted from the civil courts – and Muslims, for example, would no longer have to go through two marriage ceremonies and possibly two divorce proceedings. This would mean that a

---

[448] See Transcript of Debate of the British House of Lords of June 4, 2009, concerning, "Justice: Sharia Law," available at the official website of the British Parliament, http://services.parliament.uk/hansard /Lords/byDate/ 20090604/mainchamberdebates/part003.html (accessed September 9, 2009).

very significant form of alternative dispute resolution would be recognised not only in principle, but also in practice.[449]

Yet, the question may be asked whether an expanded recognition by English courts of Islamic law principles would provide a benefit to the larger public. As the quote, with which this chapter began, reflects, some feel uncomfortable with the creep of *shari'a* into England's judicial system. On the other hand, others have argued that the end result of such efforts may provide significant social rewards.

As Dr. Prakash Shah, a member of the faculty of London's Queen Mary University, observed in a 2006 interview with the British Broadcasting Corporation ("BBC"), tribunals imposing systems of religious or ethnic law may be "more effective" than secular courts at maintaining "social harmony" within the minority communities served.[450]

Concluding Observations

As the foregoing suggests, a number of potential models exist that may guide relations between minority Muslim communities in the West and secular systems of justice. The question that may be asked is whether any of these approaches offer potential as models employable in the U.S.

The path followed by Germany of direct recognition of *shari'a*-based legal tenets appears most problematic for U.S. policy-makers and courts. This is due to fundamental differences embedded in the laws of the two states related to the treatment of claims asserted by members of immigrant communities, particularly. Indeed, for religious law to be employed in the manner executed in Germany, a broad overhaul of U.S. law would be necessitated. The Canadian experience of flirting with an Islamic arbitration system, while technically workable in the U.S., seems challenging in practice due to the same sorts of public

---

449 "Islamic Law for Family Lawyers," *Family Law Week* (January 2007), http://www.familylawweek.co.uk/library.asp?i=2726, (accessed September 12, 2007), 6.

450 Innes Bowen, "The End of One Law for All?" report of the British Broadcasting Corporation (November 28, 2006), http://news.bbc.co.uk/1/hi/magazine/6190080.stm (accessed November 12, 2007).

relations concerns that plagued the effort in the province of Ontario. Though, as the Jewish community in the U.S. has displayed, this is a viable option and the legal mechanisms are in place to launch such a system, at least within certain state jurisdictions.

Perhaps, as a practical matter, the experience in England of the emergence of the Islamic Sharia Council, an entity formulated outside the reach of the larger secular legal system, and its application of an Anglicized version of Muslim religious law, may prove to provide the most workable immediate path for Muslims in the U.S. Yet, an effort to establish such bodies in the U.S. is fraught with challenge and difficulty. On the one hand, there will be concerns related to transparency, discrimination and the effective "ghettoization" of the Muslim community. As well, there will be hurdles especially in regard to public perception.

Indeed, the angst felt by many in the U.S. regarding issues affecting the inter-relationship between the Muslim minority community and the larger social sphere may be well reflected in an exchange that took place between U.S. Senator Sam Brownback and U.S. Attorney General Michael Mukasey during the latter's confirmation hearings before the U.S. Senate Judiciary Committee in October, 2007:

> BROWNBACK: And that's the issue that I want to get at, if we can. And it may be a difficult thing to discuss or get at. But certain countries' courts have held that sharia, or Islamic religious law trumps civil constitution. There's been a case in Malaysia. There was a case earlier this year in Germany, there a Frankfurt presiding judge over a divorce court involving two Muslim Moroccan residents in Germany put aside German divorce law and ruled, instead, on the basis of her understanding of the Koran. Case aroused considerable controversy in June. The Justice Ministry and the German state that she resided in, the judge did, decided against disciplining the judge. What would be your thoughts on this were this to arise in the United States—in a court of law in the United States?
>
> MUKASEY: I think we should not create, anywhere in this country, enclaves that are governed by any law other than the

> law that applies to everybody. We live in this country under one system of laws. And whatever may be the religious requirements of any group, we don't create enclaves where a different law applies, a different law governs and people don't have the rights that everybody else has outside that enclave. I would resist that very firmly—the creation of any such enclave.[451]

Taken on their face, the comments of Mukasey and Brownback seem to underscore a broad reluctance on the part of U.S. policy-makers and courts to lend support to any effort designed to expand the recognition of Islamic law in the U.S. On every level, it seems, the relationship between the U.S. and its minority Muslim community is marked by chronic anxiety. Thus, the point of beginning in seeking some commonality between the two groups may lie in the reshaping of opinion and impressions. The first step may be one that, through education, serves to bridge certain divides rooted in perception.

---

[451] United States Senate Committee on the Judiciary, *Hearings on the Nomination of Michael Mukasey as Attorney General*, 110th Cong., 1st Session, October 17, 2007, transcript published at the website of *The Washington Post*, http://www.washingtonpost.com/wp-srv/politics/documents/attorney_general_hearing101707.html (accessed November 17, 2007).

CHAPTER 9

Seeking Solutions

> *Nevertheless law, even though without a sanction, is not entirely void of effect. For justice brings peace of conscience, while injustice causes torment and anguish.... Justice is approved, and injustice condemned, by the common agreement of good men. But, most important of all, in God injustice finds an enemy, justice a protector. He reserves his judgments for the life after this, yet in such a way that he often causes their effects to become manifest even in this life, as history teaches by numerous examples.*[452]

What does the future hold for the Islamic community of the U.S. and, more specifically, to what extent will that future lead to a reconsideration of the role played by religious law in the lives of American Muslims? This is a difficult and challenging question. The intent here, of course, is not to predict, but to assess and propose. In that regard, these concluding thoughts constitute more of a proposal than a forecast or prophesy. Still, it is worthwhile to consider possibilities, as well as to reflect upon the potential costs associated with the embrace of alternate paths.

---

[452] Hugo Grotius, *Prolegomena to the Law of War and Peace*, Francis Kelsey, trans. (New York: Liberal Arts Press, 1957), 15.

Perhaps, any effort to propose a future course of action for U.S. Muslims demands some re-consideration of the nature of the institutions affected. Early in this work, some attention is given to the nature of Islamic law and the role it plays in the lives of Muslim adherents. It seems clear from any consideration of the Islamic system of faith that the religious law that provides an ethical and ritual structure to the tradition and its practice is of vital significance both to adherents and to the larger institutional hierarchy. Islamic law serves to set behavioral norms and to provide a framework through which the world may be interpreted. These seem to be critical components of the larger Muslim system of faith. In this regard, then, it may be questioned whether the idea of an Islamic religious system is meaningful in the absence of its internalized regime of religious law.

The question of the extent to which Islam can be separated from its legal foundations is of significance to all Muslims, but plays a role of critical practical importance for U.S. Muslims. In general, most Muslim leaders and thinkers seem to take the position that Islam cannot be separated from its system of law. As Taha Jabir al-Alwani has asserted relative to the obligation of Muslims living as minorities in non-Muslim countries, such individuals are not meant to be afforded "privileges or concessions not available to Muslim majorities."[453] That leaves Muslims, in countries like the U.S. where no form of Islamic law has received formal government sanction, often caught between institutions. As has been observed, practitioners of Islam are in a "complex position" because they are "governed by two sets of rules, one religious and the other secular."[454] This is a precarious balancing act and Muslims are increasingly unwilling to "sacrifice" their religious identities at "any secular altar." Yet, it may be asked, what is the alternative for Muslims residing in the United States and other Western countries?

In responding to this question, it is important to consider the relationship between U.S. governmental institutions and Muslims residing in the country. In seeking to determine the nature of relations

---

[453] *Toward a Fiqh for Minorities*, 3-4.

[454] Asifa Quraisha and Najeeba Syeed-Miller, "No Altars: A Survey of Islamic Family Law in the United States," website of Emory University School of Law: Law and Religion Program, http://www.law.emory.edu/ifl/index2.html (accessed September 12, 2007).

between these groups, this work has examined the historical interaction between the Muslim religious community and U.S. governmental institutions, with particular emphasis upon the judiciary. A portion of this investigation has centered upon the images of Muslims that seem to prevail within the body of decisions rendered by the U.S. judiciary. This examination raises the question of whether images of Muslims and the Islamic faith are, at least in part, the product of negative stereotyping; what some may refer to as "Orientalism." While it is unclear whether any malicious intent may lie at the heart of characterizations examined here, there is some evidence that Muslims have been subject to descriptions that are often unflattering and potentially socially damaging. It is quite possible that these curious characterizations of aspects of the Muslim Diaspora are the result of carelessness or misinformation. Still, the question may be asked whether such characterizations have damaged the image of the Muslim community held by the larger populace and the self-image of individual followers of the Islamic faith.

It is important, as well, to consider the actual experience of Muslims in U.S. courts. Through this investigation, it seems clear that issues rooted in Islamic law are increasingly finding their way into U.S. courts. Often, though not always, these claims stem from prior decisions rendered by foreign tribunals applying Islamic law. Stemming from such matters, U.S. courts face difficult decisions concerning their willingness to respect such judgments. Such cases have brought to the fore questions concerning the compatibility of Islamic religious practice and U.S. law. These cases have proved to be complicated as judges have sought to sort through the competing sets of loyalties embraced by Muslim litigants. Many of these matters have fallen into the broad area of the law of personal status and have included issues related to the validity of marriage and divorce proceedings and child custody arrangements. The only useful broad description of the outcomes of such proceedings is that they have been decidedly "mixed."

In terms of whether decisions rendered by outside tribunals imposing Islamic law should be enforced in the U.S., the courts have often disagreed. Some courts, based upon the doctrine of *comity*, have appeared open to the enforcement of such foreign judgments. Others, meanwhile, have rejected them, often citing concerns regarding the incompatibility of the foreign legal systems with domestic standards. Courts have also found room for significant disagreement as to whether basic principles associated with Islamic law are enforceable. This division among U.S. courts creates complications for Muslim litigants, as well as the larger judicial system.

For Muslims considering the utilization of U.S. courts to resolve matters that may impinge upon aspects of Islamic law, concerns regarding the volatility of decisions in this area may prompt significant hesitation. One of the important characteristics of a stable judiciary is uniformity of decision. Yet, with regard to issues related to the imposition or enforcement of Islamic law, there continues to be significant instability within the body of U.S. court opinions. For U.S. Muslims, this means that they enter the court without reasonable assurance of the manner in which their claims will be resolved. In other words, they may face not only doubts concerning any final case outcome, but even significant questions regarding the law that would be applied to the issues involved. In many instances, such uncertainties may prompt Muslims in the U.S. to avoid secular legal institutions altogether.

Against the backdrop of these inquiries concerning the treatment Muslims have received in U.S. courts loom larger questions of justice and equal treatment. If, as has been suggested above, Islamic law is interpreted by many within the Muslim leadership to be an integral part of the larger system of religious practice, the question that is begged is whether the faith can be fully followed within a social environment that does not provide some mechanism for the enforcement of such norms. Indeed, can U.S. Muslims be faithful to their chosen religious order in the absence of judicial protection of the broader system of Islamic ethical practice? In a society that through its founding legal declarations commits itself to protection of the freedom of religious practice, this question prompts important constitutional law considerations. Are Muslims being denied access to the full practice of their faith through the failure of courts to recognize and employ Islamic law?

The challenges created for Muslims by the failure of courts to enforce aspects of Islamic law may lead to further legal difficulties that extend beyond the boundaries of the United States, as well. One significant concern voiced by Muslims living in the West relates to complications produced from decisions rendered by secular courts that conflict with Islamic law. In particular, such judgments may not be recognized by religious tribunals of the home countries of Muslims, if and when such parties seek to return to these jurisdictions.

Accordingly, upon return to their countries of origin or other majority Muslim jurisdictions, practitioners of Islam may be left in a nebulous legal position and face considerable uncertainty in terms of the consequences of this state.

Yet, this is not merely a legal inquiry, but a personal one and an ethical one, as well. On a personal level, the questions considered here speak to the very self-identity of Muslims. As one Muslim commentator has observed, there is an emerging vision of an archetypal "American Muslim," for example. Yet, this archetype is confused due to the fact that it appears to embrace the seemingly contradictory loyalties that bind Muslims in the U.S.[455] Leaning upon the words of W.E.B. DuBois, these twin loyalties may be termed representative of a spirit of "double consciousness" that simultaneously guides and distracts those in the category. Thus, the maintenance of such twin loyalties may amount to an effort to "measure one's soul by the tape of a world that looks on in amused contempt."[456]

Muslims residing in the U.S. and across the West may frequently find themselves confronted with a choice between the embrace of conflicting social and religious priorities. Perhaps, some conflict of this type is inevitable. The question that may be asked is to what extent Western governments might seek avoidance of such conflict through accommodation of minority religious norms, to the extent possible without infringing upon the rights and interests of other groups.

On an ethical front, questions of justice may be strongly implicated by the experience of the Muslim community in the U.S. To what extent should Muslims or other religious minorities expect full access to the central elements of their faith? Within a social environment largely constructed and heavily influenced by practitioners of the Christian tradition, what accommodation should be made for Muslims and other religious minority communities? To what extent is the equality of treatment demanded by the concept of justice infringed upon by the prevailing status quo in the U.S.? The manner in which these questions

---

[455] Sherman Jackson, "Muslims, Islamic Law and Sociopolitical Reality in the United States," The website of Muslim Alliance of North America, http://www.mana-net.org/pages.php?ID=activism&ID2=&NUM =45 (accessed December 10, 2007).

[456] W.E.B. DuBois, *The Souls of Black Folk* (New York: Modern Library, 2000), 4.

are resolved, then, affects not only the legal status of individuals, but the manner in which they practice their faith and the contours of their self-identity. The answers to these questions may be shaped in part by knowledge of options available to lawmakers and courts to offer some meaningful accommodation of Islamic religious priorities.

This work considers potential pathways available that might afford U.S. Muslims access to some mechanism capable of enforcing religious legal norms in the future. In so doing, particular emphasis has been placed upon the consideration of arbitration as a potential vehicle for the accommodation of Islamic law in North America. In that regard, this work has considered the failed experience of political leaders in the province of Ontario, Canada to maintain a law specifically providing religious groups with the authority to establish private tribunals, applying religious law and rendering binding judgments. As well, considered here are the efforts of certain Jewish groups to establish arbitration panels, applying religious law, in the U.S.

Among the lessons learned from the Canadian experiment may be the depth of public anxiety concerning the Muslim community in North America and the political costs that may be associated with any effort to authorize the employment of Islamic legal norms in this region. The concerns that led to the demise of portions of the Ontario *Arbitration Act* were almost exclusively directed toward the Muslim community, though Jewish, Christian and other groups had made use of provisions of the *Act*. Thus, this episode highlighted the existence of a heightened public anxiety directed at Muslim groups that does not seem to affect other religious communities. As well, whether valid or not, many of the particular public concerns expressed in the debate concerning the Ontario act centered upon ways in which the *shari'a* system was asserted to be incompatible with traditional Western legal and social norms. The experience of Canadian officials in their unsuccessful efforts to defend the *Arbitration Act*, then, provides a useful reminder of the concerns and pitfalls that would likely befall any similar effort attempted in the U.S.

The experience of the Jewish community in establishing arbitration tribunals within certain jurisdictions of the U.S. offers some hints as to the legal challenges Muslims might face in any effort to fashion a broad and binding arbitration court in America. Muslims in the U.S. have not broadly embraced the path blazed by their Jewish counterparts. One may ask why this is so. Perhaps, it is partially due to the complexities of ensuring that the decisions of such panels will be observed by U.S.

courts. Indeed, it may be suspected that Muslim arbitration panel decisions might be voided on the same public policy grounds that have been invoked by U.S. courts to obviate judgments of foreign courts applying Islamic law.

Muslims may be reluctant to follow the Jewish lead, as well, because of the variations in the treatment of arbitration panels from state to state in the U.S. The law governing the use of arbitration systems is generally dictated by state legislation and, accordingly, guidelines for the use of such tribunals vary by jurisdiction. Such variation may affect the nature of matters subject to arbitration and procedures to be applied. This variation is of significance to a community that is dispersed widely, unlike certain Jewish subgroups that may generally inhabit much more confined geographical spaces.

Finally, the extensive ethnic and cultural diversity of the Muslim community of the U.S. may make it difficult to establish panels that are broadly embraced. Yet, it may still be said that arbitration offers the advantage of permitting entities to establish tribunals designed to employ rules of the litigants' own choosing. In the case of the Muslim community, such panels may be crafted to accommodate specific norms drawn from the *shari'a* system.

An additional model examined was that employed by Germany. In the case of Germany, codified choice of law provisions are written such that national courts are placed in the position of interpreting and implementing requirements of Islamic religious law under certain defined circumstances. Potentially impacted by the law are claims involving immigrants and those temporarily in Germany. Indigenous Muslims, thus, would be excluded from the reach of the law. Still, the legal regime prompts greater clarity than may be seen within the body of U.S. case law concerning matters rooted in religious law. It does so by mandating consideration of specific claims pursuant to religious law, where such law would be applied by tribunals in a litigant's native land. Ultimately, the German legal regime serves as a model that highlights the workability and advantages of a system offering a more stable environment for the consideration of such matters.

Finally, this analysis considered the efforts of Muslim groups in England to lay the foundation for the emergence of an indigenous *shari'a*. In effect, through both public activism in the sphere of politics and governance and intra-community organization, including the establishment of non-binding courts, such Muslims groups are introducing concepts stemming from Islamic law into the larger social sphere and reinforcing the necessity of adherence to such religious norms by members of the community. It is speculated by some that such efforts may lead to a gradual public embrace of such religious norms and a modification of existing law and public policy to reflect or accept them over time. Yet, at present, the primary result of this process has been the creation of a hybrid system of rules that are being applied by extra-judicial bodies. Unofficial tribunals have been established throughout England that apply a mix of Islamic law principles with basic elements of British common law.

The existence of these bodies has led some to voice apprehension. Among the concerns voiced related to such extra-judicial bodies is their apparent lack of operational transparency, the fear that the judgments issued will be affected by gender and, perhaps, even ethnic bias, and the expectation that as Muslims withdraw from secular institutions and turn inward, their communities will be effectively "ghettoized," leaving them with access to inferior judicial mechanisms and social infrastructure.

At the same time, if Muslims are going to have a larger voice within the realm of public policy, there may be a need for the construction of more organized leadership groups. Certain groups that appear to fill such a role have appeared in England. The London bombings of 2005 may have helped to expand the reach and voice of some of these groups in England. It is not clear that there are Muslims groups with comparable levels of influence either within or outside the Islamic community of the U.S. Still, it is possible that groups such as CAIR, ISNA, the Islamic Supreme Council of America, the Islamic Assembly of North America or others may evolve into broadly influential bodies over time.

Perhaps, another potential pitfall that could diminish the influence of such groups stems from broader political priorities. By entering the public sphere, such groups are subjecting themselves and their agendas to the prevailing political currents. In England, the failure of certain Muslim organizational bodies to offer sufficient support to policy proposals regarding terrorism, has led to a shifting of political support to competing entities. It may be similarly observed that the whims of the political arena in the U.S. might serve to aid or thwart the efforts of Muslim organizational bodies. Thus, a significant investment of time and resources and further maturing of organizations such as CAIR, ISNA or others may be necessary before such efforts bear significant fruit in terms of affecting U.S. public policy.

The Way Forward

What is the future for the Muslim community of the United States? To what extent is it in the interests of the U.S. government and the judiciary to work with the growing religious community? To what extent is such interaction demanded ethically? What is at stake if interaction between governmental institutions and the Muslim community fails to result in the production of a plan that would offer some accommodation of the interests of the religious community? These are the questions that seem to be begged by this analysis and the responses that may be offered to these inquiries are varied and subject to considerable debate. Still, it seems vital that these questions be entertained, and the potential consequences of the failure to give heed to these inquiries are significant.

Any adequate response to questions related to the Muslim community and the use of Islamic law in the U.S. must begin with the recognition and acceptance of the fact that present educational offerings in the U.S. on related topics are likely insufficient. The limited exposure those practicing within the field of law in the U.S. may have to Islamic religious and ethical norms is exemplified through the track record of centers of legal education. According to a 2005 article, sixty-six law schools from around the U.S. reported having offered some course or courses that focused, in whole or in part, upon some aspect of Islamic law during a five-year period.[457] The American Association of Law Schools recognizes 196 American law schools as accredited, and there are many others that would be classified as non-accreditied. Of those sixty-six identified in the survey as making some course offering focused upon the topic of Islamic law, approximately twenty-one indicated that such offerings were made on an ongoing basis. For the vast majority of law students, then, it appears that there is limited or no access to courses focused upon aspects of Islamic law. Even for those attending schools that may have made such offerings, the courses were

---

[457] John Makdisi, "A Survey of AALS Law Schools Teaching Islamic Law," *Journal of Legal Education* 55, no. 4 (December 2005): 583-588. A similar study found that approximately 30 U.S. law schools offer some type of course in Jewish law. See Samuel Levine, "Teaching Jewish Law in American Law Schools – Part II," *The Journal of International and Comparative Law Chicago-Kent* 2 (2002): 1-13.

typically available as isolated elective offerings. Only eleven law schools indicated that they had offered more than one option of courses focused upon varying aspects of Islamic law. Accordingly, it may be observed that only a very small percentage of the individuals graduating from law schools each year in the United States are afforded the option of taking a course focused upon Islamic law. Far fewer, it may be assumed, actually take such courses.

Another measure of the access U.S. legal professionals have to substantive information regarding Islamic law may come from a consideration of the process of continuing education. Based upon state rules of practice, all legal professionals are required to participate in a minimum number of hours of continuing legal education courses each year. Such courses are made available by a wide range of organizations, from state bar associations and law schools to private for-profit vendors. The best known of these organizations, however, is likely the American Bar Association ("ABA"). It offers a significant number of continuing legal education courses ("CLE") each year that are made accessible to practitioners in the field from around the country. Based upon a brief review of course offerings made by the ABA for the first half of 2008, more than 70 continuing education classes were being offered on a range of topics.[458] However, none of them related to Islamic law or even the more general topic of religious law, directly or indirectly. As an entity charged with guiding the broad community of legal professionals in the U.S., it may be observed that this failure to include topics concerning Islamic law amongst its continuing education offerings is likely reflective of a larger systematic orientation directed away from the inclusion of such topics.

As the size of the Muslim community in the U.S. grows and as courts are confronted with greater numbers of cases that touch upon issues rooted in Islamic law, it becomes increasingly important that members of the judiciary and the larger community of legal professionals have some familiarity with the nature and origins of this religious system. Such familiarity may prove important not just in the resolution of substantive legal issues, but also in the weighing of individual and expert testimony and in the efforts of justices to

---

[458] "Calendar of Events," The ABA Center for Continuing Legal Education, www.abanet.org/cle/calendar.html (accessed January 16, 2008).

appreciate and understand the social influences that bear upon Muslim litigants and the perspectives they may bring into the courtroom.

The question that may be asked is how and where this education may best be offered. Perhaps, the easiest place to begin educating jurists may be through CLE offerings. Such offerings may serve as important vehicles precisely because they attract a captive audience. Since attorneys and judges throughout the country are required to participate in a minimum numbers of hours of continuing education each year, such courses represent a useful vehicle to ensure that information on topics related to Islamic law is accessed by professionals. Moreover, it would be equally important for those who play leadership roles within the legal community, including judges and organizations like the ABA, to encourage wide participation by practitioners in such courses.

As well, specialized courses for judges may be made available that would address issues related to the treatment of concerns rooted in aspects of Islamic law within the scope of U.S. court cases. In regard to such education, it would be worthwhile to ensure that available cross-disciplinary resources are accessed. For example, faculty in such departments as religious studies, sociology and anthropology at many colleges and universities around the country offer expertise in topics related to Islamic culture, custom and ritual and ethical obligations associated with the faith. Such information may not be the typical fodder for CLE courses. Yet, this material may serve to provide insight that will allow jurists to make better judgments on issues in this area as they arise.

Peering into the more distant future, it may be anticipated that courses in Islamic law could be made available to law students on a more consistent basis at a much wider range of law schools throughout the country. In addition, it may be hoped that an expanded regime of courses might be developed. It must be recognized that short-term CLE courses can never serve as a wholesale substitute for longer-term and more detailed treatments of such subjects of the type that can be offered within a degree program.

In addition to expanding the role of education in broadening the knowledge of judges and legal professionals regarding Islamic ethical norms, the establishment of a more stable environment within which Muslim litigants may air disputes and seek resolution in accord with religious law could provide significant social benefit. Greater consistency in the manner in which U.S. courts treat such claims may serve to provide Muslim residents with an increased sense of assurance concerning the rights they may expect. This, in turn, may prompt an increased willingness to access and trust secular courts. Still, it may be asked, how may such consistency be best achieved? In part, it may be observed that greater stability in judicial judgments should be a byproduct of increased education itself. Still, increased openness by U.S. courts to the employment of the doctrine of comity for the purposes of the entertainment of disputes rooted in Islamic law may also be cultivated intentionally, through legislative action or efforts designed to build greater judicial consensus.

Such efforts to construct a more stable environment for the entertainment of issues rooted in Islamic law might be enhanced through the development of community tribunals utilizing arbitration or, perhaps, some other alternative dispute resolution process. Such tribunals afford litigants the opportunity to voluntarily choose the law that will govern the consideration of a given controversy. Yet, such tribunals still afford courts the opportunity to exercise significant oversight.

Among the key traits of such an arbitration system would be the requirement that individuals voluntarily submit to the jurisdiction of the tribunal. Thus, in theory, no one would be compelled to appear before such a religious court. In addition, procedural safeguards may be imposed upon arbitration bodies. These safeguards may include particular limitations regarding notice to opposing parties, admission of evidence and the types of matters that may be entertained. Finally, with regard to the decision of an arbitrator, there is always the option for individuals to submit a challenge to a secular court. If it is believed that the arbitrator exceeded the bounds of his authority, ignored procedural safeguards or issued a judgment that was inconsistent with public policy of the jurisdiction, challenge may be brought in a secular court to the final determination of a matter.

Of course, the establishment of such an alternative dispute resolution system is a task beset with challenge and complication, as outlined above. At some basic level, such procedures are already being employed quietly, within local mosques and communities in the U.S. Yet, if this is to grow into a recognized and broadly available venue, certainly Muslims will need to fashion more sophisticated and transparent institutions. In following this path, the Muslim community in the U.S. will need to draw lessons from the experience of their Jewish counterparts. As well, the Muslim community, the U.S.

judiciary and political and legislative leaders will have to be positioned to respond to the negative public commentary that is likely to emerge in reaction to general awareness concerning any such effort. Again, education may be a key here. If such leaders are to avoid seeing the inevitable public concern flower into public rage and outcry, it would be important that the actual dimensions of such a project be broadly communicated. Despite these constraints, some form of alternative dispute resolution mechanism may provide the most workable vehicle for Muslims to more broadly employ aspects of Islamic law in the U.S. during the near term.

It may also be observed that a federal law addressing arbitration in the context of certain subjects, including family and personal law, may provide a useful foundation for such an effort. A federal law applicable in all states would eliminate the varied treatment that arbitration panels may currently receive from jurisdiction to jurisdiction. Thus, a more stable landscape would emerge for the construction of arbitration tribunals applying religious law. As well, a substantive debate on a federal level concerning such a proposal may prompt members of the public and the legal community to consider more seriously the benefits and challenges associated with the accommodation of Islamic law versus the maintenance of status quo.

While these proposals focus upon some of the ways in which the Muslim religious system may be more fully accommodated in the U.S., it is also worthwhile to consider the cost of inaction. The complete disregard by policymakers of Muslim concern about and interest in the application of Islamic religious law may prompt increased feelings of alienation, frustration and dissatisfaction on the part of many members of the religious minority group. Such alienation may spur dissention, at least among some. Within a global environment where experiences of oppression have prompted calls for violent response within the Muslim community, it may be anticipated that action or inaction, as the case may be, in this country that fuels the passions of members of minority religious and ethnic groups has the potential of prompting anti-social outcomes. While the events of September 11, 2001, may be interpreted as a foreign-born plot that was largely unrelated to domestic affairs in the U.S., it is important that policymakers and social leaders not to lose sight of the fact that the subsequent London train bombings of 2005 were carried out precisely by home-grown assailants. Though the situations in the U.S. and England are not precisely parallel, the lessons of this latter terrorist action may be ignored only to the peril of the larger society. A plan that fully integrates religious minority communities, drawing them toward a feeling of investment in the well-being of their social community and environment, may offer the best path to the avoidance of such outcomes.

Each of the above proposals, which are aimed at achieving such desired integration of Muslims into the social fabric of their local communities, meanwhile, depends upon a broad and serious inquiry into the compatibility of essential Islamic legal and ethical norms and the demands of secular law in the U.S. In part, this inquiry is one that necessitates a comparative analysis of varying historical treatments of Islamic law by differing Muslim schools and modern attempts by foreign governments to implements or codify such standards. As well, this inquiry demands further consideration by the Muslim community of the manner in which Islamic law is to be interpreted within the modern context. Such leading Muslim figures of the modern era as Fazlur Rahman and Muhammad Iqbal voiced strong interest in the resurrection of *ijtihad* or independent analysis of Islamic law based upon reason. Such processes may lead to a reconsideration of certain Islamic norms, offering understandings that are more consistent with broadly-held notions of human rights. Yet, not all Muslims agree with the ideas articulated by Rhaman and Iqbal. Ultimately, some greater consensus within the global Muslim *ulema* on issues of interpretation and content of Islamic law may serve to open the doors for Muslims to greater acceptance of such religious norms in the U.S. and across the West.

Appendix A

Arbitration Act, 1991 (in part)
S.O. 1991, CHAPTER 17
Introductory Matters

Definitions
1. In this Act,
"arbitration agreement" means an agreement by which two or more persons agree to submit to arbitration a dispute that has arisen or may arise between them; ("convention d'arbitrage")
"arbitrator" includes an umpire; ("arbitre")
"court", except in sections 6 and 7, means the Ontario Court (General Division). ("tribunal judiciaire") 1991, c. 17, s. 1.
Application of Act

Arbitrations conducted under agreements
2. (1) This Act applies to an arbitration conducted under an arbitration agreement unless,
(a) the application of this Act is excluded by law; or
(b) the *International Commercial Arbitration Act* applies to the arbitration. 1991, c. 17, s. 2 (1).

Transition, existing agreements
(2) This Act applies to an arbitration conducted under an arbitration agreement made before the day this Act comes into force, if the arbitration is commenced after that day. 1991, c. 17, s. 2 (2).

Arbitrations conducted under statutes
(3) This Act applies, with necessary modifications, to an arbitration conducted in accordance with another Act, unless that Act provides otherwise; however, in the event of conflict between this Act and the other Act or regulations made under the other Act, the other Act or the regulations prevail. 1991, c. 17, s. 2 (3).

Transition, arbitrations already commenced
(4) Despite its repeal by section 58, the *Arbitrations Act*, as it read on the 31st day of December, 1991, continues to apply to arbitrations commenced on or before that day. 1991, c. 17, s. 2 (4).

Contracting out

3. The parties to an arbitration agreement may agree, expressly or by implication, to vary or exclude any provision of this Act except the following:

1. Subsection 5 (4) ("*Scott* v. *Avery*" clauses).
2. Section 19 (equality and fairness).
3. Section 39 (extension of time limits).
4. Section 46 (setting aside award).
5. Section 48 (declaration of invalidity of arbitration).
6. Section 50 (enforcement of award). 1991, c. 17, s. 3.

Waiver of right to object

4. A party who participates in an arbitration despite being aware of non-compliance with a provision of this Act, except one mentioned in section 3, or with the arbitration agreement, and does not object to the non-compliance within the time limit provided or, if none is provided, within a reasonable time, shall be deemed to have waived the right to object. 1991, c. 17, s. 4.

Arbitration agreements

5. (1) An arbitration agreement may be an independent agreement or part of another agreement. 1991, c. 17, s. 5 (1).

Further agreements

(2) If the parties to an arbitration agreement make a further agreement in connection with the arbitration, it shall be deemed to form part of the arbitration agreement. 1991, c. 17, s. 5 (2).

Oral agreements

(3) An arbitration agreement need not be in writing. 1991, c. 17, s. 5 (3).

"*Scott* v. *Avery*" clauses

(4) An agreement requiring or having the effect of requiring that a matter be adjudicated by arbitration before it may be dealt with by a court has the same effect as an arbitration agreement. 1991, c. 17, s. 5 (4).

Revocation
(5) An arbitration agreement may be revoked only in accordance with the ordinary rules of contract law. 1991, c. 17, s. 5 (5).
Court Intervention

Court intervention limited
6. No court shall intervene in matters governed by this Act, except for the following purposes, in accordance with this Act:
1. To assist the conducting of arbitrations.
2. To ensure that arbitrations are conducted in accordance with arbitration agreements.
3. To prevent unequal or unfair treatment of parties to arbitration agreements.
4. To enforce awards. 1991, c. 17, s. 6.

Stay
7. (1) If a party to an arbitration agreement commences a proceeding in respect of a matter to be submitted to arbitration under the agreement, the court in which the proceeding is commenced shall, on the motion of another party to the arbitration agreement, stay the proceeding. 1991, c. 17, s. 7 (1).

Exceptions
(2) However, the court may refuse to stay the proceeding in any of the following cases:
1. A party entered into the arbitration agreement while under a legal incapacity.
2. The arbitration agreement is invalid.
3. The subject-matter of the dispute is not capable of being the subject of arbitration under Ontario law.
4. The motion was brought with undue delay.
5. The matter is a proper one for default or summary judgment. 1991, c. 17, s. 7 (2).

Arbitration may continue
(3) An arbitration of the dispute may be commenced and continued while the motion is before the court. 1991, c. 17, s. 7 (3).

Effect of refusal to stay
(4) If the court refuses to stay the proceeding,

(a) no arbitration of the dispute shall be commenced; and
(b) an arbitration that has been commenced shall not be continued, and anything done in connection with the arbitration before the court made its decision is without effect. 1991, c. 17, s. 7 (4).

Agreement covering part of dispute
(5) The court may stay the proceeding with respect to the matters dealt with in the arbitration agreement and allow it to continue with respect to other matters if it finds that,
(a) the agreement deals with only some of the matters in respect of which the proceeding was commenced; and
(b) it is reasonable to separate the matters dealt with in the agreement from the other matters. 1991, c. 17, s. 7 (5).

No appeal
(6) There is no appeal from the court's decision. 1991, c. 17, s. 7 (6).

Powers of court
8. (1) The court's powers with respect to the detention, preservation and inspection of property, interim injunctions and the appointment of receivers are the same in arbitrations as in court actions. 1991, c. 17, s. 8 (1).

Questions of law
(2) The arbitral tribunal may determine any question of law that arises during the arbitration; the court may do so on the application of the arbitral tribunal, or on a party's application if the other parties or the arbitral tribunal consent. 1991, c. 17, s. 8 (2).

Appeal
(3) The court's determination of a question of law may be appealed to the Court of Appeal, with leave. 1991, c. 17, s. 8 (3).

More than one arbitration
(4) On the application of all the parties to more than one arbitration the court may order, on such terms as are just,
(a) that the arbitrations be consolidated;
(b) that the arbitrations be conducted simultaneously or consecutively; or

(c) that any of the arbitrations be stayed until any of the others are completed. 1991, c. 17, s. 8 (4).

Arbitral tribunal for consolidated arbitrations
(5) When the court orders that arbitrations be consolidated, it may appoint an arbitral tribunal for the consolidated arbitration; if all the parties agree as to the choice of arbitral tribunal, the court shall appoint it. 1991, c. 17, s. 8 (5).

Consolidation by agreement of parties
(6) Subsection (4) does not prevent the parties to more than one arbitration from agreeing to consolidate the arbitrations and doing everything necessary to effect the consolidation. 1991, c. 17, s. 8 (6).
Composition of Arbitral Tribunal

Number of arbitrators
9. If the arbitration agreement does not specify the number of arbitrators who are to form the arbitral tribunal, it shall be composed of one arbitrator. 1991, c. 17, s. 9.

Appointment of arbitral tribunal
10. (1) The court may appoint the arbitral tribunal, on a party's application, if,
(a) the arbitration agreement provides no procedure for appointing the arbitral tribunal; or
(b) a person with power to appoint the arbitral tribunal has not done so after a party has given the person seven days notice to do so. 1991, c. 17, s. 10 (1).

No appeal
(2) There is no appeal from the court's appointment of the arbitral tribunal. 1991, c. 17, s. 10 (2).

More than one arbitrator
(3) Subsections (1) and (2) apply, with necessary modifications, to the appointment of individual members of arbitral tribunals that are composed of more than one arbitrator. 1991, c. 17, s. 10 (3).

Chair
(4) If the arbitral tribunal is composed of three or more arbitrators, they shall elect a chair from among themselves; if it is composed of two arbitrators, they may do so. 1991, c. 17, s. 10 (4).

Duty of arbitrator
11. (1) An arbitrator shall be independent of the parties and shall act impartially. 1991, c. 17, s. 11 (1).
Disclosure before accepting appointment
(2) Before accepting an appointment as arbitrator, a person shall disclose to all parties to the arbitration any circumstances of which he or she is aware that may give rise to a reasonable apprehension of bias. 1991, c. 17, s. 11 (2).

Disclosure during arbitration
(3) An arbitrator who, during an arbitration, becomes aware of circumstances that may give rise to a reasonable apprehension of bias shall promptly disclose them to all the parties. 1991, c. 17, s. 11 (3).

No revocation
12. A party may not revoke the appointment of an arbitrator. 1991, c. 17, s. 12.

Challenge
13. (1) A party may challenge an arbitrator only on one of the following grounds:
1. Circumstances exist that may give rise to a reasonable apprehension of bias.
2. The arbitrator does not possess qualifications that the parties have agreed are necessary. 1991, c. 17, s. 13 (1).

Idem, arbitrator appointed by party
(2) A party who appointed an arbitrator or participated in his or her appointment may challenge the arbitrator only for grounds of which the party was unaware at the time of the appointment. 1991, c. 17, s. 13 (2).

Procedure for challenge
(3) A party who wishes to challenge an arbitrator shall send the arbitral tribunal a statement of the grounds for the challenge, within fifteen days of becoming aware of them. 1991, c. 17, s. 13 (3).

Removal or resignation of challenged arbitrator
(4) The other parties may agree to remove the challenged arbitrator, or the arbitrator may resign. 1991, c. 17, s. 13 (4).

Decision of arbitral tribunal
(5) If the challenged arbitrator is not removed by the parties and does not resign, the arbitral tribunal, including the challenged arbitrator, shall decide the issue and shall notify the parties of its decision. 1991, c. 17, s. 13 (5).

Application to court
(6) Within ten days of being notified of the arbitral tribunal's decision, a party may make an application to the court to decide the issue and, in the case of the challenging party, to remove the arbitrator. 1991, c. 17, s. 13 (6).

Arbitration may continue
(7) While an application is pending, the arbitral tribunal, including the challenged arbitrator, may continue the arbitration and make an award, unless the court orders otherwise. 1991, c. 17, s. 13 (7).

Termination of arbitrator's mandate
14. (1) An arbitrator's mandate terminates when,
(a) the arbitrator resigns or dies;
(b) the parties agree to terminate it;
(c) the arbitral tribunal upholds a challenge to the arbitrator, ten days elapse after all the parties are notified of the decision and no application is made to the court; or
(d) the court removes the arbitrator under subsection 15 (1). 1991, c. 17, s. 14 (1).

Significance of resignation or agreement to terminate
(2) An arbitrator's resignation or a party's agreement to terminate an arbitrator's mandate does not imply acceptance of the validity of any reason advanced for challenging or removing him or her. 1991, c. 17, s. 14 (2).

Removal of arbitrator by court
15. (1) The court may remove an arbitrator on a party's application under subsection 13 (6) (challenge), or may do so on a party's

application if the arbitrator becomes unable to perform his or her functions, commits a corrupt or fraudulent act, delays unduly in conducting the arbitration or does not conduct it in accordance with section 19 (equality and fairness). 1991, c. 17, s. 15 (1).

Right of arbitrator
(2) The arbitrator is entitled to be heard by the court if the application is based on an allegation that he or she committed a corrupt or fraudulent act or delayed unduly in conducting the arbitration. 1991, c. 17, s. 15 (2).

Directions
(3) When the court removes an arbitrator, it may give directions about the conduct of the arbitration. 1991, c. 17, s. 15 (3).

Penalty
(4) If the court removes an arbitrator for a corrupt or fraudulent act or for undue delay, it may order that the arbitrator receive no payment for his or her services and may order that he or she compensate the parties for all or part of the costs, as determined by the court, that they incurred in connection with the arbitration before his or her removal. 1991, c. 17, s. 15 (4).

Appeal re penalty
(5) The arbitrator or a party may, within thirty days after receiving the court's decision, appeal an order made under subsection (4) or the refusal to make such an order to the Court of Appeal, with leave of that court. 1991, c. 17, s. 15 (5).

No other appeal
(6) Except as provided in subsection (5), there is no appeal from the court's decision or from its directions. 1991, c. 17, s. 15 (6).

Appointment of substitute arbitrator
16. (1) When an arbitrator's mandate terminates, a substitute arbitrator shall be appointed, following the procedure that was used in the appointment of the arbitrator being replaced. 1991, c. 17, s. 16 (1).

Directions

(2) When the arbitrator's mandate terminates, the court may, on a party's application, give directions about the conduct of the arbitration. 1991, c. 17, s. 16 (2).

Court appointment

(3) The court may appoint the substitute arbitrator, on a party's application, if,

(a) the arbitration agreement provides no procedure for appointing the substitute arbitrator; or

(b) a person with power to appoint the substitute arbitrator has not done so after a party has given the person seven days notice to do so. 1991, c. 17, s. 16 (3).

No appeal

(4) There is no appeal from the court's decision or from its directions. 1991, c. 17, s. 16 (4).

Exception

(5) This section does not apply if the arbitration agreement provides that the arbitration is to be conducted only by a named arbitrator. 1991, c. 17, s. 16 (5).

Jurisdiction of Arbitral Tribunal

Arbitral tribunal may rule on own jurisdiction

17. (1) An arbitral tribunal may rule on its own jurisdiction to conduct the arbitration and may in that connection rule on objections with respect to the existence or validity of the arbitration agreement. 1991, c. 17, s. 17 (1).

Independent agreement

(2) If the arbitration agreement forms part of another agreement, it shall, for the purposes of a ruling on jurisdiction, be treated as an independent agreement that may survive even if the main agreement is found to be invalid. 1991, c. 17, s. 17 (2).

Time for objections to jurisdiction

(3) A party who has an objection to the arbitral tribunal's jurisdiction to conduct the arbitration shall make the objection no later than the

beginning of the hearing or, if there is no hearing, no later than the first occasion on which the party submits a statement to the tribunal. 1991, c. 17, s. 17 (3).

Party's appointment of arbitrator no bar to objection
(4) The fact that a party has appointed or participated in the appointment of an arbitrator does not prevent the party from making an objection to jurisdiction. 1991, c. 17, s. 17 (4).

Time for objections that tribunal is exceeding authority
(5) A party who has an objection that the arbitral tribunal is exceeding its authority shall make the objection as soon as the matter alleged to be beyond the tribunal's authority is raised during the arbitration. 1991, c. 17, s. 17 (5).

Later objections
(6) Despite section 4, if the arbitral tribunal considers the delay justified, a party may make an objection after the time limit referred to in subsection (3) or (5), as the case may be, has expired. 1991, c. 17, s. 17 (6).

Ruling
(7) The arbitral tribunal may rule on an objection as a preliminary question or may deal with it in an award. 1991, c. 17, s. 17 (7).

Review by court
(8) If the arbitral tribunal rules on an objection as a preliminary question, a party may, within thirty days after receiving notice of the ruling, make an application to the court to decide the matter. 1991, c. 17, s. 17 (8).

No appeal
(9) There is no appeal from the court's decision. 1991, c. 17, s. 17 (9).

Arbitration may continue
(10) While an application is pending, the arbitral tribunal may continue the arbitration and make an award. 1991, c. 17, s. 17 (10).

Detention, preservation and inspection of property and documents

18. (1) On a party's request, an arbitral tribunal may make an order for the detention, preservation or inspection of property and documents that are the subject of the arbitration or as to which a question may arise in the arbitration, and may order a party to provide security in that connection. 1991, c. 17, s. 18 (1).

Enforcement by court

(2) The court may enforce the direction of an arbitral tribunal as if it were a similar direction made by the court in an action. 1991, c. 17, s. 18 (2).

Conduct of Arbitration

Equality and fairness

19. (1) In an arbitration, the parties shall be treated equally and fairly. 1991, c. 17, s. 19 (1).

Idem

(2) Each party shall be given an opportunity to present a case and to respond to the other parties' cases. 1991, c. 17, s. 19 (2).

Procedure

20. (1) The arbitral tribunal may determine the procedure to be followed in the arbitration, in accordance with this Act. 1991, c. 17, s. 20 (1).

Idem

(2) An arbitral tribunal that is composed of more than one arbitrator may delegate the determination of questions of procedure to the chair. 1991, c. 17, s. 20 (2).

Evidence

21. Sections 14, 15 and 16 (protection of witnesses, evidence at hearings, notice of facts and opinions) of the *Statutory Powers Procedure Act* apply to the arbitration, with necessary modifications. 1991, c. 17, s. 21.

Time and place of arbitration

22. (1) The arbitral tribunal shall determine the time, date and place of arbitration, taking into consideration the parties' convenience and the other circumstances of the case. 1991, c. 17, s. 22 (1).

Meetings for special purposes

(2) The arbitral tribunal may meet at any place it considers appropriate for consultation among its members, for hearing witnesses, experts or parties, or for inspecting property or documents. 1991, c. 17, s. 22 (2).

Commencement of arbitration

23. (1) An arbitration may be commenced in any way recognized by law, including the following:

1. A party to an arbitration agreement serves on the other parties notice to appoint or to participate in the appointment of an arbitrator under the agreement.
2. If the arbitration agreement gives a person who is not a party power to appoint an arbitrator, one party serves notice to exercise that power on the person and serves a copy of the notice on the other parties.

3. A party serves on the other parties a notice demanding arbitration under the agreement. 1991, c. 17, s. 23 (1).

Exercise of arbitral tribunal's powers

(2) The arbitral tribunal may exercise its powers when every member has accepted appointment. 1991, c. 17, s. 23 (2).

Matters referred to arbitration

24. A notice that commences an arbitration without identifying the dispute shall be deemed to refer to arbitration all disputes that the arbitration agreement entitles the party giving the notice to refer. 1991, c. 17, s. 24.

Procedural directions

25. (1) An arbitral tribunal may require that the parties submit their statements within a specified period of time. 1991, c. 17, s. 25 (1).

Contents of statements

(2) The parties' statements shall indicate the facts supporting their positions, the points at issue and the relief sought. 1991, c. 17, s. 25 (2).

Documents and other evidence
(3) The parties may submit with their statements the documents they consider relevant, or may refer to the documents or other evidence they intend to submit. 1991, c. 17, s. 25 (3).

Changes to statements
(4) The parties may amend or supplement their statements during the arbitration; however, the arbitral tribunal may disallow a change that is unduly delayed. 1991, c. 17, s. 25 (4).

Oral statements
(5) With the arbitral tribunal's permission, the parties may submit their statements orally. 1991, c. 17, s. 25 (5).

Directions of arbitral tribunal
(6) The parties and persons claiming through or under them shall, subject to any legal objection, comply with the arbitral tribunal's directions, including directions to,
(a) submit to examination on oath or affirmation with respect to the dispute;
(b) produce records and documents that are in their possession or power. 1991, c. 17, s. 25 (6).

Enforcement by court
(7) The court may enforce the direction of an arbitral tribunal as if it were a similar direction made by the court in an action. 1991, c. 17, s. 25 (7).

Hearings and written proceedings
26. (1) The arbitral tribunal may conduct the arbitration on the basis of documents or may hold hearings for the presentation of evidence and for oral argument; however, the tribunal shall hold a hearing if a party requests it. 1991, c. 17, s. 26 (1).

Notice
(2) The arbitral tribunal shall give the parties sufficient notice of hearings and of meetings of the tribunal for the purpose of inspection of property or documents. 1991, c. 17, s. 26 (2).

Communication to parties

(3) A party who submits a statement to the arbitral tribunal or supplies the tribunal with any other information shall also communicate it to the other parties. 1991, c. 17, s. 26 (3).

Idem

(4) The arbitral tribunal shall communicate to the parties any expert reports or other documents on which it may rely in making a decision. 1991, c. 17, s. 26 (4).

Party's failure to act

Failure to submit statement

27. (1) If the party who commenced the arbitration does not submit a statement within the period of time specified under subsection 25 (1), the arbitral tribunal may, unless the party offers a satisfactory explanation, make an award dismissing the claim. 1991, c. 17, s. 27 (1).

Idem

(2) If a party other than the one who commenced the arbitration does not submit a statement within the period of time specified under subsection 25 (1), the arbitral tribunal may, unless the party offers a satisfactory explanation, continue the arbitration, but shall not treat the failure to submit a statement as an admission of another party's allegations. 1991, c. 17, s. 27 (2).

Failure to appear or produce evidence

(3) If a party fails to appear at a hearing or to produce documentary evidence, the arbitral tribunal may, unless the party offers a satisfactory explanation, continue the arbitration and make an award on the evidence before it. 1991, c. 17, s. 27 (3).

Delay

(4) In the case of delay by the party who commenced the arbitration, the arbitral tribunal may make an award dismissing the claim or give directions for the speedy determination of the arbitration, and may impose conditions on its decision. 1991, c. 17, s. 27 (4).

Jointly commenced arbitration
(5) If the arbitration was commenced jointly by all the parties, subsections (2) and (3) apply, with necessary modifications, but subsections (1) and (4) do not. 1991, c. 17, s. 27 (5).

Counterclaim
(6) This section applies in respect of a counterclaim as if the party making it were the party who commenced the arbitration. 1991, c. 17, s. 27 (6).

Appointment of expert
28. (1) An arbitral tribunal may appoint an expert to report to it on specific issues. 1991, c. 17, s. 28 (1).

Information and documents
(2) The arbitral tribunal may require parties to give the expert any relevant information or to allow him or her to inspect property or documents. 1991, c. 17, s. 28 (2).

Hearing
(3) At the request of a party or of the arbitral tribunal, the expert shall, after making the report, participate in a hearing in which the parties may question the expert and present the testimony of another expert on the subject-matter of the report. 1991, c. 17, s. 28 (3).

Witnesses and taking of evidence
Notice to witness
29. (1) A party may serve a person with a notice, issued by the arbitral tribunal, requiring the person to attend and give evidence at the arbitration at the time and place named in the notice. 1991, c. 17, s. 29 (1).

Service of notice
(2) The notice has the same effect as a notice in a court proceeding requiring a witness to attend at a hearing or produce documents, and shall be served in the same way. 1991, c. 17, s. 29 (2).

Power of arbitral tribunal

(3) An arbitral tribunal has power to administer an oath or affirmation and power to require a witness to testify under oath or affirmation. 1991, c. 17, s. 29 (3).

Court orders and directions

(4) On the application of a party or of the arbitral tribunal, the court may make orders and give directions with respect to the taking of evidence for an arbitration as if it were a court proceeding. 1991, c. 17, s. 29 (4).

Restriction

30. No person shall be compelled to produce information, property or documents or to give evidence in an arbitration that the person could not be compelled to produce or give in a court proceeding. 1991, c. 17, s. 30.

Awards and Termination of Arbitration

Application of law and equity

31. An arbitral tribunal shall decide a dispute in accordance with law, including equity, and may order specific performance, injunctions and other equitable remedies. 1991, c. 17, s. 31.

Conflict of laws

32. (1) In deciding a dispute, an arbitral tribunal shall apply the rules of law designated by the parties or, if none are designated, the rules of law it considers appropriate in the circumstances. 1991, c. 17, s. 32 (1).

Designation by parties

(2) A designation by the parties of the law of a jurisdiction refers to the jurisdiction's substantive law and not to its conflict of laws rules, unless the parties expressly indicate that the designation includes them. 1991, c. 17, s. 32 (2).

Application of arbitration agreement, contract and usages of trade

33. The arbitral tribunal shall decide the dispute in accordance with the arbitration agreement and the contract, if any, under which the dispute arose, and may also take into account any applicable usages of trade. 1991, c. 17, s. 33.

Decision of arbitral tribunal
34. If an arbitral tribunal is composed of more than one member, a decision of a majority of the members is the arbitral tribunal's decision; however, if there is no majority decision or unanimous decision, the chair's decision governs. 1991, c. 17, s. 34.

Mediation and conciliation
35. The members of an arbitral tribunal shall not conduct any part of the arbitration as a mediation or conciliation process or other similar process that might compromise or appear to compromise the arbitral tribunal's ability to decide the dispute impartially. 1991, c. 17, s. 35.

Settlement
36. If the parties settle the dispute during arbitration, the arbitral tribunal shall terminate the arbitration and, if a party so requests, may record the settlement in the form of an award. 1991, c. 17, s. 36.

Binding nature of award
37. An award binds the parties, unless it is set aside or varied under section 45 or 46 (appeal, setting aside award). 1991, c. 17, s. 37.

Form of award
38. (1) An award shall be made in writing and, except in the case of an award made on consent, shall state the reasons on which it is based. 1991, c. 17, s. 38 (1).

Idem
(2) The award shall indicate the place where and the date on which it is made. 1991, c. 17, s. 38 (2).
Formalities of execution
(3) The award shall be dated and shall be signed by all the members of the arbitral tribunal, or by a majority of them if an explanation of the omission of the other signatures is included. 1991, c. 17, s. 38 (3).

Copies
(4) A copy of the award shall be delivered to each party. 1991, c. 17, s. 38 (4).

Extension of time limits
39. The court may extend the time within which the arbitral tribunal is required to make an award, even if the time has expired. 1991, c. 17, s. 39.

Explanation
40. (1) A party may, within thirty days after receiving an award, request that the arbitral tribunal explain any matter. 1991, c. 17, s. 40 (1).

Court order
(2) If the arbitral tribunal does not give an explanation within fifteen days after receiving the request, the court may, on the party's application, order it to do so. 1991, c. 17, s. 40 (2).

Interim awards
41. The arbitral tribunal may make one or more interim awards. 1991, c. 17, s. 41.

More than one final award
42. The arbitral tribunal may make more than one final award, disposing of one or more matters referred to arbitration in each award. 1991, c. 17, s. 42.

Termination of arbitration
43. (1) An arbitration is terminated when,
(a) the arbitral tribunal makes a final award in accordance with this Act, disposing of all matters referred to arbitration;
(b) the arbitral tribunal terminates the arbitration under subsection (2), (3), 27 (1) (claimant's failure to submit statement) or 27 (4) (delay); or
(c) an arbitrator's mandate is terminated, if the arbitration agreement provides that the arbitration shall be conducted only by that arbitrator. 1991, c. 17, s. 43 (1).

Order by arbitral tribunal
(2) An arbitral tribunal shall make an order terminating the arbitration if the claimant withdraws the claim, unless the respondent objects to the termination and the arbitral tribunal agrees that the respondent is entitled to obtain a final settlement of the dispute. 1991, c. 17, s. 43 (2).

Idem

(3) An arbitral tribunal shall make an order terminating the arbitration if,

(a) the parties agree that the arbitration should be terminated; or

(b) the arbitral tribunal finds that continuation of the arbitration has become unnecessary or impossible. 1991, c. 17, s. 43 (3).

Revival

(4) The arbitration may be revived for the purposes of section 44 (corrections) or subsection 45 (5) (appeal), 46 (7), 46 (8) (setting aside award) or 54 (3) (costs). 1991, c. 17, s. 43 (4).

Death

(5) A party's death terminates the arbitration only with respect to claims that are extinguished as a result of the death. 1991, c. 17, s. 43 (5).

Corrections and additional awards

Errors, injustices caused by oversights

44. (1) An arbitral tribunal may, on its own initiative within thirty days after making an award or at a party's request made within thirty days after receiving the award,

(a) correct typographical errors, errors of calculation and similar errors in the award; or

(b) amend the award so as to correct an injustice caused by an oversight on the part of the arbitral tribunal. 1991, c. 17, s. 44 (1).

Additional awards

(2) The arbitral tribunal may, on its own initiative at any time or at a party's request made within thirty days after receiving the award, make an additional award to deal with a claim that was presented in the arbitration but omitted from the earlier award. 1991, c. 17, s. 44 (2).

No hearing necessary

(3) The arbitral tribunal need not hold a hearing or meeting before rejecting a request made under this section. 1991, c. 17, s. 44 (3).

Remedies

Appeals

Appeal on question of law

45. (1) If the arbitration agreement does not deal with appeals on questions of law, a party may appeal an award to the court on a question of law with leave, which the court shall grant only if it is satisfied that,

(a) the importance to the parties of the matters at stake in the arbitration justifies an appeal; and

(b) determination of the question of law at issue will significantly affect the rights of the parties. 1991, c. 17, s. 45 (1).

Idem

(2) If the arbitration agreement so provides, a party may appeal an award to the court on a question of law. 1991, c. 17, s. 45 (2).

Appeal on question of fact or mixed fact and law

(3) If the arbitration agreement so provides, a party may appeal an award to the court on a question of fact or on a question of mixed fact and law. 1991, c. 17, s. 45 (3).

Powers of court

(4) The court may require the arbitral tribunal to explain any matter. 1991, c. 17, s. 45 (4).

Idem

(5) The court may confirm, vary or set aside the award or may remit the award to the arbitral tribunal with the court's opinion on the question of law, in the case of an appeal on a question of law, and give directions about the conduct of the arbitration. 1991, c. 17, s. 45 (5).

Setting aside award

46. (1) On a party's application, the court may set aside an award on any of the following grounds:

1. A party entered into the arbitration agreement while under a legal incapacity.
2. The arbitration agreement is invalid or has ceased to exist.
3. The award deals with a dispute that the arbitration agreement does not cover or contains a decision on a matter that is beyond the scope of the agreement.

4. The composition of the tribunal was not in accordance with the arbitration agreement or, if the agreement did not deal with that matter, was not in accordance with this Act.
5. The subject-matter of the dispute is not capable of being the subject of arbitration under Ontario law.
6. The applicant was not treated equally and fairly, was not given an opportunity to present a case or to respond to another party's case, or was not given proper notice of the arbitration or of the appointment of an arbitrator.
7. The procedures followed in the arbitration did not comply with this Act.
8. An arbitrator has committed a corrupt or fraudulent act or there is a reasonable apprehension of bias.
9. The award was obtained by fraud. 1991, c. 17, s. 46 (1).

Severable parts of award

(2) If paragraph 3 of subsection (1) applies and it is reasonable to separate the decisions on matters covered by the arbitration agreement from the impugned ones, the court shall set aside the impugned decisions and allow the others to stand. 1991, c. 17, s. 46 (2).

Restriction

(3) The court shall not set aside an award on grounds referred to in paragraph 3 of subsection (1) if the party has agreed to the inclusion of the dispute or matter, waived the right to object to its inclusion or agreed that the arbitral tribunal has power to decide what disputes have been referred to it. 1991, c. 17, s. 46 (3).

Idem

(4) The court shall not set aside an award on grounds referred to in paragraph 8 of subsection (1) if the party had an opportunity to challenge the arbitrator on those grounds under section 13 before the award was made and did not do so, or if those grounds were the subject of an unsuccessful challenge. 1991, c. 17, s. 46 (4).

Deemed waiver

(5) The court shall not set aside an award on a ground to which the applicant is deemed under section 4 to have waived the right to object. 1991, c. 17, s. 46 (5).

Exception

(6) If the ground alleged for setting aside the award could have been raised as an objection to the arbitral tribunal's jurisdiction to conduct the arbitration or as an objection that the arbitral tribunal was exceeding its authority, the court may set the award aside on that ground if it considers the applicant's failure to make an objection in accordance with section 17 justified. 1991, c. 17, s. 46 (6).

Connected matters

(7) When the court sets aside an award, it may remove the arbitral tribunal or an arbitrator and may give directions about the conduct of the arbitration. 1991, c. 17, s. 46 (7).

Court may remit award to arbitral tribunal

(8) Instead of setting aside an award, the court may remit it to the arbitral tribunal and give directions about the conduct of the arbitration. 1991, c. 17, s. 46 (8).

Time limit

47. (1) An appeal of an award or an application to set aside an award shall be commenced within thirty days after the appellant or applicant receives the award, correction, explanation, change or statement of reasons on which the appeal or application is based. 1991, c. 17, s. 47 (1).

Exception

(2) Subsection (1) does not apply if the appellant or applicant alleges corruption or fraud. 1991, c. 17, s. 47 (2).

Declaration of invalidity of arbitration

48. (1) At any stage during or after an arbitration, on the application of a party who has not participated in the arbitration, the court may grant a declaration that the arbitration is invalid because,

(a) a party entered into the arbitration agreement while under a legal incapacity;

(b) the arbitration agreement is invalid or has ceased to exist;

(c) the subject-matter of the dispute is not capable of being the subject of arbitration under Ontario law; or

(d) the arbitration agreement does not apply to the dispute. 1991, c. 17, s. 48 (1).

Injunction
(2) When the court grants the declaration, it may also grant an injunction against the commencement or continuation of the arbitration. 1991, c. 17, s. 48 (2).

Further appeal
49. An appeal from the court's decision in an appeal of an award, an application to set aside an award or an application for a declaration of invalidity may be made to the Court of Appeal, with leave of that court. 1991, c. 17, s. 49.

Enforcement of award
Application
50. (1) A person who is entitled to enforcement of an award made in Ontario or elsewhere in Canada may make an application to the court to that effect. 1991, c. 17, s. 50 (1).

Formalities
(2) The application shall be made on notice to the person against whom enforcement is sought, in accordance with the rules of court, and shall be supported by the original award or a certified copy. 1991, c. 17, s. 50 (2).

Duty of court, award made in Ontario
(3) The court shall give a judgment enforcing an award made in Ontario unless,
(a) the thirty-day period for commencing an appeal or an application to set the award aside has not yet elapsed;
(b) there is a pending appeal, application to set the award aside or application for a declaration of invalidity; or
(c) the award has been set aside or the arbitration is the subject of a declaration of invalidity. 1991, c. 17, s. 50 (3).

Duty of court, award made elsewhere in Canada
(4) The court shall give a judgment enforcing an award made elsewhere in Canada unless,

(a) the period for commencing an appeal or an application to set the award aside provided by the laws of the province or territory where the award was made has not yet elapsed;
(b) there is a pending appeal, application to set the award aside or application for a declaration of invalidity in the province or territory where the award was made;
(c) the award has been set aside in the province or territory where it was made or the arbitration is the subject of a declaration of invalidity granted there; or
(d) the subject-matter of the award is not capable of being the subject of arbitration under Ontario law. 1991, c. 17, s. 50 (4).

Pending proceeding
(5) If the period for commencing an appeal, application to set the award aside or application for a declaration of invalidity has not yet elapsed, or if such a proceeding is pending, the court may,
(a) enforce the award; or
(b) order, on such conditions as are just, that enforcement of the award is stayed until the period has elapsed without such a proceeding being commenced, or until the pending proceeding is finally disposed of. 1991, c. 17, s. 50 (5).

Speedy disposition of pending proceeding
(6) If the court stays the enforcement of an award made in Ontario until a pending proceeding is finally disposed of, it may give directions for the speedy disposition of the proceeding. 1991, c. 17, s. 50 (6).

Unusual remedies
(7) If the award gives a remedy that the court does not have jurisdiction to grant or would not grant in a proceeding based on similar circumstances, the court may,
(a) grant a different remedy requested by the applicant; or
(b) in the case of an award made in Ontario, remit it to the arbitral tribunal with the court's opinion, in which case the arbitral tribunal may award a different remedy. 1991, c. 17, s. 50 (7).

Powers of court
(8) The court has the same powers with respect to the enforcement of awards as with respect to the enforcement of its own judgments. 1991, c. 17, s. 50 (8).

Appendix B

Dispute Resolution in Family Law:
Protecting Choice, Promoting Inclusion
December 2004
Report prepared by Marion Boyd (Former Attorney General of the Canadian Province of Ontario)

Executive Summary

On June 25, 2004, the Attorney General, the Honourable Michael Bryant, and the Minister Responsible for Women's Issues, the Honourable Sandra Pupatello asked Marion Boyd to conduct a review of the use of arbitration in family and inheritances cases and to examine the impact that the use of arbitration has on vulnerable people, including women, persons with disabilities and elderly persons.

The Review began as a result of public concern expressed in the media and through groups and individuals about the use of Muslim personal law (often referred to as Sharia) in arbitrations. There was significant confusion in the media and public consciousness about a plan by the Islamic Institute of Civil Justice to establish a "Sharia Court" in Ontario. These public concerns led to a need to address the issue of the use of arbitration in family and inheritance cases in a comprehensive and constructive way. Ms. Boyd, a former Attorney General, and former Minister Responsible for Women's Issues, was asked to gather and articulate the concerns of Ontarians, and provide recommendations to the government. This report is the result of the Review process, and contains Ms. Boyd's conclusions and recommendations.

There was a high level of consensus about the remedies that respondents proposed to safeguard Ontario's arbitration process and permit the continued use of alternatives to court for family law and inheritance cases. In this context, the report concludes that tolerance and accommodation of minority groups who seek to engage in alternative dispute resolution must be balanced against a firm commitment to individual autonomy. It is important to seek solutions that respect not only the rights of minority groups within Ontario, but also help individuals within that minority exercise their individual rights with ease.

Arbitration

Arbitration is a dispute resolution method in which people participate only by choice. The court system is the only mandatory dispute resolution process in which people can be compelled to participate without their agreement. The Review heard that arbitrated decisions may be more acceptable to the parties, and more reflective of some elements of the parties' shared values. Religious arbitration can allow the people in dispute to select a shared set of values and rules that may be different than Ontario law. Use of the *Arbitration Act* by minority communities is a way of engaging with the broader community by formalizing a method of decision-making which currently occurs in an informal manner.

Family Law

Family law is an area of shared jurisdiction between the federal and provincial governments. Most family law disputes are resolved without court action, but increasingly alternative dispute resolution is used. Arbitration can only resolve disputes that the parties could agree about themselves; it cannot change a person's status by granting a divorce, or by concluding that they are a parent. Domestic contracts, such as separation agreements, are a common means of resolving family law disputes and the law has some built-in safeguards for these types of contracts. The Review heard concerns about polygamy and child abduction, but these issues are not affected by arbitration. Criminal law and child welfare law protect children from abuse, and people have a duty to report children in need of protection.

The Importance of the *Charter*

Ontarians believe deeply in the *Canadian Charter of Rights and Freedoms'* aims of justice, fairness and equality. They do not see multiculturalism to be an unlimited concept, but rather one that must be balanced against individual freedoms. All participants in the Review articulated a desire to protect and enhance access to justice, but took very different perspectives on what this would look like. All participants in the Review had a high level of interest in the *Charter,* but the application of many of the provisions of the *Charter* in the context of arbitration is not clear. Nonetheless, the Review did not conclude that the *Charter* prohibits the use of arbitration for resolving disputes about family law and inheritance.

Violence Against Women

Exposing and ending violence against women is a pressing public policy concern in most parts of the world. This concern is expressed and supported by the *United Nations Declaration on the Elimination of Violence Against Women*. Addressing domestic violence is impossible when attitudes and beliefs that condone violence persist. Alternative dispute resolution may provide a venue for continued abuse after the breakdown of a relationship, and therefore safeguards must be in place. Many respondents to the Review recognized the need for the Muslim community to counter traditional attitudes that may condone violence against women.

Personal Law

Personal law is the law that pertains to an individual's status and membership in a community or family group. Family and inheritance matters fall within a category of personal law that developed primarily from religious sources. Personal law has been used throughout history to allow groups to maintain their cultural identity, by allowing them to continue to control their definitions of family and community. In parts of Europe, the practice of applying the personal law of an individual's country of origin continues until today. For example, the citizenship laws of France and Germany mean that people may not be subject to the laws of their country of residence, but rather their country of origin.

Themes in the Submissions

There were a number of different themes expressed by those consulted, which were often contradictory. Some thought that arbitration should not be permitted in family law and inheritance cases because it would offend the *Charter* and perpetuate an imbalance of power in cases of abuse. Others argued that arbitration should be permitted because it is less costly and more effective. Still others submitted that religiously-based arbitration must be permitted because it is protected by freedom of religion, and is integral to a faithful person's life.

In fact, religious arbitration is already being conducted by several different faiths. Although some participants in the Review fear that the use of arbitration is the beginning of a process whose end goal is a separate political identity for Muslims in Canada, that has not been the experience of other groups who use arbitration. As well, Canada's First Nations people are the only minority group that has a defined right to negotiate with the Canadian state about political autonomy.

Canada is a multicultural society and the fundamental tension that must be addressed is between respect for the minority group and protection of a person's individual rights within that minority. The Review found that secular state laws do not treat everyone equally because people's individual backgrounds lead to differences in the impact of these laws. If the state allows cultural groups complete freedom to define family and inheritance matters those groups may trample on the rights of individuals within the group and may discriminate in ways that are unacceptable to Canadian society. The Review concluded that cultural groups should not be permitted to stop people from having access to laws and processes that are available to all.

Summary of Recommendations

1. Arbitration should continue to be an alternative dispute resolution option that is available in family and inheritance law cases, subject to the further recommendations of this Review.

2. The *Arbitration Act* should continue to allow disputes to be arbitrated using religious law, if the safeguards currently prescribed and recommended by this Review are observed.

Legislative

3. Section 51 of the *Family Law Act* should be amended to add mediation agreements and arbitration agreements to the definition of "domestic contracts" to bring these agreements into the general protections of Part IV of the Act. Therefore these agreements would be required to be in writing, signed by the parties and witnessed.

4. When Part IV of the *Family Law Act* applies, a mediation agreement or arbitration agreement should be able to be set aside on the same grounds as other domestic contracts.

5. Part IV of the *Family Law Act* should be amended so that if a co-habitation agreement or marriage contract contains an arbitration agreement, that arbitration agreement is not binding unless it is reconfirmed in writing at the time of the dispute and before the arbitration occurs.

6. The reconfirmation in writing should not be required for an arbitration conducted:

(a) under a separation agreement;
(b) as a consequence of an award made in an arbitration that was itself agreed to contemporaneously; or
(c) as a consequence of a judgment of a court.

7. Section 55 (2) of the *Family Law Act* should be amended to require prior court approval of a domestic contract entered into by a minor in Ontario.

8. Section 33 (4) of Part III of the *Family Law Ac*t, permitting the Court to set aside a domestic contract or paternity agreement for provision of support, should be amended to permit a court to set aside an arbitral award on the same grounds (unconscionability, person owed support is receiving social assistance, or the support is in arrears).

9. The *Arbitration Act* should be amended to permit a court to set aside an arbitral award in a family or inheritance matter if:

(a) the award does not reflect the best interests of any children affected by it;
(b) a party to it did not have or waive independent legal advice;
(c) the parties do not have a copy of the arbitration agreement, and a written decision including reasons; or
(d) applicable, a party did not receive a statement of principles of faith-based arbitration.

10. The *Arbitration Act* or the *Family Law Act* should be amended to provide regulation-making powers for family law and inheritance arbitrations and to require the use of regulated forms and procedures.

11. The *Child and Family Services Act* s. 72 (5) should be amended to explicitly include mediators and arbitrators in the class of professionals who have an enforceable duty to report a child in need of protection.

Regulatory

12. Regulations in the *Arbitration Act* or the *Family Law Act* should require that arbitration agreements of family law and inheritance cases must be in writing and must set out:

•a detailed list of issues that are submitted to arbitration;
•whether the arbitration is binding or advisory;
•the form of law, if not Ontario law, which will be used to decide the dispute, and in the case of religious law, which form of the religious law;
•if the arbitration is under religious law, an acknowledgement that the party has received and reviewed the statement of principles of faith-based arbitration prior to signing the agreement;
•explicit details of any waiver of any rights or remedies under the *Arbitration Act*;
•an explicit statement that judicial remedies under s. 46 and the right to fair and equal treatment under s. 19 of the *Arbitration Act* cannot be waived;
•an explicit statement recognizing that judicial oversight of children's issues cannot be waived and that s. 33 (4) of the *Family Law Act* continues to apply; and
•an explicit statement that s. 56 of the *Family Law Act* applies to the agreement and cannot be waived and therefore a party can apply to set the agreement aside for additional reasons including if it is not in the best interests of any children affected by the agreement, there was not full and frank financial disclosure, or a party did not understand the nature or consequences of the agreement.

13. Regulations in the *Arbitration Act* or the *Family Law Act* should require arbitration agreements in family law and inheritance cases to contain either a certificate of independent legal advice or an explicit waiver of independent legal advice.

14. Regulations in the *Arbitration Act* or the *Family Law Act* should require mediators and arbitrators in family law and inheritance cases to

be members of voluntary professional organizations, or fall into an excluded [6] class defined by the regulation, in order to have their decisions enforced by Ontario courts.

15. Regulations under the *Arbitration Act* should define the concept of a fair and equal process in the context of family law or inheritance arbitrations.

16. Regulations in the *Arbitration Act* or the *Family Law Act* should require that arbitrators who apply religious law in family law and inheritance arbitrations develop a statement of principles of faith-based arbitration that explains the parties' rights and obligations and available processes under the particular form of religious law.

17. Regulations in the *Arbitration Act* or the *Family Law Act* should require religiously-based arbitrators to distribute their statement of principles of faith-based arbitrations to all prospective clients.

18. Regulations in the *Arbitration Act* or the *Family Law Act* should require mediators and arbitrators in family law and inheritance cases to screen the parties separately about issues of power imbalance and domestic violence, prior to entering into an arbitration agreement, using a standardized screening process.

19. Regulations under the *Arbitration Act* or the *Family Law Act* should require mediators and arbitrators in family law and inheritance cases to certify that they have screened the parties separately for domestic violence, that they have reviewed the certificates of Independent Legal Advice or the waiver of Independent Legal Advice, and are satisfied that each party is entering into the arbitration voluntarily and with knowledge of the nature and consequences of the arbitration agreement.

20. Regulations under the *Arbitration Act* or the *Family Law Act* should state that if the records required by Recommendations 37, 38 and 39 are not maintained, a party can apply to have an arbitral award set aside.
Independent Legal Advice 21. The certificate of Independent Legal Advice in family law and inheritance cases should state that the party has received advice about the Ontario and Canadian law applicable to his or her fact situation, the law of arbitration, and the remedies available to both parties under Ontario family and arbitration law.

22. Arbitration services which conduct family law and inheritance arbitrations should distribute the statement of principles of faith-based arbitrations required under Recommendations 16 and 17 to potential clients, in advance of the clients seeing a lawyer.

23. If religious law is chosen under the arbitration agreement in a family law or inheritance case, the Independent Legal Advice certificate should explicitly state that the lawyer reviewed the statement of principles of faith-based arbitration and the lawyer is satisfied that the person has sufficient information to understand the nature and consequences of choosing the religious law.

24. Waivers of Independent Legal Advice in family law and inheritance cases should state that the party has waived the right to receive advice about Canadian and Ontario family law and Ontario arbitration law, and if religious law is chosen should state that the party has received and reviewed the statement of principles of faith-based arbitration required by Recommendations 16 and 17.

Public Legal Education

25. The Government of Ontario should develop, in collaboration with community organizations and experts, a series of public education initiatives, aimed at creating awareness of the legal system, alternative dispute resolution options, and family law provisions.

26. The initiatives in Recommendation 25 should be linguistically and culturally designed to suit the diverse needs of different communities, as well as any communications challenges faced by members of the community (e.g. blindness, deafness, etc.).

27. Any public education campaign that is developed should include, but not limit itself to, information on the following topics:

- General rights and obligations under the law;
- Family law issues;
- Alternative forms of dispute resolution;
- *Arbitration Act;*
- Immigration law issues; and

•Community supports.

28. Public legal information programs funded by the government of Ontario should include an overview of the options for resolving a family law dispute, including the arbitration process.

29. Public legal information programs in family law funded by the government of Ontario should be available to all community members who wish to attend, whether or not they have a matter before the court.

30. Family Law Information Centres should provide information that has been developed by and for specific ethno-cultural communities and in community languages about their rights and responsibilities under Ontario and Canadian law.

Training and Education for Professionals

31. The Government of Ontario should work together with professional bodies to develop a standardized screening process for domestic violence for use in family law and inheritance mediations and arbitrations.

32. The Ministry of the Attorney General, the Law Society of Upper Canada and LawPro should strike a joint task force to examine the use of arbitration in family law and inheritance cases, to develop and deliver continuing education to lawyers about arbitration and Independent Legal Advice, and to examine the insurance and public compensation issues as they impact on the public interest.

33. The Government of Ontario should work with voluntary professional associations for mediators and arbitrators to provide training on issues of power imbalance in family law and inheritance cases, use of the prescribed screening process from Recommendation 18, and the process for an arbitrator to certify the material for a family law or inheritance case as required by Recommendation 19.

34. The guidelines of voluntary professional associations for training, conduct and competence of mediators and arbitrators should clearly explain their professional duty to report children in need of protection.

35. Voluntary professional associations for mediators and arbitrators should require that in family law and inheritance cases, if mediators practise arbitration during mediation sessions, the agreement to arbitrate must precede the commencement of the mediation, and all the obligations of arbitrators under Recommendations 16, 17, 18 and 19 must be met before the commencement of any arbitration.

Oversight and Evaluation of Arbitrations

36. The Ministry of the Attorney General should work with professional organizations to review existing codes of professional conduct and assess whether they apply when a member of a profession conducts an arbitration or mediation.

37. Decisions of arbitrators in family law and inheritance cases should be delivered to the parties in writing and include a copy of the arbitration agreement, and any attachments required by the regulations. Decisions should include written reasons.

38. The arbitrator in family law and inheritance cases should maintain copies of the decision for a period of at least 10 years.

39. Arbitrators should be required to keep a record of each arbitration in family law and inheritance cases including the names of the parties and their representatives (if any), the arbitration agreement, the certificates or waivers of Independent Legal Advice, any documents filed by the parties, a summary of the facts of the case and the written decision. Copies of these files should be made available to the parties upon request. If an arbitrator does not maintain these files, or make the file available when requested, the arbitral decision may be set aside.

40. Arbitrators of family and inheritance matters should be required to report annually to the Ministry of the Attorney General, the following aggregated and non-identifying information:

- Number of arbitrations conducted;
- Number of appeals or motions to set aside and the outcome, if known (e.g. pending, award set aside, court refers back to arbitrator, etc.); and

•Any complaints or disciplinary actions they are aware of that have been taken against them during that year by their professional body or the courts.

41. Arbitrators in family law and inheritance cases should be required to provide the Government of Ontario with summaries of each decision, free of identifying information, and the Government should make these summaries available upon request for research, evaluation and consumer protection purposes. If in the future arbitrators become a self-regulating profession, the inventory of summaries of decisions should be transferred to the regulatory body for that profession.

42. Voluntary registration organizations should consider failure to make decisions available and file decisions in accordance with Recommendations 40 and 41 grounds for the deregistration of the arbitrator.

Community Development

43. The Government of Ontario should encourage and fund community organizations who run arbitration services to develop information materials about rights and obligations under religious law.

44. The Government of Ontario should encourage and fund community organizations to work with experienced public legal education providers and the legal community to research and develop effective public information materials which explain rights under Ontario and Canadian law in a way that is likely to be comprehensible to people of diverse backgrounds and culture.

Further Policy Development

45. The Ministry of the Attorney General should set a long-term goal of professional self-regulation of mediators and arbitrators who deal with family law and inheritance cases. The Ministry should work with professional organizations including the Law Society of Upper Canada and voluntary mediation and arbitration organizations to develop a consultation process which will lead to guidelines for conduct and competency for these professionals.

46. The Ministry of the Attorney General should conduct further policy analysis of the legality and desirability of providing a higher level of court oversight to settlements of family and inheritance cases based on religious principles than is available to non-religiously based settlements under Part IV of the *Family Law Act* in addition to the several additional grounds set out in these recommendations under which arbitral awards may be challenged.

Bibliography

Abdal-Haqq, Irshad. "Islamic Law: An Overview of Its Origins and Elements." *Journal of Islamic Law and Culture* 7 (2002): 27-49.

Abdul-Rauf, Muhammad. "The Future of the Islamic Tradition in North America." In *The Muslim Community of North America*. Edited by Earle Waugh, Baha Abu-Laban and Regula B. Qureshi. Edmonton: University of Alberta Press, 1983.

Abedin, Syed Z. and Saleha M. Abedin. "Muslim Minorities in Non-Muslim Societies." *The Oxford Encyclopedia of the Modern Islamic World*. Edited by John Esposito. Oxford: Oxford University Press, 1994: 112-117.

Abou El Fadl, Khaled. *The Authoritative and the Authoritarian in Islamic Discourses: a ContemporaryCase Study*. Austin, TX: Dar Taiba, 1997.

_____. "Striking a Balance: Islamic Legal Discourse on Muslim Minorities," in *Muslims on the Americanization Path?* Edited by Yvonne Haddad and John Esposito. Oxford: Oxford Press, 2000.

_____. "Constitutionalism, Human Rights and the Rule of Law in Iraq." A statement before the United States Senate Committee on the Judiciary, June 25, 2003.

Abraham, Nabeel. "Arab Detroit's American Mosque." In *Arab Detroit: From Margin To Mainstream*. Edited by Nabeel Abraham. Detroit: Wayne State Univ. Press, 2000.

Abramson, Jeffrey. *Minerva's Owl: The Tradition of Western Political Thought*. Cambridge, Mass.: Harvard Univ. Press, 2009.

Adelson, Roger. *London and the Invention of the Middle East: Money, Power, and War, 1902-1922*. New Haven: Yale University Press, 1995.

Ahmad, Akbar. *Postmodernism and Islam: Predicament and Promise*. London: Routledge, 1992.

Ahmed, Akbar and Hastings Donnan, eds. *Islam, Globalization and Postmodernity*. London: Routledge Press, 1994.

Ahmed, Imad-ad-Dean. "Reconciling Secular Government with Islamic Law." A Paper for the 6th Annual Conference of the Center for the Study of Islam and Democracy: Democracy and Development—Challenges for the Islamic World, April 22-23, 2005, Washington D.C. http://www.minaret.org.

Ahmed, Parvez. "American Muslims: Integration and Disenfranchisement." In *Changing Identities--Evolving Values Is There Still a Transatlantic Community?* Esther Brimmer, ed. Washington D.C.: Brookings Press, 2006.

Ainain, Badran Abdul. *Huquq ul Awlad-fish-Shariat-il-Islamiyya wal Wanoon.* Alexandria, 1981.

Al-Alwani, Taha Jabir. "The Crisis in Fiqh and the Methodology of Ijtihad." 8 *American Journal of Islamic Social Science* 2 (1991): 317-337.

_____. "Fiqh of Minorities I." *Milli Gazette* 5, no. 9 (May 1, 2004). http://www.milligazette.com/Archives/2004/01-15May04-Print-Edition/0105200444.htm.

_____. Al-Alwani blog, President of the Graduate School of Islamic and Social Sciences, on "Problems facing Muslim communities in the West," posted April 10, 2005, http://www.islamonline.net/ livedialogue/english/browse. asp?hGuestID=9Vgi9m.

_____. *Usul al Fiqh al Islami.* http://www.witness-pioneer.org/vil/Books/TA_uaf (Sept. 18, 2007).

Al-Azami, M. Mustafa. *On Schacht's Origins of Muhammadan Jurisprudence.* Cambridge: The Islamic Texts Society, 1996.

Al-Hibri, Azizah. "Muslim Marriage Contracts in American Courts." A speech to the Minaret of Freedom Institute banquet, Bethesda, Maryland (May 20, 2000).

Al-Qaradawi, Yusef. *Priorities of the Islamic Movement in the Coming Age.* http://www.witness-pioneer.org/vil/books/Q_Priorities.

An-Na'im, Abdullahi Ahmed. "The Foundations of Law: Globalization And Jurisprudence: An Islamic Law Perspective." *Emory Law Journal* 54 (2005): 25-49.

_____. "Shari'a and Basic Human Rights." In *Liberal Islam.* Edited by Charles Kurzman. Oxford: Oxford University Press, 1998.

Anderson, J.N.D. *Islamic Law in the Modern World.* New York: New York University Press, 1959.

Anderson, Norman. *Law Reform in the Muslim Worl*d. London: The Athlone Press, 1976.

Andrews, Danielle. "Non-Muslim Mothers v. Egyptian Muslim Fathers: The Conflict between Religion and Law in International Child Custody Disputes and Abductions." *Suffolk Transnat't Law Review* 23 (Summer 2000): 595-628.

Antoun, Richard T. "The Islamic Court, the Islamic Judge, and the Accomodation of Tradition," *International Journal of Middle East Studies* 12 (1980): 455-67.

Asadulla, Abubakr. *Islam vs. West: Fact or Fiction?* Bloomberg, Ind.: iUniverse Pub., 2009.

Asani, Ali. "On Pluralism, Intolerance and the Qur'an." *American Scholar* 71, no. 1 (Winter 2002): 52-60.

Ashcroft, Bill and Pal Ahluwaila. *Edward Said: The Paradox of Identity*. London: Routledge, 1999.

Aslan, Reza. *How to Win a Cosmic War: God, Globalization and the End of the War on Terror*. New York: Random House, 2009.

Aswad, Barbara. "Arab Muslim Families in the United States." In *Middle Eastern Diaspora Communities in America*. Edited by Mehdi Bozorgmehr. New York: New York University Press, 1996.

Athar, Shahid. *Reflections of an American Muslim*. Chicago: Kazi Publications, 1994.

Bagby, Ihsan, Paul Perl, and Bryan T. Froehle. "The Mosque in America: A National Portrait." *Report of the Mosque Study Project*. Council of American-Islamic Relations, April, 2001.

Bannerman, Patrick. *Islam in Perspective: A Guide to Islamic Society, Politics, and Law*. London: Routledge for the Royal Institute of International Affairs, 1988.

Bassiouni, M. Cherif and Gamal M. Badr. "The Shari'ah: Sources, Interpretation, And Rule-Making." *UCLA Journal Islamic & Near Eastern Law* 1 (2002): 135-162.

Beekum, Rafik Issa. *Islamic Business Ethics*. Herndon, VA: International Institute of Islamic Thought, 1997.

Bell, Richard. *The Origin of Islam in its Christian Environment*. London: Routledge, 1968.

Benda-Beckmann, Franz von, Keebet von Benda-Beckmann, and Anne Griffiths. *The Power of Law in a Transnational World*. London: Berghahn Books, 2009.

Blenkhorn, Lindsey. "Islamic Marriage Contracts in American Courts: Interpreting *Mahr* Agreements as Prenuptials and Their Effect on Muslim Women." *Southern California Law Review* 76, no. 1 (Nov. 2002): 189-226.

Bonney, Richard. *Jihad: From Qur'an to bin Laden*. London: Palgrave Macmillan, 2004.

Bostom, Andrew G. *The Legacy of Jihad: Islamic Holy War and the Fate of Non-Muslims*. Amherst, N.Y.: Prometheus Books, 2005.

Bourdieu, Pierre. "The Force of Law: Toward a Sociology of the Juridical Field." *Hastings Law Journal* 38 (1987): 805-829.

Bowen, James R. Can Islam be French? Pluralism and Pragmatism in a Secularist State. Princeton: Princeton Univ. Press, 2009.

Bowker, John. *Voices of Islam.* Oxford: OneWorld Publications, 1995.

Brachear, Manya. "Torn between Cross and Crescent." *Beliefnet.com* (Feb., 14, 2003) http://www.beliefnet.com/story/119/story_11987.html (November 12, 2007), re-printed with permission from *The Dallas Morning News.*

Brockopp, J.E. *Early Maliki Law: Ibn 'Abd al-Hakam and his major Compendium of Jurisprudence.* Leiden: Brill, 2000.

Brown, Daniel. *A New Introduction to Islam.* West Sussex, England: Wiley-Blackwell, Pub., 2009.

Bulliet, Richard. *Islam: The View from the Edge.* New York: Columbia University Press, 1994.

Burton, John. *Introduction to the Hadith.* Edinburgh: Edinburgh University Press, 1994.

Calder, Norman. "Accomodation and Revolution in Imami Shi`i Jurisprudence: Khumayni and the Classical Tradition," *Middle Eastern Studies* 18 (1982): 3-20.

Cardin, Lara. "The Hague Convention on the Civil Aspects of International Child Abduction as Applied to Non-Signatory Nations: Getting to Square One." *Houston Journal Int'l Law* 20 (1997): 141-182.

Cheragh Ali, Moulavi. *A Critical Exposition of the Popular Jihad: Showing that all the Wars of Mohammad were Defensive, and the Aggressive War, or Compulsory Conversion, is not allowed in the Koran.* Calcutta, India, 1885; reprinted Karachi, Pakistan, 1977.

Cook, David. *Understanding Jihad.* Berkeley: University of California Press, 2005.

Cooper, John, Ronald L. Nettler and Muhammad Mahmoud, editors. *Islam and Modernity : Muslim Intellectuals Respond.* London : I. B. Tauris, 2000

Coulson, Noel J. *Conflicts and Tensions in Islamic Jurisprudence.* Chicago: University of Chicago Press, 1964.

______. *A History of Islamic Law.* Edinburgh: Edinburgh University Press, 1964.

Christelow, Allan. "Islamic Law and Judicial Practice in Nigeria: An Historical Perspective," *Journal of Muslim Minority Affairs* 22, no. 1 (2002): 185-204.

Crone, Patricia. *Roman, Provincial and Islamic Law: The Origins of the Islamic Patronate*. Cambridge: Cambridge University Press, 1987.

Daigle, Dorothy C. "Due Process Rights of Parents and Children in International Child Abductions: An Examination of the Hague Convention and Its Exceptions." *Vanderbilt Journal of Transnat'l Law* 26 (1993): 865-893.

Davies, Merryl Wyn. "Wilful Imaginings: Merryl Wyn Davies Shows how Orientalism Feeds both Islamophobia and Muslim Fundamentalism." *New Internationalist*, no. 345 (May 12, 2002): 22-24.

Dien, Mawil Izzi. *Islamic Law: From Historical Foundations to Contemporary Practice*. Edinburgh: Edinburgh University Press, 2004.

DeLorenzo, Yusuf Talal. "The Fiqh Councilor in North America." In *Muslims on the Americanization Path?* Edited by Yvonne Yazbeck Haddad and John Esposito. Atlanta: Scholars Press, 1998.

_____. "Fiqh and the Fiqh Council of North America." http://www.islamicity.com/politics/SHARIAH.HTM#S2 (Accessed July 24, 2007).

Doi, A. Rahman I. *Non-Muslims under Shari'ah*. Lahore: Kazi Publications, 1981.

Donaldson, William J. *Sharecropping in the Yemen: A Study of Islamic Theory, Custom and Pragmatism*. Leiden: Brill, 2000.

Du Pasquier, Roger. *Unveiling Islam*. Cambridge: Islamic Texts Society, 1992.

El Alami, Dawoud S. *The Marriage Contract in Islamic Law in the Shari`ah and Personal Status Laws of Egypt and Morocco*. London: Graham and Trotman, 1992.

El Alami, Dawoud S. and Doreen Hinchcliffe. *Islamic Marriage and Divorce Laws of the Arab World*. London: Kluwer Law International, 1996.

Elkholy, Abdo. *The Arab Muslims in the United States*. New Haven: College and University Press, 1966.

Emon, Anver. "Toward a Natural Law Theory in Islamic Law: Muslim Juristic Debates on Reason as a Source of Obligation." *UCLA Journal of Islamic and Near Eastern Law* 3, no. 1 (2003-2004).

Esposito, John L. and Azzam Tamimi, eds. *Islam and Secularism in the Middle East*. New York: New York University Press, 2000.

Esack, Farid. *Qur'an. Liberation and Pluralis: An Islamic Perspective of Interreligious Solidarity against Oppression*. Oxford: OneWorld 1997.

Fahmy, Khaled. "The Anatomy of Justice: Forensic Medicine and Criminal Law in Nineteenth-Century Egypt," *Islamic Law and Society* 6, no. 2 (June, 1999): 224-271.

Fareed, Muneer Goolam. *Legal Reform in the Muslim World: the Anatomy of a Scholarly Dispute in the 19 th and 20 th Centuries on the Usage of Ijtihad as a Legal Tool.* San Francisco: Austin and Winfield, 1996.

Firestone, Reuven. *Jihad: The Origin of Holy War in Islam*. Oxford: Oxford University Press, 1999.

Fishman, Shammai. "Fiqh al-Aqalliyyat: A Legal Theory for Muslim Minorities." Research Monographs on the Muslim World Series, No. 1, Paper 2. Washington D.C.: Hudson Institute. (October 2006).

_____. "Some Notes on Arabic Terminology as a Link Between Tariq Ramadan and Sheikh Dr. Taha Jabir al-Alwani, Founder of the Doctrine of 'Muslim Minority Jurisprudence'(*Fiqh al-Aqaliyyat al-Muslimah*)." http://www.e-prism.org. (Accessed September 30, 2007).

Forte, David F. *Studies in Islamic Law: Classical and Contemporary Application*. New York: Austin & Winfield Publishers, 1999.

Freamon, Bernard K. "Slavery, Freedom, and the Doctrine of Consensus in Islamic Jurisprudence." *Harvard Human Rights Journal* 11 (Spring, 1998): 1-64.

Fuller, Graham and Ian Lesser. *A Sense of Siege: The Geopolitics of Islam and the West*. Boulder. Col.: Westview Press, 1995.

Gatje, Helmut. *The Qur'an and its Exegesis*. Translated by Alford Welih. Berkeley: University of California Press, 1976.

Geiger, Abraham. *Judaism and Islam.* F.M. Young, trans. New York: Ktav Publishing House, 1970.

Gerber, Heim. "Rigidity versus Openness in Late Classical Islamic Law: the Case of the Seventeenth-Century Palestinian Mufti Khayr al-Din al-Ramli." *Islamic Law and Society* 5, no. 2 (1998): 165-195.

_____. *State, Society and Law in Islam: Ottoman Law in Comparative Perspective.* Albany: State Univ. of New York Press, 1994.

Gerges, Fawaz. *America and Political Islam: Clash of Cultures or Clash of Interests*? New York: Cambridge University Press, 1999.

Goldziher, Ignáz. *Introduction to Islamic Theology and Law.* Translated by Andras and Ruth Hamori. Princeton, N.J.: Princeton University Press, 1981.

Gordon, David C. *Images of the West: Third World Perspectives.* Savage, Maryland: Rowman & Littlefield Pub., 1989.

Gradeva, Rossitsa. "Orthodox Christians in the Kadi Courts: The Practice of the Sofia Sheriat Court, Seventeenth Century," *Islamic Law and Society* 4, no. 1 (1997): 37-69.

Haddad, Yvonne Yazbeck. *The Muslims of America.* Oxford: Oxford Univ. Press, 1991.

___________ and Jane Idleman Smith, eds. *Muslim Communities of North America.* Albany: State University of New York, 1994.

___________. *Muslim Minorities in the West: Visible and Invisible.* New York: Altamira Press, 2002.

___________ and Barbara Freyer Stowasser. *Islamic Law and the Challenge of Modernity.* Walnut Creek, California: Alta Mira Press, 2004.

Hadhrami, Abu Amal. "Muslims Need Own Outlook." *Islamic Horizons*. (Jan.-Feb. 2000): 48-53.

Haeri, Shahla. *Law of Desire: Temporary Marriage in Shi'i Iran.* Syracuse University Press, 1989.

Hammad, Ahmad Zaki. *Islamic Law: Understanding Juristic Differences.* Indianapolis: American Trust Publications, 1992.

Hasan, Asma Gull. *American Muslims: The New Generation.* New York: Continuum, 2000.

Hekmat, Anwar. *Women and the Qur'an.* Amherst, N.Y.: Prometheus Press, 1997.

Henderson, Monica. "U.S. State Court Review of Islamic Law Custody Decrees – When are Islamic Custody Decrees in the Child's Best Interest?" *Brandeis Journal of Family Law 36* (Summer 1997/98): 423-456.

Huxley, Andrew. *Religion, Law and Tradition: Comparative Studies in Religious Law.* Routledge/Curzon, 2002.

Ibn Warraq. *Defending the West: A Critique of Edward Said's Orientalism.* New York: Prometheus Books, 2007.

Iqbal, Walid. "Dialogue and the Practice of Law and Spiritual Values: Glimpses into the Islamic Tradition," *Fordham Urban Law Journal* 28 (April 2001): 1035-81.

Irwin, Robert. *Dangerous Knowledge: Orientalism and its Discontents.* New York: Overlook Press, 2006.

Izetbegovic, Alija Ali. *Islam Between East and West.* Plainfield, Indiana: American Trust Pub., 1999.

Johansen, Baber. *Contingency in Sacred Law: Legal and Ethical Norms in the Muslim Fiqh.* Leiden: Brill, 1998.

Kamali, Mohammad. *Principles of Islamic Jurisprudence.* New York: New York University Press, 1999.

Keane, John. "The Limits of Secularism." In *Islam and Secularism in the Middle East*, Edited by John Esposito and Azzam Tamimi. New York: New York University Press, 2000.

Keller, Nuh Ha Mim, trans. *Reliance of the Traveler: A Classic Manual of Islamic Sacred Law.* Beltsville, Md.: Amana Pub., 1994.

Kepel, Gilles. *Muslim Extremism in Egypt.* Sacramento: Univ. of California Press, 1997.

___________. *Allah in the West: Islamic Movements in America and Europe.* Cambridge: Polity Press, 1997.

Kerr, Malcolm H. "Review of 'Orientalism'." *International Journal of Middle Eastern Studies* 12, no. 4 (1980): 544-47.

Khadduri, Majid and Herbert J. Liebesny, eds. *Law in the Middle East.* Clark, N.J.: The Lawbook Exchange, Ltd., 2008.

Khadduri, Majid. "Nature and Sources of Islamic Law." *The George Washington Law Review* 22 (1953): 3-23.

Khan, Mohammed A. Muqtedar. "Islam as an Ethical Tradition of International Relations." *Islam and Christian-Muslim Relations* 8, no. 2 (1997): 173-188.

Kourides, P. Nicholas. "Traditionalism and Modernism in Islamic Law." *Columbia Journal of Transnational Law* 11 (1972): 497-505.

Kroncke, Jed. "Substantive Irrationalities and Irrational Substantivities: The Flexible Orientalism of Islamic Law." *UCLA Journal of Islamic and Near Eastern Law* 4 (2004/2005): 41-77.

Kurzman, Charles, ed. *Liberal Islam.* New York: Oxford University Press, 1999.

Lane, Jan-Erik and Hamadi Redissi. *Religion and Politics: Islam and Muslim Civilizations.* Surrey, England: Ashgate Pub. 2009.

Lang, Jeffrey. *Struggling to Surrender: Some Impressions of an American Convert to Islam*. Beltsville, Md.: Amana Publications, 1994.

Lapidu, Ira M. *A History of Islamic Societies*. Cambridge: Cambridge University Press, 1988.

Laroui, Abdallah. "Western Orientalism and Liberal Islam: Mutual Distrust?" *Middle East Studies Association Bulletin* 31, no. 1 (July 1997): 3-10.

Leonard, Karen Isaksen. *Muslims in the United States: The State of Research*. New York: Russell Sage Foundation, 2003.

Lev, Daniel S. *Islamic Courts in Indonesia: A Study in the Political Bases of Legal Institutions*. Los Angeles: University of California Press, 1972.

Lewis, Reina. *Gendering Orientalism: Race, Femininity and Representation*. New York: Routledge, 1995.

Liebesny, Herbert J. *The Law of the Near and Middle East*. Albany, N.Y.: State University of New York Press, 1975.

Lincoln, E. Eric. *The Black Muslims in America*. Grand Rapids: Eerdmans Press, 1994.

Little, Douglas. *American Orientalism: The United States and the Middle East Since 1945*. Chapel Hill: University of North Carolina Press, 2002.

Madigan, Daniel. *The Qur'an's Self-Image*. Princeton: Princeton University Press, 2001.

Makdisi, John. "The Islamic Origins of the Common Law." *North Carolina Law Review* 77 (June 1999): 1635-80.

Mallat, Chibli. *The Renewal of Islamic Law*. Cambridge: Cambridge University Press, 1993.

Mamood, Saba. "Modern Power and the Reconfiguration of Religious Tradition," Interview with Tala Asad. *Stanford Humanities Review* 5, no. 1 (1996), http://www.stanford.edu/group/SHR/5-1/text/asad.html.

Maqdisi, George. *Religion, Law and Learning in Classical Islam*. Collected Studies Series. London: Variorum, 1991.

March, Andrew F. *Islam and Liberal Citizenship: The Search for an Overlapping Concensus*. Oxford: Oxford Univ. Press, 2009.

Marsh, Clifton. *From Black Muslims to Muslims*. Metuchen: Scarecrow Press, 1984.

Masih, Hazrat Mirza Bashiruddin Mahmood Ahmad II. *The Holy Qur'an*. Vol. 1-5. Islamabad: Islam International Publications, 1988.

Mayer, Ann Elizabeth. *Islam and Human Rights: Tradition and Politics*. Boulder: University of Colorado Press, 1995.

McAuliffe, Jane Dammen. *Qur'anic Christians: An Analysis of Classical and Modern Exegesis*. Cambridge: Cambridge University Press, 1991.

Melton, Gordon and Michael Koszegi, eds. *Islam in North America: A Sourcebook*. New York: Garland Press, 1992.

Mernissi, Fatima. *Islam and Democracy: Fear of the Modern World.* Reading, Mass.: Addison Wesley Publishing Co., 1992.

Miller, Jane. *Seductions: Studies in Reading and Culture.* London: Virago, 1990.

Mir-Hosseini, Ziba. *Marriage on Trial: a Study of Islamic Family Law: Iran and Morocco Compared.* London, New York: I.B. Tauris, 1993.

Modarressi, Hossein. *Introduction to Shi`i Law: a Bibliographical Study.* London: Ithaca Press, 1994.

Moore, Kathleen. *Al-Mughtaribun: American Law and the Transformation of Muslim Life in the United States*. Albany: State University of New York, 1995.

Moustafa, Tamir. "Conflict and Cooperation Between the State and Religious Institutions in Contemporary Egypt." *International Journal of Middle East Studies* 32 (2000): 3-22.

Muqtedar Khan, Mohammad A. *American Muslims: Bridging Faith and Freedom.* Beltsville, Md.: Amana Pub., 2002.

Nasr, Seyyed Hossein. *A Young Muslim's Guide to the Modern World.* Chicago: Kazi Publishing, 1994.

Neubauer, Stephen S. *Judicial Process: Law, Courts and Politics in the United States*. Boston: Wadsworth Press, 2010.

Neusner, Jacob and Tamara Sonn. *Comparing Religions Through Law.* London: Routledge Press, 1999.

Noorani, A.G. *Islam and Jihad: Prejudice Versus Reality.* London: Zed Books, 2002.

Nu'man, Fareed. *The Muslim Population in the United States*. Washington D.C.: The American Muslim Council, 1992.

Olmstead, Matthew. "Are things Falling Apart?; Rethinking the purpose and Function of International Law." *Loyola of Los*

Angeles International & Comparative Law Review 27 (Summer 2005): 401-427.

Oren, Michael. *Power, Faith and Fantasy: America in the Middle East 1776 to Present.* New York: W.W. Norton & Co., 2007.

Osman, Fathi. The Other: A Restructuring of the Islamic Concept. Walnut, Cal.: Pharos Foundation, 2009.

Owsia, Parviz. *Formatin of Contract: a comparative study under English, French, Islamic and Iranian Law.* Graham and Trotman, 1994.

Parfrey, Adam, ed. *Extreme Islam: Anti-American Propaganda of Muslim Fundamentalism.* Los Angeles: Feral House, 2001.

Parolin, Gianluca P. *Citizenship in the Arab World: Kin, Religion and Nation-State.* Amsterdam: Amsterdam Univ. Press, 2009.

Pearl, David. *Textbook on Muslim Law.* Oxford: Oxford Univ. Press, 1964.

Peters, Rudolph. *The Jihad in Classical and Modern Islam.* Princeton: Princeton University Press, 1996.

Philips, Abu Ameenah Bilal. *The Evolution of Fiqh (Islamic Law & the Madh-habs).*Riyadh: Tawheed Publications, 1988.

Powers, David S. *Law, Society and Culture in the Maghrib, 1300-1500.* Cambridge: Cambridge University Press, 2002.

Qutb, Sayyid. *Milestones.* Kuwait: International Islamic Federation of Student Organizations, 1978.

_____. *Social Justice in Islam.* John Hardie, trans. Oneonta, N.Y.: Islamic Publications International, 2000.

Ramadan, Tariq. *To be a European Muslim.* Leicester: The Islamic Foundation, 1999.

Rashid, Samoy. "Divergent Perspectives on Islam in America." *Journal of Muslim Minority Affairs* 20 (Jan. 2000): 75-90.

Reese, N. "The Status in the Country of Judgments Rendered Abroad." *Columbia Law Review* 50 (Spring 1950): 783-802.

Reinhart, A. Kevin. *Before Revelation: the Boundaries of Muslim Moral Thought.* Albany: State University of New York Press, 1995.

Reiter, Ytizhak. *Islamic Institutions in Jerusalem: Palestinian Muslim Organization under Jordanian and Israeli Rule.* Jerusalem: Kluwer Law Intl., 1997.

Renard, John, ed. *Windows on the House of Islam: Muslim Sources on Spirituality & Religious Life.* Berkeley: University of California Press, 1998.

Rippin, Andrew, ed. *The Qur'an: Formative Interpretations.* Aldershot: Aldersgate Publishing, 1999.
Robinson, Neal. *Discovering the Qur'an: a Contemporary Approach to a Veiled Text.* London: SCM Press 1996.
Rosen, Lawrence. *The Anthropology of Justice: Law as Culture in Islamic Society.* New York: Cambridge University Press, 1989.
______. *The Justice of Islam.* Oxford: Oxford University Press, 2000.
Rotter, Andrew. "Saidism Without Said: Orientalism and U.S. Diplomatic History." *American Historical Review* 105, no. 4 (October 2000): 1-25.
Sachedina, Abdulaziz. *The Islamic Roots of Democratic Pluralism.* New York: Oxford University Press, 2001.
Safi, Louai. "The Creative Mission of Muslim Minorities in the West." A paper presented at the Conference *Fiqh Today: Muslim as Minorities*, Westminister University, London, England, February 21, 2004.
Said, Edward. *Orientalism.* New York: Vintage Books, 1978.
______. *Culture and Imperialism.* New York: Vintage Books, 1994.
______. *Covering Islam.* New York: Vintage Books, 1997.
Salai, Sean. "Islam Convert Loses Custody of Her Son." *The Washington Times* (July 11, 2002): A-2.
Sayyid, Bobby. *A Fundamental Fear.* London: Zed, 1997.
Schacht, Joseph. *An Introduction to Islamic Law.* Oxford: Clarendon Press, 1964.
Shaham, Ron. "Custom, Islamic Law, and Statutory Legislation: Marriage Registration and Minimum Age at Marriage in the Egyptian Shari`a Court." *Islamic Law and Society* 2, no. 3 (1995): 258-281.
Sherif, Faruq. *A Guide to the Contents of the Qur'an.* Reading: Ithaca Press, 1995.
Siddiqi, Muzammil. "Muslims in a Non-Muslim Society." *Islamic Horizons* (May-June 1986): 22-24.
Singh, N.K. *Social Justice and Human Rights in Islam.* Delhi: Guyan Press, 1998.
Sonbol, Amira. "Women in Shari'ah Courts: A Historical and Methodological Discussion." *Fordham Int'l L.J.* 27 (Dec. 2003): 225-259.
Spellberg, D.A. *Politics, Gender and the Islamic Past: the Legacy of 'A'isha Bint Abu Bakr.* New York: Columbia University Press, 1994.

Springer, Devin R., James L. Regens, and David N. Edger. *Islamic Radicalism and Global Jihad.* Washington D.C.: Georgetown Univ. Press, 2009.

Stahnke, Tad and Robert Blitt. *The Religion-State Relationship and the Right to Freedom of Religion or Belief: A Comparative Textual Analysis of the Constitutions of Predominantly Muslim Countries.* Washington D.C.: U.S. Commission on International Religious Freedom, March 2005.

Stowasser, Barbara Freyer. *Women in the Qur'an, Traditions, and Interpretation.* Oxford: Oxford University Press, 1994.

Suleiman, Michael, ed. *Arabs in America: Building a New Future.* Philadelphia: Temple University Press, 1999.

Tamimi, Azzam. "The Origins of Arab Secularism." In *Islam and Secularism in the Middle East.* Edited by John Esposito and Azzam Tamimi. New York: New York University Press, 2000.

Termine, Kori. "Should Courts Really Enter the Thicket of Theology?" *Quinnipiac Law Review* 24 (2005): 187-209.

Turner, Richard Brent. *Islam in the African-American Experience.* Bloomington: University of Indiana Press, 1997.

Tweed, Thomas and Stephen Prothero. *Asian Religions in America: A Documentary History.* New York: Oxford Press, 1999.

Voll, John Obert. *Islam, Continuity and Change in Modern Islam.* Syracuse: Syracuse University Press, 1994.

Wadud, M. *The Qur'an and Women.* Oxford: Oxford University Press.

Wansbrough, John. *Qur'anic Studies: Sources and Methods of Scriptural Interpretation.* London Oriental Series, Vol. 31. Oxford: Oxford University Press, 1977.

_____. *The Sectarian Milieu.* Oxford: Oxford University Press, 1978.

Warraq, Ibn, ed. *The Origins of the Qur'an.* Amherst, N.Y.: Prometheus Publishing, 1998.

Watt, Montgomery. *Companion to the Qur'an.* London: George Allen & Unwin, Ltd., 1967.

______ and Richard Bell. *Introduction to the Qur'an.* Edinburgh: Edinburgh University Press, 1970.

Wegner, Judith Romney. *Chattel or Person?: The Status of Women in the Mishna*h. New York: Oxford University Press, 1988.

_____. "Islamic and Talmudic Jurisprudence: the four roots of Islamic Law and their Talmudic counterparts." *The American Journal of Legal Histor*y 26 (1983): 25-71.

Wormser, Richard. *American Islam: Growing up Muslim in America.* New York: Walker and Co. Press, 1994.

Yilmaz, Ihsan. *Muslim Laws, Politics, and Society in Modern Nation States: Dynamic Legal Pluralisms in England, Turkey, and Pakistan.* Burlington, Vermont: Ashgate Pub., 2005.

Zaman, Muhammad Qasim. "The Caliphs, the 'Ulama', and the Law: Defining the Role and Function of the Caliph in the Early 'Abbasid Period." *Islamic Law and Society* 4, no. 1 (1997): 1-36.

Ziadeh, Farhat. "Compelling Defendant's Appearance at Court in Islamic Law," *Islamic Law and Society* 3, no. 3 (1996): 305-315.

Zubaida, Sami. *Law and Power in the Islamic World.* London: I.B. Tauris, 2003.

<u>Codified Acts</u>

Hague Convention on the Civil Aspects of International Child Abduction, Oct. 25, 1980, art. 5, 99 U.S.T. 11 (codified as 42 U.S.C. §§ 11601-11610 (2001)).

Uniform Child Custody Jurisdiction and Enforcement Act, § 105 (c) (1997), available at http://www.law.upenn.edu/bll/ulc/uccjea/final1997act.htm.

<u>Court Decisions</u>

Federal Decisions:

Alosio v. Iranian Shipping Lines, 426 F. Supp. 687 (S.D.N.Y. 1976).

Bakshandeh v. American Cyanamid Co., 211 F. Supp. 803 (S.D.N.Y. 1962).

Clay v. U.S., 403 U.S. 698; 91 S. Ct. 2068; 29 L. Ed. 2d 810 (1971).

Couch v. Mobil Oil Corp., 327 F. Supp. 897 (S.D. Tex. 1971).

Hillcrest Foods, Inc. v. United Food and Commercial Workers Union, AFL-CIO Local No. 576, 753 F. Supp. 1541 (Dist. Ct. Kan. 1990).

Hilton v. Guyot, 159 U.S. 113 (1894).

Miller Brewing Co. v. Brewery Workers Local No. 9, AFL-CIO, 739 F. 2d 1159 (7th Cir. 1984).

Nakhleh v. Chemical Construction Co., 359 F.Supp. 357 (S.D.N.Y. 1973).

National Group for Communications, Ltd. v. Lucent Technologies International, Inc., 331 F. Supp. 2d 290 (Dist. Ct. N.J. 2004).

New Alliance Party v. Dinkins, 743 F. Supp. 1055 (So. Dist. N.Y. 1990).
Olivieri v. Ward, 801 F.2d 602 (2nd Cir. 1986).
Shikoh v. Murff, 257 F.2d 306 (2d Cir. 1958).
Stewart v. Thorpe Holding Co. Profit Sharing Plan, 207 F.3d 1143 (9th Cir. 2000).
Terminiello v. Chicago, 337 U.S. 1; 93 L.Ed. 1131; 69 S.Ct. 894 (1949).
U.S. v. Abdel Rahman, 189 F.2d 88 (2nd Cir. 1999).
U.S. v. Khan, 309 F. Supp. 2d 789 (Eastern Dist. Vir. 2004).
Walton v. Arabian American Oil Co., 233 F.2d 541 (2d Cir. 1955).

State Court Decisions:

Abouzahr v. Matera-Abouzahr, 361 N.J. Super. 135, 824 A.2d 268 (2003).
Aghili v. Saadatnejadi, 958 S.W. 2d 784 (Tenn. Ct. App. 1997).
Akileh v. Elchahal, 666 So. 2d 246 (Flor. Ct. App. 1996).
Al-Ali v. Al-Saba, No. 93-CA-2297-MR, slip op. (Ky Ct. App. March 10 1995).
Ali v. Ali, 652 A. 2d 253 (N.J. Super. Ct. 1994).
Amin v. Bakhaty, 798 So.2d 75 (Louisiana Sup. Ct., 2001).
Arain v. Arain, 209 A. 2d 406; 619 N.Y.S.2d 591 (N.Y. Sup. Ct. 1994).
Aziz v. Aziz, 853 N.E. 2d 229; 819 N.Y.S. 2d 860 (N.Y. Ct. App. 2006).
Chaudry v. Chaudry, 159 N.J. Super. 566, 388 A. 2d 1000 (1978).
Credit Union Central Falls v. Lawrence S. Groff, *871 A.2d 364* (R.I. Sup. Ct. 2005).
Dexter v. Idaho State Bar Board of Commissioners, 116 Idaho 790; 780 P.2d 112 (Idaho Sup. Ct. 1989).
Espy v. Espy, 191 Cal. App. 3d 1163; 236 Cal. Rptr. 755 (Cal. Ct. App. 1987).
Farah v. Farah, 16 Va. App. 329; 429 S.E. 2d 626 (Vir. Ct. App. 1993).
First Federal Savings and Loan v. Vandygriff, 639 S.W.2d 492 (Tex. Ct. App. 1982).
Garg v. Garg, 163 Md. App. 546, 881 A.2d 1180 (Maryland Ct. App. 2005).
Hassan v. Hassan, Slip Op. No. FA010632261; 2001 Conn. Super. LEXIS 2959 (Sept. 30, 2001).
Hosain v. Malak, 108 Md. App. 288 (1996).
Hunt v. Coastal States Gas, 570 S.W.2d 503 (Tx. Ct. App. 1978).

In the Matter of Sonia Ramadan and Samer Ramadan, 891 A.2d 1186 (N.H. Sup. Ct. 2006).
In re Dajani, 204 Cal. App. 3d 1387; 251 Cal. Rptr. 871 (Cal. Ct. App. 1988).
In re Noghrey, 169 Cal. App. 3d 326; 215 Cal. Rptr. 153 (Cal. Ct. App. 1985).
In re the Marriage of Awatef and Nabil A. Dajani, 204 Cal. App. 3d 1387; 251 Cal. Rptr. 871 (Cal. Ct. App. 1988).
In re the Marriage of Farima and Kambiz Noghrey, 169 Cal. App. 3d 326; 215 Cal. Rptr. 153 (Cal. Ct. App. 1985).
In re the Marriage of Fereshteh R. and Speros Vryonis, Jr. 202 Cal. App. 3d 712; 248 Cal. Rptr. 807 (Cal. Ct. App. 1988).
In re the Marriage of Malak, 182 Cal. App. 3d 1018, 227 Cal. Rptr. 841 (1986).
In re Petition of Elliot Rothenberg for Review of a Decision of the Board of Continuing Legal Education, 676 N.W. 2d 283 (Minn. Sup. Ct. 2004).
In re Vyronis, 202 Cal. App. 3d 712; 248 Cal. Rptr. 807 (Cal. Ct. App. 1988).
Jabri v. Jabri, 83 N.Y.2d 954; 639 N.E.2d 419; 615 N.Y.S.2d 878 (N.Y. Ct. App. 1994).
Malak v. Malak, 182 Cal. App.. 3d 1018, 227 Cal. Rptr. 841 (1986).
Malik v. Malik, 638 A.2d 1184 (Maryland Court Spec. App. 1994).
McManus v. Fulton, 85 Mont. 170; 278 P. 126 (Mont. Sup. Ct. 1929).
Noordin v. Abdulla, 88 Wash. App. 746, 947 P. 2d 745 (1997).
Odatalla v. Odatalla, 355 N.J. Super. 305; 810 A.2d 93 (N.J. Super. Ct. 2002).
Samman v. Samman, Slip Op. No. 249877; Lexis 3089 (Mich. Ct. App., Nov. 9, 2004).
Seth v. Seth, 694 S.W.2d 459 (Tex. Ct. App. 1985).
Shaban v. Shaban, 88 Cal. App. 4th 398; 105 Cal. Rptr. 2d 863 (Cal. Ct. App. 2001).
Shike v. Shike, Slip Op. No. 14-97-00888-CV; 2000 Tex. App. LEXIS 2733 (Tex. Ct. App., April 27, 2000).
Shikoh v. Murff, 257 F.2d 306 (2nd Cir. Ct. App. 1958).
Sullivan v. Chafee, 703 A.2d 748 (R.I. Sup. Ct. 1997).

Index